Jennifer Kavanagh worked in publishing for nearly thirty years, the last fourteen as an independent literary agent. Books she represented included world rights for *Chinese Lives*, an oral history of China just before the Tiananmen Square atrocity, and the British rights for classic American oral historian Studs Terkel.

'During my long years as a hostage I had no books and no contact whatsoever with the outside world. Using my imagination I walked along the streets of London and had many imaginary conversations with the people I met there. If only I had had this book with me then. Jennifer Kavanagh has actually walked the length and breadth of this great city and recorded the many conversations she had with people. Apart from being a fascinating snapshot of London in the 21st century, it's a valuable social commentary.' Terry Waite

'What shines through this wonderfully engaging book is the author's genuine assumption that every life matters and, if we care to listen, has important things to tell us about our own.' *Guardian*

'The openness of the people she spoke to, and the empathy and skill she devised in winning their trust, are remarkable features of this humane and attractive book.' *Times Literary Supplement*

'Jennifer Kavanagh's [work is a] richly detailed mapping of the stories of those who have least, are often invisible, and bear the brunt of market forces they cannot influence.' *OnLondon*

T0008383

Let Me Take You by the Hand

True Tales from London's Streets

Jennifer Kavanagh

Drawings by Rosie Wyllie

ABACUS

First published in Great Britain in 2021 by Little, Brown
This paperback edition published in 2022 by Abacus

1 3 5 7 9 10 8 6 4 2

ISBN 978-0-349-14424-5

Typeset in Baskerville by M Rules
Printed and bound in Great Britain by
Clays Ltd, Elcograf S.p.A.

Papers used by Abacus are from well-managed forests
and other responsible sources.

Abacus
An imprint of
Little, Brown Book Group
Carmelite House
50 Victoria Embankment
London EC4Y 0DZ

An Hachette UK Company
www.hachette.co.uk

www.littlebrown.co.uk

In memory of Henry Mayhew
1812–87

Contents

III: What's Enough?

IV: Survival

V: My Time

Acknowledgements

First, an immense thank you to all the people who generously gave of their time, and opened their hearts. This is your book. To Alastair Murray and Mat Amp, without whose expertise and experience this book would not have happened. Thank you for your valuable contributions and generous support.

Thanks too to all those others who helped me in innumerable ways, including Fred Ashmore, The Connection at St Martin's, Crisis at Christmas, Rob Francis, Groundswell, Housing Justice, International Workers of Great Britain, Jean Jameson, Neil Jameson, Michael Jardine, Jesuit Refugee Service, London Catholic Worker, Ruby Maw, The Passage, The Pavement, St Martin-in-the-Fields, St Mungo's, Susan Oudot, Quaker Homeless Action, Rosa Schling, Trust for London and Margaret Waterworth.

Preface

The research for this book was done from the end of 2018 to spring 2020. This was a period in which Brexit loomed large and then, at the end, the outbreak of coronavirus changed the lives of us all. At the time we stopped interviewing, it was too early to tell the effects on those on the street, but the plight of those already disadvantaged by having no sick pay, those whose pay stopped if they stopped, was becoming clear. And, in common with others in the retail trade, traders were suffering from a drop-off in custom. People were staying at home and buying online. And as for working from home – that simply wasn't possible for most of the people we interviewed. One woman said: 'As a door-to-door interviewer that really isn't an option, so I have no idea how I will live over the next few months. I don't think I qualify for sick pay, my firm have shown no leadership or transparency in how they are going to treat staff. I'm deeply worried.'

As we go to press in February 2021, we are in a third lockdown, and it is hard to know how things will be when we emerge. Except for increased numbers of delivery cyclists, the streets are almost empty. Some well-established markets have been able to remain open, but most businesses inside and out have closed their doors. Akim, the coffee seller, has disappeared, as has the stall outside Goodge Street station. It is unlikely that either will return. There are few people to buy the *Big Issue*, or 'give a little change' to buskers or those desperate enough to continue begging. Some of those sleeping on the streets were moved into hotels and emergency accommodation by the well-publicised 'Everyone In' operation during the first lockdown, but that has not been repeated, and the laying off of staff by cafés and shops has led to a large influx of newly homeless people.

But during this period, as we learn that it is safer to be outside than in, as we are encouraged to spend time out of doors, so the outside life of London has come into its own: the cafés with outside seating and, above all, the parks, where Londoners exercise, spend more of their time alone and, when permitted, in socially distanced meetings with friends. As one woman said to me, 'It's the only thing that keeps me sane.'

In the 1980s I was a literary agent, and was selling the translation rights to an oral history of China – a hundred interviews with 'ordinary' Chinese people. It was a portrait of a country opening up to the outside world, but by the time the paperback version came out in the UK, the events of Tiananmen had stamped on those new freedoms. In January 2021, even the BT Tower was broadcasting 'Stay Home. Protect the NHS. Save Lives'. I hope that by the time this book comes out, it will not be telling the tale of a London that has gone into history.

Another way of looking at it is that the pandemic has brought into focus the very subject of this book. The crisis has exposed the vulnerabilities and inequalities that are embedded in our society, but usually hidden from public view.

Whatever the situation, however individual lives might change, the picture of London revealed by these rarely heard voices is one that will endure. It is a reminder of our common humanity and the invaluable contribution of those who have least and are often invisible.

Introduction

Let me take you by the hand and lead you
through the streets of London

London has been described as the world in one city. In some dark
tunnels leading out of Waterloo station on the South Bank is an
extraordinary series of mosaics portraying just that idea. David
Tootill, the project director of Southbank Mosaic, which created it,
wrote: 'Mosaic is a metaphor for bringing together all the peoples,
tribes, creeds, cultures, colours, clans, faiths and freedoms to make
a brilliant whole.'

There have been other points of view. David Copperfield considered London to be 'fuller of wonders and wickedness than all
the cities of the earth'. In January 2020, the Sutton Trust released
a report, based on research from the London School of Economics,
describing London as 'the epicentre of the elites . . . London is essentially off-limits to ambitious people from poorer backgrounds who
grow up outside the capital.' This, it says, is exacerbated by practices
such as unpaid internships, which are available only to those who can
afford to live and work in London without earning. The paradox of
a great, vibrant and diverse city riven with inequalities is the context
of this book.

Its inspiration is an extraordinary work of investigative journalism
from the nineteenth century. Henry Mayhew's ground-breaking
study, *London Labour and the London Poor*, was published first in
weekly instalments in the *Morning Chronicle* from December 1850
to February 1852, and then in volume form: volumes one to three

in 1861 and volume four a year later. The total came to some 2000 pages, nearly two million words.

Mayhew interviewed hundreds of people who lived or worked on the streets of London, from market traders and entertainers to thieves and beggars, uncovering a city of stark inequality and precarious lives. These detailed and intimate stories, in turn moving, funny and inspiring, are rendered with a sympathy and immediacy that makes *London Labour and the London Poor* a literary work that can stand alongside the best of Victorian fiction.

Mayhew was born in the same year as Charles Dickens, and is widely regarded as an influence on him, the two writers covering similar ground and each revealing a similar passion for social justice. And recognising that, as Judith Flanders says in her book *The Victorian City*:

> These streets that Dickens drew on ... were a hive of activity, a route for commuters, a passage from home to work and from work to home. But they were also a place of work itself, as well as one of leisure and amusement. The streets had purpose to them; they were a destination as well as a means of reaching a destination.

A climate change protester living on the streets today said: 'It's perfectly normal to work on the streets. There are people digging the road, people who have stalls, charities raising money on the street. The street in my opinion is no more dangerous than anywhere else.'

Superficially, the streets of London in 1861 and in 2020 may seem entirely different places. Tower blocks have appeared; older houses have been refurbished or have disappeared. Gone are the horses and their manure; the advent of the internal combustion engine has transformed the streets into thoroughfares where the automobile holds sway. For those working on the streets, much has changed too. Many tasks such as refuse collection and street cleaning now fall under the aegis of local councils; dustmen are no longer men collecting coal dust from houses to sell on, but refuse collectors employed by the council. Bus companies employ bus drivers;

some markets are run by larger collectives. For those sleeping in the streets, things have changed too – notably because of the introduction of the National Health Service, and of the benefit system which has provided a safety net for some of those on low incomes.

But under the surface the similarities are striking and, in many cases, shocking. This book explores the changes and continuities by collecting and mapping stories from today's London, finding startling similarities in the work carried out on the streets, even if in some cases the terminology and the moral perspective have changed. Beggars, street entertainers, stalls selling food, clothes or second-hand goods, thieves and the sex trade still hold sway. The rise of the gig economy has brought a multitude of drivers and cyclists, delivering and moving goods, transporting meals and people, all organised through smartphones but using the same streets as Mayhew's informants. The precarious existence faced by this new workforce would be familiar to the street-sellers of Mayhew's day.

In the preface to Volume I of his great work, Mayhew said, 'My earnest wish is that the book may serve to give the rich a more intimate knowledge of the sufferings, and the frequent heroism under those sufferings, of the poor. The condition of a class of people whose misery, ignorance and vice, amidst all the immense wealth and great knowledge of the first city in the world is, to say the least, a national disgrace to us.'

What is exceptional about Mayhew's approach is that he put his interviewees centre stage. People normally ignored or even unseen are given a voice. Like Mayhew, I've tried to reveal the person behind the uniform or the anonymous role: cleaner, doorman, delivery man. People who are so close to us – and too often beneath our notice.

Although starting from the standpoint of the categories in Mayhew's book, I have not followed the same structure.

Method of working

London Labour and the London Poor is famous for its poignant stories: of the Returned Convict and the Watercress Girl. *Let Me*

Take You by the Hand also has powerful and poignant stories to tell, but I struggle to categorise individuals in terms of the job that they do – because they often do more than one, and as people they are so much more than their work. Categorisation can too easily become the source of our prejudices. So, on the whole, the categories I use are broader and the people have their unique and complex stories.

Some interviewees welcomed the chance to talk about their lives. Some found telling their stories, often for the first time, helpful. Friends have asked how I knew if they were telling the truth. The answer is, I didn't. But like the rest of us, they have found ways of telling their stories that they can live with.

Not all the interviews were carried out by me: I needed the experience and expertise of my colleagues, Mat and Alastair. Most interviews were recorded. For those that were not, it was either because people didn't want to be recorded, or because the conversation came from a more informal chat, with notes taken at the time or immediately afterwards. Interviewees each signed a consent form. Many names have been changed.

Given the number of nationalities we knew we would be working with, our intention was to work with interpreters. In the event, it proved not to be practicable. We never knew what language someone would speak, or whether they would be found in the same spot when we visited again. We had to make do with a combination of English, a smattering of other languages, and sign language.

Where?

This book focuses on the London known by Mayhew. That is largely what we now regard as inner London, namely the boroughs of Camden, City of London, Hackney, Hammersmith & Fulham, Islington, Kensington & Chelsea, Lambeth, Southwark, Tower Hamlets, Wandsworth and Westminster. In this way it is possible to make some interesting, if not absolute, comparisons between the city then and now.

Who?

It was important to present a balance of gender, ethnicity and age as well as giving a fair portrait of the diversity of activities. Without making any effort, I find we have interviewed people from some twenty-five nationalities. I decided not to interview people working for large organisations such as the NHS, Transport for London, the Royal Mail, or the police. Although many of their workers may not be well off, most of these organisations are already paying the National Living Wage and conforming to statutory conditions of work. We could not class their employees as living 'on the edge'.

The nature of our interviewees was that they were hard to pin down. Many led erratic lives and might not be able to stick to an appointment. So it took perseverance. On the whole, it was easiest to interview those who had, as one put it, their own spot: independent or solitary traders, and homeless people.

To some extent, the interviewees were self-selecting: people who were willing to be interviewed either because the money offered was an overwhelming attraction, or because sharing their story was in itself a pleasure, a chance to talk to someone. The most difficult were those whose work is peripatetic: for instance delivery drivers, and those working under the radar, without a licence, or leading a life of illegality. Even with the promise of anonymity, such people were suspicious of anyone who might reveal or report their activities to the authorities.

No, thanks

Many, of course, refused to be interviewed. People have different reasons for keeping quiet, and find different ways to avoid being interviewed. Some politely said 'No', or 'I'm not interested'. And some, especially those on the wrong side of the law, although willing enough to speak, were unwilling to be recorded, even with an offer of anonymity. One man, a market trader for many years, poured out stories with alacrity but when I started to read out the consent form – he is illiterate – alarm bells sounded and he backed off. Mention of 'personal details' had him running for cover and, despite the offer of anonymity, he refused a formal interview.

A man giving away *Time Out* magazine outside Holborn tube twice gave me the same exact time to turn up to interview him, and on both occasions he had gone (although I had seen him half an hour before). It was hard to escape the feeling that he deliberately gave me a time when he knew he would be finished. A peanut seller vehemently – fearfully? – refused, and practically ran away, and a young motorcycle driver for a pizza company, who was probably in his late teens or early twenties, with limited and accented English, was parking his bike when I politely enquired whether he was self-employed. 'No,' he said, seemingly terrified, 'no, no, I'm not self-employed,' and fled.

And the reasons for the fear? Sometimes people mistook me for someone in authority, or prepared to report them for some infringe-ment. I learned later from a flower seller that the peanut seller did not have the necessary licence; others might be working while on benefits or with no right to remain. Supposition in these cases, but

they are real enough reasons. Some people simply didn't want to talk, which was their prerogative; others – civil enforcement officers (CEOs, previously called traffic wardens), some security guards and a couple of street sweepers told us that they were forbidden to give interviews. Which was enough to raise questions about whether some hidden exploitation was taking place.

An old man with sparse hair and rheumy eyes, pushing along a supermarket trolley that held his possessions, including several newspapers, near Great Portland Street station one day, near Mortimer Street the next, courteously declined to be interviewed. We must keep them in mind, these private and silent souls, who hide away from outreach and the rest, and retain stories that are not for sharing.

*

It is important to stress that not all the voices are negative. Far from it. I was struck, and touched, by how few people complained. People who are struggling to make enough to live on, who sleep on the pavement or who get up at 2 a.m. to travel into London to work, show extraordinary resilience and positivity. Yes, there are desperate, heart-breaking voices, but that's not the whole story.

The interest in an interview is not always in the personal story of the person being interviewed, but on the light it sheds on life on the streets around them. Like Mayhew, I am not giving answers, just an ear, with an invitation to let go of our preconceptions, not least about what we consider lousy jobs and our assumptions that those doing them must be unhappy.

Reasons for being on the street are varied and individual, and constitute one of the major subjects of this exploration. As Mayhew says, 'Among the street-folk there are many distinct characters of people – people differing as widely from each in tastes, habits, thoughts and creed, as one nation from another.' He talks of some 'unable to find employment in their own trade' and it is true that the life of people on the streets is often about a contrast with a previous existence – they may have fallen from stability to precarity or run away from abuse and danger; or they may have given up a stable life for a greater expression of their true selves.

References in the text to Henry Mayhew's *London Labour and the London Poor* come from the full Gutenberg text online, unless otherwise noted, in which case they are from abridged versions, published by Penguin or Oxford University Press (details in references at the end of the book).

I

The World Outside

1

The changing city

By the last census return [1841] the metropolis
covered an extent of nearly 45,000 acres, and
contained upwards of two hundred and sixty
thousand houses, occupied by one million
eight hundred and twenty thousand souls,
constituting not only the densest, but the busiest
hive, the most wondrous workshop, and the
richest bank in the world. A strange incongruous
chaos of wealth and want – of ambition and
despair – of the brightest charity and the darkest
crime, where there is more feasting and more
starvation, than on any other spot on earth.

In the nineteenth century, London was one major construction site.
Apart from the continuing work needed for the repair and updating
of utilities – laying gas mains, renewing sewers, changing water pipes
from wood to iron – there was the building of the first underground
lines and the creation of hundreds of new streets. During the building of Holborn Viaduct, Holborn was for three years reduced to
one lane of traffic. The *Daily News* reported, 'The remainder of the
roadway is . . . a place given up to contractors, diggers, and builders,
to navvies and bricklayers, to carts and wheelbarrows, to piles of
materials for masonry, and huge frames of timber.'

Contemporary Londoners will be familiar with this picture.
Crossrail, the east–west trainline from Reading to Shenfield,

running through central London, is currently the biggest railway infrastructure project in Europe. It began construction in May 2009. After many delays, it is hoped that the central portion of the Elizabeth Line, as it is now called, will open in 2021. That is over ten years of disruptive works around the centre of the city. At the time of writing, the disruption is compounded by the West End Project, which includes turning the north–south highways of Gower Street and Tottenham Court Road into two-way roads. Like many major cities, London is in a constant state of transition.

In 2020 the closure alternately of the southbound and north-bound routes on Regent Street caused yet another diversion for buses, taking long-suffering drivers and less patient passengers on very circuitous routes. On one of these diverted (but not diverting) journeys, I commiserated with the bus driver.

'I don't know how you cope.'

'I don't know how I'm still alive. They get one lot to dig up the road, then the gas, electricity, fibre broadband people or whoever come and do their bit, and then they have to wait for the hole fillers-in. And then they dig it up all over again.'

The surrounding roads are jammed by frustrated drivers. Pedestrians contend with long, uneven and changing walkways, caged in metal netting to keep them from the ongoing roadworks. An obstacle race that is hard for any pedestrian, let alone someone whose sight or other faculties are impaired.

On a smaller, but still significant scale, the demolition and refur-bishment of buildings are adding to the changing face of the city and disruption to residents' lives. History is ever-present in such work. One man, working on the refurbishment of a nineteenth-century pub, complained that all the floors and walls in the building were tilting. He pointed over the road and said, 'There was bomb damage there.'

Development provides a big opportunity for work. Mayhew esti-mated that there were 80,000 construction workers in London. By the 1860s more than 10 per cent of the city's adult male population was employed in the building trade. Today, too, the streets are full of those working in construction. According to a parliamentary briefing paper in December 2019, there are 346,000 construction industry jobs in London.

The larger contractors generally promote environmental policies and have active corporate social responsibility programmes. Pay varies considerably. At the high end, skilled labourers typically earn from £120 to £150 per day. The unskilled workforce consists almost exclusively of foreign labour; in 2018, 28 per cent of workers in the industry were from EU countries and 7 per cent were non-EU nationals. The pay for unskilled labour ranges from the National Minimum Wage (as of April 2020, £8.72 per hour for those aged twenty-five and over) to the London Living Wage (£10.75); the workers are provided with reasonable welfare facilities on site, including subsidised canteens. They are expected to work hard and are often hired through umbrella companies, which means that, while they have basic employment rights, they have no job security or guaranteed employment. But, for most of these workers, the pay is still significantly higher than anything they can get in their home countries.

Apart from the big companies, the sector includes an unusually high number of 'unregistered' businesses, typically self-employed contractors. As a result, it's difficult to get accurate figures for average weekly earnings in the industry. It is also hard to know whether there will be enough workers from these sources once the post-Brexit changes to migration are in force.

It seems that there are plenty of casual labouring jobs around. Andrew is a tall, young, lightly bearded man from a close-knit London family. He lives with his mum in a central London basement flat. We met in his family's pub, where he was doing a double shift to make up for time when a bad back prevented him from working, and he needed to stay behind the bar.

'I'm twenty-seven years old. Lived in London my entire life. I worked in a range of places from a huge council estate in Wapping to houses worth several million pounds in um just near Great Ormond Street.' When asked how he got the work, he said, 'Word of mouth, people in the pub, friends. Found out they were . . . one bloke, you would never have thought he was a painter-decorator from the way he dresses. He dresses very smart, and I've worked for him several times; family friends have got work.

'Yeah, I enjoy it. Not in the winter, when you're getting up and it's dark and you come home from work and it's dark. In the summer it's good, and you're working outdoors and the weather's nice. But it's not something I really want to make a career of.

'Hired by the day. Pay depends on the job. Just casual labour, but as I've been doin' it for several years now, I'm probably more . . . I mean I can paint. I've been left on jobs before just to do the painting, so obviously it's dependent on what I'm doing.'

'How easy is it to get casual work?'

He pauses to think.

'Um, I'd say it was easy enough. Like, you've just got to look at London. There's building work taking place all over the shop, and I'm quite fortunate in the people I've worked for are a) good to work for and b) always pay – there's never a hassle about getting paid.

'I mean I'm lucky in that I don't have to find it, but I can't imagine it would be hard, because you've just got to look all over London, and there's nothing but builders. Round here, everywhere you look there's builders, building sites, so I think it's just a case of . . . it's easy enough ter . . . there's work out there. Whether or not you'll be doing something you enjoy, maybe it's not something you want to do.'

He said no qualifications were needed. 'That depends on what you're doing, doesn't it? Look, let's be honest, people on a site doing menial jobs probably don't have many qualifications. I can't imagine if they were Cambridge or Oxford they'd be doing something like that.'

And the people he worked with came from various places. 'Depends on the firm. One firm I did work for, all the people working there were British, whereas some firms obviously employ more Eastern Europeans. I can't say what they get paid, they may think they can pay them less, but I can't comment, I don't know anything about that. My experience is that all the people I've worked with have been British, but I'd say I'd be more of a rare case. I mean when you're walking past, you hear the accents, and they're very seldom British.'

A man who has worked in the construction industry for many years told me that 'jobbing builders will either have a regular crew who are paid often in cash, or they spot hire them on street corners for a day's work. These guys work hard in generally poor conditions without much H&S provision but it does provide an income for people who otherwise would find it difficult to work.' A friend whose father was a builder said it had always been like that – men wandering from site to site in search of work. Nowadays, with all sorts of health and safety and insurance requirements, she said, it's not the same.

Robert, from Hungary and currently homeless, struck lucky.

'When I was first here, on Seven Sisters Road there is a B&Q and in front of that there are a lot of foreigners waiting for jobs, some people come and pick them up, for day jobs. You need to be there in the morning. You can find some good ones. Painting. I usually got nice jobs, inside jobs like this guy was doing a house and he asked me to come in and you know the frame? With the sandpaper I just had to make it smooth, ready to paint. I done it, he checked it, he said, "Can you paint?" So I did. He said to me first of all it was just for one day, £50. I painted it and he liked it and he actually gave me two weeks' job. So it was quite good. Of course, when you have no money you'll take anything, but I was lucky.'

It's perhaps not surprising that so much work in this area is advertised by word of mouth. It can be hard to find people who are reliable, reasonable and good at their work, so it is important to employ someone who comes recommended.

Even in more established jobs, it seems that word of mouth can do the trick: I came across Stefan, a short, broad, dark-haired man, sitting on a digging machine in the middle of the building site that is the West End Project, staring into space. He works for highway maintenance, which in Westminster is contracted out to Eurovia Contracting, and he lives in north London. When I explained about the book, he got out of his cab and we chatted through the netting that divided the building site from the temporary walkway for pedestrians. He talked fluently about his life and work, without any prompting from me.

'I am not English. I'm from Romania. I come eleven years ago. London better for jobs, and way of life. Before I come I imagine London like you see on TV – all those tall buildings.' He gestured around him. 'A friend from my country was working like this and asked if I was interested. I thought I would just come for a few months, make some money and go back. That was in January. In April I asked my girlfriend, now my wife, if she'd like to come. She did and got work as a cleaner for good money. We buy a house in our country and then the kids come, and we ask ourselves shall we stay here or go back? We think here – a better future for our children.

'This is a mini digger. Can lift up to ten tons. If you want to lift more, you need a bigger digger. Yes, training course for this, different course for bigger digger. Yes, we work together, we are colleagues. We are a team of three. I am in charge. If the supervisor wants something, he asks me. But I am not better than them. If they ask me to do something, I do it.

'We work eight to four, with two breaks. Not like an office. You are free – I can walk around, talk to people, take a break. When we work in Oxford Street, all those shops, they needed their entrances' – he makes a sign with his hands of a very narrow entrance – 'We talk to them.' He shakes his head. It had obviously been a difficult negotiation.

Fred and Bill

It was 10 a.m. on a mild January day. The pair of builders were sitting in paint-splattered dungarees, enjoying a break and a cigarette at an outside café table behind Tottenham Court Road. I didn't ask their names, but I will call them Bill and Fred. Fred was perhaps in his forties; Bill was younger, maybe late thirties, with tattoos running all over his neck up to his chin.

I explained the concept of the book.

Fred: 'We don't work outside.'

Bill: 'Too cold.'

Fred: 'Painting, yes, and ...' he nods towards some buildings over the road 'office refurbs.'

'Is it your own company?'

Bill: 'No, wish it was.'

'What's it like?'

Fred: 'Boring. Very boring.'

'What would you like to do?'

Fred: 'If I knew that, I'd be doing it.'

'Why did you go into it?'

Fred: 'Me dad was a painter.'

Bill: 'To pay the bills, same as everyone.'

'Does it?'

Bill: 'Just about.'

'How are you paid? Monthly, weekly, by the job?'

Bill: 'Weekly.'

'Do you have guaranteed work?'

Bill: 'No, we're self-employed. If we don't work we don't get paid.'

'And if you're sick?'

Both together: '*We don't get paid.*'

Bill: 'No holiday pay.'

'Unions?'

Fred: 'No, there used to be, but we don't hear about them these days.'

Noise

Mayhew wrote of the noise of the city, 'the riot and tumult of the traffic of London at once stun and terrify'. With most road surfaces being cobbles or tarmacadam, the din from rattling carriages and omnibuses and horses' hooves must have been terrible. Combined with the construction work, the chattering crowds and the piercing cries of competing street traders – what Mayhew's later work *The Great World of London* called 'the riot, the struggle, and the scramble for a living' – the cacophony can only be imagined.

Modern London is rarely quiet either. Along the busier roads, there is the sound of moving traffic, of impatient horns as the traffic grinds to a halt, of the sirens of emergency services, and, hovering above with insistent noise, the occasional helicopter keeping an eye on possible disturbances. Alarms go off in houses and cars. Music systems blast out from loudspeakers in cars and vans as drivers sit and wait, scrolling through their phones. And, increasingly, delivery cyclists accompany their journeys with music for the rest of us to hear. Meanwhile, the seemingly constant construction work and digging up of our roads provides not only dust and disruption but the noise of drills, of thumpers, of hammering on metal.

But side roads can be surprisingly quiet and the West End Project is apparently to include noise reduction barriers in its new paving. Maybe someone is paying attention.

Neighbourhoods

Walking along Old Compton Street, the heart of Soho, though it is still a bustling place, and there are still individual shops selling everything from lengths of material to timber, it is easy to see the changes. Yes, down a little passage are a couple of massage parlours and a sex shop, reminders of a different era, but it's a faint memory of what in my childhood was considered a 'naughty' place. Bustling traffic, lorries unloading beer barrels outside a gay bar. Cyclists, people drinking coffee or eating breakfast outside cafés or pubs, in the narrow streets. One building covered from top to bottom in a Pride poster, a remnant of the huge march a few weeks ago. One beggar accosting me for 'a little change'. Two homeless men: one, topless, sleeping on the pavement; one, in a poignant contrast, outside the elegant Patisserie Valerie.

A few hundred yards from Soho, across Charing Cross Road, is the rather nondescript area of Seven Dials. Mayhew quotes Dickens's description:

> The stranger who finds himself in 'The Dials' for the first time, and stands, Belzoni-like, at the entrance of seven obscure passages, uncertain which to take, will see enough around him to keep his curiosity and attention awake for no inconsiderable time. From the irregular square into which he has plunged, the streets and courts dart in all directions, until they are lost in the unwholesome vapour which hangs over the house-tops, and renders the dirty perspective uncertain and confined ... The peculiar character of these streets, and the close resemblance each one bears to its neighbour, by no means tends to decrease the bewilderment in which the unexperienced wayfarer through 'the Dials' finds himself involved. He traverses streets of dirty, straggling houses, with now and then an unexpected court, composed of buildings as ill-proportioned and deformed as the half-naked children that wallow in the kennels.

Seven Dials is a very different place now. These days it's just a road junction, a roundabout for traffic, in a sought-after residential area. There are also a few stalls. On a hot Tuesday morning in July, there were only three, just setting up at 10 a.m.: one selling shirts, another scarves and hats, and the third a variety of stickers and badges. This is tourist land, on the edge of Shaftesbury Avenue, and round the corner from the Palace Theatre at Cambridge Circus where clumps of tourists in shorts are taking photos of the frontage advertising *Harry Potter*.

Other parts of London have undergone similar changes. When I was growing up, Notting Hill, now an extremely affluent area, was almost a slum, with a mainly Afro-Caribbean population in houses of multiple occupancy, the centre of the notorious exploitative activities of landlord Peter Rachman. Camden Town, now very fashionable, was decidedly scruffy. My father used to take me to Parkway once a month or so, to visit the stamp shop and the pet shop (which was still there until recently), and to buy fish and chips.

The East End too has changed a lot over the centuries as different groups of migrants have come and gone, from the Huguenots in the seventeenth century onwards. Much of the area around Spitalfields and Bishopsgate was still very run down in the 1980s: a wasteland of bombsites and derelict buildings, the result of the sustained bombing of the East End during the Second World War. The war photographer Don McCullin documented some of the homeless people and meths drinkers who lived there in squats and derelict basements.

In the 1980s Shoreditch began attracting younger squatters on the dole, up-and-coming artists and a more upwardly mobile set. It was cheap and there were plentiful spaces like warehouses and workshops to squat or rent. With the growing wealth of the City and escalating property prices in the early 1990s, Bishopsgate saw a huge redevelopment. The Bangla town restaurants of Brick Lane started to become known for cheap and authentic curries, and gradually the East End began its transformation. Shoreditch became clubbing central in the early 1990s, with its mixed working- and middle-class and multiracial community on the edge of the City. And some things, like the twenty-four-hour Bagel Bakery, simply haven't changed.

Peter, a sound engineer who has lived in London since the early 1990s, talked about what he has observed. 'We were saying how things have changed over the years around Oxford Street and uptown, and one of my friends who many, many years ago was working in the centre of town as a street trader was saying that there used to be tons of street traders. When the IRA bombs started they all got cleared off by the authorities.

'He met one of the guys who used to walk round Leicester Square. You probably remember him, he used to walk round with big sandwich boards that said "don't eat eggs or protein, it'll lead to sin", it'll lead to having sex, basically. The tourists used to love him. He had a little pamphlet. Eddie saw him in this café and couldn't resist saying, "How's it going, mate?" And he said, "Oh, pretty good, sold like, fifty pamphlets today, that's two hundred quid." And it was just a scam, he wasn't really religious! It was literally his act. There's lots of people like that. He had a book, and that's what he made his money on. He printed it and he sold it for like, five quid a pop. The tourists would pay him because they thought he was a genuinely religious nutter and just wanted to interact with him.

'There's been rises and changes in the streets. Around Waterloo there used to be the homeless city, the cardboard city, where the IMAX [cinema] is now. There used to be hundreds of people living in ... and then that all got cleared out, didn't it? And then we had the economic boom of the nineties. Now we've started to see recently, I've noticed, 'cause I'm there walking through town every day, I've noticed more and more people on the streets.'

In few cities do the population and character of the streets change so quickly as in central London. Architecturally, the historic exists alongside the new, as in the square mile of the City of London, where the massive height of skyscrapers vies with the ancient glory of churches designed by Wren and Hawksmoor. Areas and individual streets go up and down, but the general tendency is to increased affluence and gentrification, as investors realise the potential of valuable real estate.

And the population changes too. Today, as in Mayhew's day, 'once an area "improved" ... its original residents were priced out, and the problem was simply moved elsewhere'. In his era, though, without inexpensive public transport, workers were forced to live within walking distance of 'their bread'; if labourers were not near their work, they were not in work. Now, too, most of the people working in central London have been priced out, but they are forced to move away and travel in – at considerable expense, both in time and money.

2

Which Londoners?

According to the 1861 census, the population of inner London was 2,808,494. In 2011 it was 3,231,901 – not such a great difference. The enormous population growth (the estimate for Greater London's population in 2021 is over 9 million) has taken place entirely in the outer boroughs. Central London is vibrant, yes, but few can afford to live there.

The 1841 census was the first to record people's birthplace, as well as their name, age, sex and occupation. In 1851, over 38 per cent of Londoners were born somewhere else. At 109,000, the Irish, escaping the Great Famine of 1846–9, made up the single largest immigrant group, with 26,000 from the rest of the world. These included refugees from France, Spain, Italy and Germany, many of whom had been forced to flee after the revolutions of 1830 and 1848, and smaller groups of sailors from Africa, China and India. There was also a large and thriving Jewish community.

There are, however, few mentions of non-English people in Mayhew. A few Italians, one American, some Scots, one born in Jamaica but who counted himself English, and mostly Irish. Also Jews, mostly in the East End. And mention of 'Hindoo' preachers.

Astonishingly, according to the 2011 census, at 37 per cent the percentage of people in London born outside the UK is almost the same as in 1851 (although in 2011 we are speaking about

Greater London). The percentage is however made up of different nationalities.

In our time, Greater London is home to an amazing 270 nationalities, with 300 languages. Modern London not only draws tourists from all over the world, but people who come to study, and to work, live, marry, and bring up their families. And some of them end up working or living on the streets; I did not have to make an effort to interview people of a variety of nationalities.

London is rightly proud of its multiculturalism. Even forty years ago, my children's inner-city school had twenty-seven nationalities. Now, I imagine it is more. Everywhere we go, on the tube, in the street, we hear a splendid medley of languages, sometimes ones that I can't even identify. A film at the Venezuelan embassy in Fitzrovia brings out the South American population; a concert at the Hellenic Centre in Marylebone the Greeks; and Indians flock to the Nehru Centre for exhibitions of Indian dance. As do we all, grateful for such a rich supply of cultural activity from all corners of the world. Despite a shameful past, and some hidden prejudice, marriage between people of different nationalities and ethnicities is now standard, taken for granted.

Racism

Even so, prejudice is still to be found. I recently overheard an American call Westminster Bridge 'the Gypsy bridge', a reference to the number of Roma people, mainly from Romania, who were congregating there at the time. In a sense, the Roma are the absent people in this book. There are large numbers of Roma people in London, many homeless. People often referred to them – mainly in derogatory terms – and I have failed to present their voices. This is largely because they were unwilling to engage, either with me or with any of the services supporting homeless people. But there is no doubt that they are the main targets of racism in the capital. A Bulgarian woman selling the *Big Issue* said, 'Many people are nice.' Some, when new to her, are not. 'They think I am Gypsy,' she said, running her hands down her skirt. 'I look Romanian. They are scared of me.'

One elderly man didn't specify, but he spoke for many British rough sleepers when he expressed his resentment. 'The trouble is too many immigrants coming into this country and it's spilling out at the edges. You've got more foreign nationals on the streets than there ever have been. And I don't know the conditions, don't know how it is, but it seems a bit crazy that there are more of them than there used to be. You can hardly find any British people on the streets . . . I mean down the Strand there's one beggar every ten feet.'

A man of Kenyan origin wondered about his lack of success in portrait painting. Was he too young, did he just not have the right face – or for some people could it be that he was black? But in general, even when asked directly, few of the people we interviewed reported any racism. Viorica, a Romanian cleaner in her fifties, worked for a while in Italy. She found people there very racist. 'But here, I never meet racist people. No. When I read something about racists here, I can't believe it, because I never meet the person like that. Never.'

Anthony, a Jamaican caricaturist working in Trafalgar Square, spoke of how attitudes have changed.

'I've always lived in north London. You know Kensal Rise? I was brought up there. We first moved to Paddington when we came to this country. Then my mum and dad bought a house in Kensal Rise. And we were about the third black people up there, on our street. No, it wasn't a problem for me, because I was a kid, I had my mates. It didn't really affect me, because I was a child. But when I grew up, I realised that, er, because where I lived, there were a lot of Cockneys living there, cab drivers from the East End, you know, they were the indigenous people in Kensal Rise. They've all gone. They didn't die out. They moved. Because black people moved in, they moved out. Because they didn't want to live next door to a black person.

'When we came to England, there used to be signs which said no blacks, no Irish, no dogs. That was the kind of environment that I grew up in. My dad used to work for Rootes, the car company, which was in Ladbroke Grove. And every evening he would have to run home from work because of the Teddy Boys. Teddy Boys and rockers – they used to beat up black people. Then, in Ladbroke Grove, they fought back and from then it subsided: the violence between black people and whites.

'Now through the years, Kensal Rise has changed immensely. because all the Cockneys – you know the programme *EastEnders*? It was predominantly about East Enders. Now, it's completely bloody different – you've got all sorts in *EastEnders*. The Cockneys – they've all gone. Leave it to the immigrants, leave it to the foreigners – I've heard them say that.

'Even at school we had racism. Once you stood up to that person and beat him up, he's your friend for life. That was the situation. So nowadays I don't come across racism. The racism I come across now is from these Eastern Europeans that come over here. They think the – their attitude towards us now is different from the indigenous English people. They're used to us. But the Eastern Europeans aren't used to us, and they're fucking, they've got an attitude towards us, and that's a fact.

'The future? For myself? Well, I haven't got much time, my time's going to come up soon, but I hope the next generation will have a better time. The Windrush situation – what a bloody farce that is. They asked us to come and build the motherfucking country here, then they pull that card on us about, you know. There's people been here for fifty years, forty years, and they want to deport 'em. What kind of situation is that? They wouldn't do that to white people.

'They wouldn't fucking chase white people, but they do it to black people, that shows that the attitude of this country is racist. It's down on black people. Look at South Africa – how the fuck can you have eight per cent of the people, white people, in Africa, owning all the fucking land. It's ridiculous. And white people don't seem to understand that it is fucking taking a liberty with black people. The ones in power. The ones on the street understand because they suffer just like us, but the ones in power do not seem to grasp the fact that what they're doing to black people is not right. You see what I'm saying?'

Susie, a gardener in Regent's Park, told me she had not had negative experiences. '[As] a woman who is of … mixed race, I've been in London like over ten years all in all. I grew up in the countryside, in Norfolk, and it was OK, but I know that in some parts of the countryside there's not a lot of diversity, and people can be quite racist. But in London, even though there is some racism, there's more of an awareness of people who have their privilege as white people and they help to raise that around the community, if that makes sense?'

But racism shows itself in many less obvious ways. There is no doubt that a large proportion of low-paid jobs are done by people of BAME background. And the attitude is institutionalised. McGinlay, also of mixed race, spoke of her time in care. 'Basically I said to them I wasn't coping with being in foster care. From fourteen to sixteen, they've moved me around in four different foster homes, none of which was mixed race. They were either black families or white families and no one asked me how I was feeling or how I was coping. And at that age, between fourteen and sixteen, my hormones were raging because puberty has kicked in, I'm trying to get my head around GCSEs, I'm already standing out like a sore thumb 'cos I'm the only child in my class who's in foster care, and back in the nineties that particular school that I went to didn't have a school uniform, so if you wasn't in the latest gear you was a target for bullying as well.

'You know what, when I was younger, I used to hear these old-timers like from different communities talk about, like, institutionalised racism and I thought errm, nah, maybe they're just a little bit bitter because their parents or their grandparents has been ranting on about the old days of slavery and what have you. Let's fast forward to 2019, I still question how I was able to go through so many care systems through my teens and my adulthood and yeah, there was no emotional support or support surrounding my needs and I do believe there's an element of institutionalised racism involved.' She laughs nervously. 'There was times when I try and assert myself and they'd be like, Oh, she's demanding, she's challenging, she's rude, she's difficult to cope with. It's like, No, I'm freaking out here because I'm having a panic attack.'

'Me no go school'

It is surprising how many people in London and trying to make a living have not the most basic language tools to do it. An Eastern European *Big Issue* seller understands 'Have you got change?' but either can't or won't understand, 'You're here early. What time did you start?' or, perhaps more problematically, 'Where do you come from?' An Italian market stallholder selling a few fish doesn't understand 'Where do you get the fish from?' He didn't even react to 'Billingsgate?', so presumably he did not get it from there. And attempts to engage with people begging often reveal a complete lack of English, which makes it hard to offer help.

Some people I met, both English and of other nationalities, are illiterate. One stallholder at Ridley Road Market was from the UK and in his seventies. He said he'd picked up bits and pieces over the years, but when he went to the post office to fill in a form, he had to pretend he'd forgotten his reading glasses. On a second visit to his stall, remembering that he had literacy problems, I read out the consent form. As soon as I mentioned personal details and the internet, he absolutely refused to sign it or to go any further. So did a key cutter, who came from elsewhere but had some spoken English. Again, trying to read out the consent form led to failure. He didn't want to know.

Livia, from Romania, sells the *Big Issue*. At the mention of £10, her face lit up. 'Ten pounds? That's real money!' I had to read out the consent form. She could sign her name but could scarcely write or read. Both before and after her interview, she expressed a desperate wish not to be on TV. Running her hand over her *Big Issue* tabard, she repeated, 'Not TV, not TV.' Her English was limited; sometimes she misunderstood questions. Against a background of loud traffic from Tottenham Court Road, I asked her at what age she had left school. 'Me no go school, me never go school.'

'You can't read and write?'

'No. Like this' – she pointed at some capital letters – 'yes, but the other letters no.'

Those who had come out of the care system often revealed a lack of education. A former soldier told me, 'We wasn't educated. I wasn't educated. I never went to school. I was brought up in children's homes, you know.'

Race is a tall lanky man in his sixties. Sitting in his usual spot in Regent Street, he said, 'Well, I never had any skills, since I left school in 1971. I had fifteen jobs in two years. Couldn't keep a job down. I was in a bakery for four years, worked in there '75 to '79, and then in 1991 the retina slipped out me eyes, so I had operations, then I was disabled, partially sighted. So I never picked up no skills . . .

'No, I had no training or anything. The only thing I was any good at was smiling, and I had to give that out. Oh yeah, and a memory for dates. Dates and colours. Always put dates with colours. Tuesday is grey, always a grey colour, silver grey. February is red and nineteen is dark, a dark colour. So I've always put them together. I suppose it was from as a kid when they used to show us the date with colours. Tuesday was grey, Wednesdays were black and I remember them, so I kept those colours in my head. Always days with colours. And Sundays is green. Bright green.'

A black cab driver blamed his lack of success on a poor level of education. He was the archetypal cabbie – couldn't stop talking from the moment we got into the cab till the end of the journey. 'Bin doing it about seven years, before that, commercial vans.' He complained so much about traffic, roadworks and other drivers that I asked him whether he liked the job.

'I hate it. It's me own fault, I should've got educated. I was one of fourteen, and me dad died when I was ten, so me mum had to cope with all of us. My older brothers looked after us, but they were no kind of role models. We weren't brought up. None of us went to school, well I left when I was about fourteen. Fair enough if you're foreign and you've got no education, but no excuse if you're British. We was animals. One brother went to prison – he burnt a house down – and another burgled the house next door. "Well," he said, "they left the door open." We wasn't brought up to think that thieving was wrong. But if we questioned anything at home, we got the belt. We needed it – it was all we understood.'

Lack of education crops up again and again in the stories of people's lives, resulting not only in a lack of success but a lack of self-esteem. Denis, formerly homeless, is now a case worker. 'I was born in Bow. Went to school all over the country. I went to boarding school 'cause I had dyslexia, so they thought I was a dunce and plus I came from a broken-down family. Mad upbringing. I went to different boarding schools. I got chucked out of one of them.'

Ben, a van driver and car boot seller, is in his thirties: 'When I was young, I was a bit of a bad boy, didn't stick it at school, so didn't get any qualifications, I didn't do my exams, so I can't go and work in an office or do any kinda proper job or make decent money, so it's always been a struggle. But I'm trying my hardest to build a life.

'In five years' time? That's a bit of a hard question. Because as I said I've no qualifications. I've been told all my life that I'm thick and stupid, you know, because I was bad. Nowadays if you're bad and frustrated, you've got ADHD. When I was younger, you were stupid. ADHD didn't exist, autism didn't exist, it was only that you were stupid. You were bad, you know, so I been told that all my life, so it's really been drummed into me.'

3

The world outside

Despite the unreliable British climate, a lot of London's life goes on out of doors. Over recent years, more and more cafés have added outside tables, giving some areas an almost Parisian feel. Even in winter, a few hardy souls – or, since the 2007 ban on smoking in all enclosed public spaces, those with a need for a smoke – can be found drinking their coffees or breakfasting outside. Some more sophisticated restaurants have outside heaters to take off the chill.

Some people treat the street as their office. Walking down the road, leaning against a tree or a lamp post, working at café tables, conducting business, even dictating letters on their phones, laptops and other devices. Never off-duty. Sometimes we hear a snatch of a conversation, get a glimpse of someone's business or personal life – 'I told her I didn't want to come back.'

Sometimes the division between inside and outside is almost porous. While their main job is not outside, cleaners, hotel door-keepers, security personnel spend time out of doors sweeping up, polishing brass, watching out.

Those doing building and odd jobs often use the pavement for tasks inconvenient to perform inside. One man lay on the ground as he worked inside a fridge. Elsewhere a man sat at a little port-able table on the pavement on which he did metalwork with a well-compartmentalised box of equipment beside him. And, to top it, I saw two men outside an imposing column-fronted house manoeuvring a door to continue sawing. They had a table and a little pergola-shaped cover over a variety of tools. 'Yes,' one told me, 'we do often do this. It's more convenient and there's more room.' The fact that so much work is being done outside is also a reflection of the high cost of workshops and offices in central London.

Parks

London is a city of squares, gardens and parks, free and open to the public all the year round: it's one of the greenest cities in the world. Indeed, you can walk through central London by way of its parks from Notting Hill in the west to Whitehall and the river. And there are only a few streets to cross to reach Regent's Park to the north. The five Royal Parks in central London – St James's Park, Hyde Park, Kensington Gardens, Green Park and Regent's Park – provide over 1000 acres of green space. And, beyond them are other substantial parks like Victoria Park, which opened in the East End in 1845, Holland Park in Kensington, and Hampstead Heath in Camden, which, at 790 acres, is London's largest ancient parkland, and was first mentioned historically in AD 974.

The parks are full, especially on summer weekends, as Londoners revel in their opportunities for picnics, walking, boating, jogging and sports activities, as well as organised events from the Open Air Theatre and jazz concerts to local stargazing and bird-watching groups.

But we take for granted the care that is needed to maintain them. The people who work there – maintenance people, gardeners and deckchair attendants – are, like so many people who provide our comfort, largely invisible.

Susie is thirty-five, a tall young woman with very long dark hair, working in the gardens of Regent's Park. I chatted to her one day, and agreed to return the following day with my recorder. A sunny October morning. I asked if she could spare ten minutes.

Susie looked down the path. 'If my boss comes, I'll have to say goodbye.' The gardeners work for ID Verde, a landscaping and grounds maintenance service provider contracted to the Royal Parks. Susie is an apprentice, working forty hours a week on a permanent contract, with pension, holiday and statutory sick pay.

'I've been here about a month. I was doing office admin for about ten years, and decided I wanted to move outside and do horticulture and then started doing it, so that's why the apprentice programme. The programme is about three years, and I get a qualification at the end and all training is paid for and there's also an option to do an RHS course in the third year, which would be excellent. I just thought em I didn't like office work, it's mentally strenuous and stressful, and I felt I would be . . . feel better for working in an out-side environment. And also I want to put my hands in and make the environment better, and the parks, they're really important, green spaces, and a lot of people say how they like what we do.'

What she likes about it is 'literally getting your hands dirty, learning about the plants and how different they are and what each plant is used for in a design perspective. I like talking to people I've just met. It's very social as well. I like the sun on my skin' – she rubs her face – 'getting some Vitamin D, and the general wellbeing that is created through gardening. I don't feel stressed. My body can get stressed physically, but my psyche is a lot better and that, and I'm very happy now.

'I suppose in the summer, when we do lots of weeding, that can get a bit strenuous on your hands. I thought I would be a bit scared, a bit worried about early mornings: we start at seven in the morning. I get up at five but I actually quite enjoy it. It's so peaceful in the morning. I find it's good to work as well. I cycle in from north-west London, in Kilburn. It takes me about twenty-five minutes. I work seven till three thirty.'

She likes working with others. 'Oh yes, yes. There's a lot of dif-ferent characters here, um, it's predominantly male, there's a few women, but we all get along, and there's no aggravation from what I've seen towards anyone. The men are really – I was a bit appre-hensive to be honest, to work in a male-dominated environment, but they appear to be posh. Everyone seems really nice. There's one apprentice per park, so it's a three-year apprenticeship, and there are two other apprentices in Regent's Park, I think. But the rest of the people are either agency staff or employed full time. I'll be in this park for three years.

'Because it's an apprentice programme, I get paid the apprentice-ship wage for my age, which is £8.21. That's set by the government. Yeah, just enough for my rent and my food and things. I live with my partner so it's manageable. It's not much, no, but that's the government. My goal is to fully qualify, to become a professional gardener, either create my own business so I can garden in private houses, private residences, or I'd like to work at an RHS garden, because they're really lovely.

'In the course you learn about different aspects of gardening and the business study side of things, so I'm looking forward to learning about that. And permaculture. I really like the idea of permaculture and there's quite a few people on my course who have the same ideas as well about what they want to do in the future, so maybe we could collaborate together to make one. If we stay in London. My partner and I are thinking about moving, probably after four years' time. Can't buy a house in London, unless you have a stable ... Yeah, I do love London. It's a great place, there's a lot here. But it's hard. Just the pace of it, too much traffic. Ideally, everyone would cycle everywhere in suburban areas, but that's not likely to happen. But that would be my ideal. All the speed limits would go down to 20 mph everywhere – it's quite scary on a bike.'

In answer to my question: 'Yes, we're on a rota. Told what to do. We're clearing beds at the moment.'

Getting around

London is a city where people walk. In nothing like the numbers before the age of mass public transport, but still exceptional com-pared with most major cities of the world. Narrow streets and the difficulties of parking contribute to making walking a more efficient and pleasurable way to get around. And the distances in central London, between areas of very different nature and use, are surprisingly small.

In a congested city like this, cycling has always been a speedy and flexible option and is growing in popularity. The Santander bikes, which anyone can hire from a number of docking stations, were introduced in 2010, and more recent additions include electrically controlled lime-green bikes and Uber red ones, which can be picked up and dropped off anywhere with the injection of a pound coin. Bikes are increasingly used for deliveries too, even by giant international couriers such as Fedex and DHL.

However, cycling has always been a dangerous activity, with a number of fatalities each year, and riders' behaviour is variable; cyclists sometimes ride on pavements, go the wrong way down one-way streets or cross red lights. For greater ease and safety, Transport for London (TfL) has introduced a number of cycleways (formerly called 'superhighways') and are planning a further 450 km of new routes by 2024.

And however much we complain, this is a city with excellent public transport, with a large network of tubes and buses run by TfL and a variety of other companies. Some buses run all night, and in 2016 night tubes were introduced on some Underground lines.

Stations

In the Victorian period, competing railway companies built a number of railway stations in London, from London Bridge in 1836 to Paddington in 1899. By Mayhew's time, the railways were fully operational and making a considerable difference to the life and work of London. Thousands travelled into the city by train; goods were being brought in, changing the pattern of buying. Surprisingly, the only mention of stations that I found in Mayhew was of newspapers being sold in railway stations. As he says, stations aren't really the streets, but they do act as a kind of halfway house.

Since his day all the stations have undergone substantial redevelopment, but many retain original architectural features including impressive roof spans. Now, too, both Underground and mainline stations are a hub for all sorts of money-making activities. From chains of shops to tiny cubbyholes selling sweets and chocolate, from flower sellers to buskers, the point of departure or arrival provides a potential source of income. Commuters, travellers and tourists come through in great numbers and, in the case of mainline stations, often spend some time there. Main-line stations such as Euston and Victoria have a full range of shops and cafés, to suit people who often have time to wait. And on the London trains themselves, both Underground and overground, travellers provide a captive audience for the plaintive stories – true or otherwise – of people asking for money.

The nature and quality of tube station shops, whether inside or outside, vary with their local population, as do their prices. Some in poorer areas with scruffy stations have little to offer, whereas smarter stations in business districts offer a range of eateries and coffee shops. Holborn, a station located on a very busy junction, and serving a lot of office workers, has just a few individual stalls outside, including some selling flowers and fruit. Downstairs at Old Street, another busy city station, there are a number of stalls, mostly for food and drink, but as the area was being renovated at the time of my visit, some, including a bookshop, were shut. Appropriately, Leicester Square, in theatreland, has a cut-price ticket stall and, more unexpectedly, a little shop selling cup cakes – a very pretty display, but rarely a customer in sight.

At Camden, there is no separation between the station and Camden Lock Market on its doorstep, a mecca for young tourists from all over the world and one of the top-rated destinations in London. Selling clothes of all kinds – Eastern, vintage, punk – as well as fruit juice, jewellery and pottery, hundreds of stalls spill out over a wide area.

Marylebone is an old-fashioned, rather charming station, dating from 1899, the last of London's main-line termini to be built, and one of the smallest. Announcements over the loudspeaker are surprisingly given in languages which include Arabic and Chinese, for the many visitors who are heading for the Bicester Village shops further up the line.

Along with the usual station shops, it has a number of other features, such an old weighing machine, a coffee cup recycling service, and a shoeshine service with a notice of the prices:

Shoe Shine Express
Premium economy – £5.99
Business class – £6.99
New shoelaces (including fitting) – £3.99
Extra for knee-high boots

In front of a platform bearing two high-backed leather chairs with straps rather reminiscent of the electric chair, is a young Asian man, standing alone, staring into space, apart from the hurly-burly of the station.

John's name was touted to me as the best watch repairer in London. Unusually, he is neither employed nor a franchisee, but a lone operator, and works out of what he calls 'a cupboard' in the Underground station at Piccadilly Circus. A slightly bent, elderly man with a very mobile face, he talks in a strong London accent, in a manner alternately confiding and with an expression which says, 'should I be telling you this?' Leaving his new assistant in charge, John takes me to Costa for a cup of tea. 'You haven't even got a watch on. You're losing your street cred.' He starts to tell me his story and, wanting to save it for the recording, I say, 'Don't say anything.' 'What do you mean, don't say anything? I'll say what I bloody well like!' The interview is interspersed with long pauses, as he thinks about what to say.

'I've been a watch repairer here in Piccadilly Circus for twenty-five years and maybe a consequence of that . . . is the broad range of people you'll see in Piccadilly Circus from everywhere in the world. That's the best part of down here, it's seeing all the people. Not a love of watches. Fixing watches is just a job, maybe cynical about watches. Truly, the best part of it is seeing people. But now, I'm pulling out. I'm old, sixty-seven, not long left. Suddenly erm, tumours are appearing in me and it's time to diminish, so I'm coming in one day a week and young Joel up here, he's having a go.

'Yeah, yeah, I do mind. Every day I come in I have a laugh, and I miss that. I miss the social. I don't miss the watches at all. Why did I come into it? I started at Garrard, the Crown Jewellers up in Regent Street, in 1968 so I was sixteen then. Everything's interesting when you're sixteen, isn't it? Now, maybe I've got so much work because there's no watch repairers here. Training? Yeah, I was an apprentice up in Garrard's for three or four years, I think, and then I've been in the watch business ever since. Even fixing clocks on London Underground.

'I've been active all my life collectively, an activist, socialist, organising the trade union sector of workplaces, involved in all sorts of things. Raised in Highbury, north London, look at how Highbury is now. Now, live in Dartford, south-east London.'

I ask if it's his own business.

'You put it rather grandly. It's a cupboard,' he says with a laugh. 'Do I have to pay for it? Very much so. A thousand quid a month? For a cupboard? If I wasn't here, they'd be keeping brooms in it. How much do I make a week?' He laughs again. 'How much do I want to tell yer? I had a till in there. New guys that come in, and they transform the place.' He asks himself a different question. 'How much has it changed? I had a till there, it never worked, and if I closed it, I couldn't open it again so the till stayed open. I only took cash, didn't take cards. Isn't that the envy of every business in the world? Maybe. Things have changed. I see myself now.' Pause. 'Do you know who you are? No, you don't. Neither does anyone else know who they are. I kinda get to know who I am when I see someone else operating my business. It gave me an insight into who I was. He's been there a year now.' Pause.

'All that business had to do was feed me. Joel's come in and I'm sure with youth and enthusiasm he thinks he can operate a much-improved business than what he's come into. For his father, who's a watchmaker as well. It only had to feed me before. Prices have gone up and I didn't have the business enthusiasm, the petty bourgeois . . . ' Another laugh. 'I didn't have that drive, so maybe twenty per cent of people I would charge nothing at all. It was a small job, why was it worth charging a pound or something? Suddenly I see how they think they can do things better. That sounds pompous, dunnit?

'What am I going to do? I'm doing something at the moment, actually. Maybe street art? On me house, down in the town I live in. An artist? God, no, I'm just a bloke who's trying to provoke the council.' He laughs mischievously. 'Unionised? A hundred per cent unionised, there's only me! All turn up for the Christmas party!' This time we both laugh.

'But when I started, I didn't think I'd be there beyond six months. I stayed because it picked up and twenty-five years ago, before the days of social networks and everything that goes with it, you're advertising in the Yellow Pages, thirty quid a month, you're getting the postman to deliver leaflets in people's letterboxes round here. Back then I was raising two kids by myself, trying to pay a mortgage. So lucky me, I've been here twenty-five years. Most businesses pack up within a year, don't they? I guess I was a hit, yeah. Otherwise I'd have moved on somewhere else.

'There's a customer come down, whom I've known for ages, and he invited me down to dinner there, and he said you'll need to wear a suit 'n' tie, and I said I haven't got one. He was the ex-secretary of the Carlton Club, a gentlemen's club in Mayfair. The Carlton Club is the spiritual home of the Conservative Party.'

I laugh.

'I thought fuck it, does he know who I am? I've never hidden who I am, I thought I won't be cowed, submissive, I consciously went there with that attitude. I've got to say I thought I'd have a laugh. And I know the guy now – I mean, we'll go out. That's Piccadilly Circus, you'll get people of that sort, like him, nothing special. That's what I'd miss here.

'The last couple of years I've been in the hospital, I need to get out while I'm still capable. I will miss that aspect ... I'm concerned about going away myself, going into the park and feeding the ducks. The end is near if that happens. They can feed themselves!

'I've got a hundred things I want to do. We could make a film about a couple of things here in Piccadilly Circus. Things I could direct you to. Maybe a film would tell you more about me than me sitting here talking to you. I'm conscious about losing a spark. I'm conscious about beating myself up here. Why do I need to do that? I feel like I'm doing that. To you. You're a stranger, for fuck's sakes.'

After the interview, John opens his phone and shows me his street art – paintings on the side of his house, including a huge anti-fascist mural (which, amazingly, was eventually passed by the council), and some of his spray painting on local bridges and walls in protest against Trump's visits, as well as a big black painting of Che Guevara on six-inch white tiles. And his other interests: sewing, collecting cacti. He tells me of his Republican activist parents from Northern Ireland, and how when he was twenty-one, in his first job at Seiko, he and some others occupied the office. He was raised an activist, and still is one. Stories pour out, and it's hard to leave.

He's about to go into hospital for his fourth operation in eighteen months. 'Never been in hospital in me life.' He is very emotional as I leave. 'You've got me looking at meself.' And he gives me a hug.

'The book won't be out for a couple of years.'

'I'll be dead by then.'

London is not an ideal city for driving, parking or keeping a car. In fact, only 39 per cent of inner London households have access to a car, with Islington, at 26 per cent, having the lowest level of car ownership. The congestion charge in inner London – currently covering the area within the London Inner Ring Road – was introduced in 2003, applying to vehicles entering the zone between 7 a.m. and 6 p.m. Mondays to Fridays, the cost at the time of writing being £11.50 per day. The congestion charge has reduced the volume of private cars passing through central London, but it creates traffic jams in streets such as Euston Road which border it. Like the new cycle lanes, it's a source of resentment for professional drivers, self-employed people dependent on their vans or cars for work. It also creates an extra cost for any work being undertaken in the area, which can be a barrier for smaller businesses who have to pass on the cost to their customers.

Air quality

In the mid-1800s, London was probably the most polluted city in England:

> It was noon, and an exquisitely bright and clear spring day; but the view was smudgy and smeared with smoke. Clumps of building and snatches of parks looked through the clouds like dim islands rising out of the sea of smoke. It was impossible to tell where the sky ended and the city began; and as you peered into the thick haze you could, after a time, make out the dusky figures of tall factory chimneys plumed with black smoke; while spires and turrets seemed to hang midway between you and the earth, as if poised in the thick grey air.

When I was growing up, London was renowned for its fog and, indeed, its smog, brought on largely by the burning of fossil fuels. As a result of the Clean Air Act it's a different city now, but it still has a problem with air quality – mostly from traffic, but also as a result of the dust and dirt from continuous demolition and roadworks. Despite the low level of car ownership, air pollution is worst in the inner London boroughs. Parts of Westminster have recorded some of the worst air pollution levels in Europe. Some people were wearing masks in public even before the coronavirus outbreak in 2020. I saw one man begging with a green mask covering his mouth and nose. It is hard to imagine that he attracted much money.

The Mayor of London has made tackling air pollution one of his priorities. It is hoped that an increase in the use of electric cars will improve the air quality in the capital, and April 2019 saw the introduction of the Ultra Low Emission Zone (ULEZ), applying to vehicles which do not meet emissions standards. From 2021, the congestion charge exemption will apply only to pure electric vehicles and from 2025 there will be no discounts for electric vehicles.

And now we come to the factor which most affects the lives of those working or living on the streets. Nearly everyone I interviewed said: 'The worst thing about this life? The weather.'

The weather

Now of all modes of obtaining subsistence, that of street-selling is the most precarious. Continued wet weather deprives those who depend for their bread upon the number of people frequenting the public thoroughfares of all means of living; and it is painful to think of the hundreds belonging to this class in the metropolis who are reduced to starvation by three or four days successive rain ... 'Three wet days,' I was told by a clergyman, who is now engaged in selling stenographic cards in the streets, 'will bring the greater part of 30,000 street-people to the brink of starvation.'

For some occupations, there seems to be no such thing as good weather. A Soho stallholder said, 'If it's raining, it's bad, if the weather is too hot, it's bad, everyone's facing the same issues. If people are selling fresh produce, the last thing you need is ten weeks of burning heat and drought.'

For a street sweeper: 'When it's wintertime and it's raining, it's really hard, really really hard. You have to get out and do the job, because we are paid for that, so we try to clean as much as we can but when it's raining, it's really hard, honestly. And when it's hot, it's less hard, but even when it is hot, even that time is going to be very busy ... full of people drinking, chucking things on the floor.'

And in some jobs if you don't work, you don't get paid. An outdoor charity fundraiser, one of those often referred to by the rather derogatory term of 'chuggers' (charity muggers), told me: 'Never worked in snow, but I've worked when it's been torrential rain – you just have to be prepared, bring an umbrella. And you have to work, so . . . ' She laughs.

'So if you can't work, if you're sick or something, you don't get paid?'

'You have holiday pay, you can ask, take it out of my holiday pay.'

A motorbike delivery driver complained: 'Yeah, weather's tough. Very tough. In the summer, it's way too hot, with all the protective gear, and you're sitting on an engine, basically, it's very hot. And in winter, the cold can be, I mean wind chill, you can take ten degrees off what the normal temperature is. If you're going at seventy miles an hour, the wind chill really brings it down.' Not only difficult, but dangerous. 'Snow is lethal on a motorcycle. Ice is horrible. I do stop, but I've been caught out in snow a few times. Rain, as well. Wet roads slow us down by about fifty per cent – it's quite dangerous in the wet on a motorcycle.'

Even vendors at the top end of the market have to contend with the weather. When interviewed in January, an organic butcher at Broadway Market in Hackney said: 'The biggest challenge is honestly just the weather. I think that's part of the atmosphere and part of the energy of the market as well. It's always great fun trying to hold on to the produce whilst they're flying down the street! The weather is our biggest enemy. Every day, every morning I look at what the weather is going to be like in Hackney to Broadway Market. The closer to Saturday it gets we can make a decision on how much or what type of produce we're going to bring, 'cause the weather impacts that greatly. Obviously the closer to Saturday the more accurate you'd think the weather forecast is, but also the closer it gets to Saturday the less time you've got to make it and pack it. The rain could almost halve what we take ourselves at the weekend.'

But for him, cold weather works. 'This cold snap, the first three weekends that we've had so far in January for us have been great, they've been very busy. The weekend just gone in particular was probably in our top five for the last year and a half, not counting

Christmas weekends. I know at the moment in this month there's a lot of talk of veganism and vegetarians, people maybe eating less meat or cutting it out for a month. The cold weather definitely does bring people out to that comfort food, going home, putting something in the oven, warming up the house. Maybe people have given up their two-week health routine and are being a bit more naughty as well.' He laughs.

It's the rain that is the cause of most complaints. A homeless *Big Issue* seller gave a typical response: 'Worst thing? Rain. Hate rain! Being out in the rain is horrible.'

A bike courier gave a graphic description of how it affects him. 'The worst part is like last week it was raining quite a bit. On those days we need to work and then this week it is going to rain as well. But there's nothing you can do, just bring another change of clothes with you. Even with the waterproofs you get soaked 'cause you sweat inside. It's just impossible. Some days it doesn't stop raining for the whole day. On your break you go to a place to dry yourself, while you're waiting for the next job. Some days I'm working like ten-hour shifts and if you get soaked first job in the morning you're going to be soaked all day long. The whole day. Makes it quite hard.

'And on those kinds of days usually we tend to be short of staff, right, because people will find any excuse not to come to work or that kind of thing.'

It's not just the discomfort. Bad weather affects business. Jeremy, a magician in Covent Garden, has a realistic approach: 'If you get into a period of, you know, two or three weeks when you've got rain pretty much every day, then you've got enforced holiday when you can't make any money. Can't do it when it's raining, people just won't stop. It's interesting, because when the rain stops, that first half hour or so, that first show after the rain, can be really good. I mean people are happy to be able to walk around and not be trapped inside. So rain is not necessarily the enemy for a busker, as long as it doesn't last too long. An hour or two won't necessarily ruin the day. But if you've got rain all day then you know, just go home.'

For Luke, a street poet, rain makes work impossible. He has to take shelter. As we spoke, a few drops of rain fell, and he had to protect his typewriter. Busking can be hard too. Michael worries about his amp, and a busker setting up on Regent Street one March afternoon talked about the previous day, when it rained for the whole day. 'No, couldn't work. I'd have been drownded. Blown up, actually, because this [his guitar] is electric.'

A building manager is only worried about his pocket: 'If it rains after, say, noon, I 'ave to pay 'em half a day's work.' And some people are not bothered at all. A woman at a car boot sale stood in the rain in a zipped-up parka with a hood, in the middle of the car park, a small tarpaulin with a few items at her feet. 'I've just driven twenty-three miles to come and deliver a birthday card, so I thought I'd come and chance my arm. I knew it was going to rain. It's only rain. Won't do us any harm. We're human beings, and rather timid.'

A bulky middle-aged scaffolder, holding the ropes and pulling planks up to the top, was also philosophical. 'Rain? I don't mind it. I'm not made of sugar. There's plenty of me.'

It's not just wet weather, but the cold. You can see security men stamping their feet to keep the circulation going. And everyone has their layers on. In late November a fruiterer told me: 'Got me long johns on. Will have 'em on till March.' So has Susie in Regent's Park. And so, under his smart uniform, has Daniel, the doorman at the five-star Langham Hotel.

'Get my thermals on, get my stockings and suspenders,' he says with a laugh, 'and whatever else I put on ... but, er, yeah, put everything on when it's cold outside. All my kit on. When I'm on twelve to twelve, when I get home I just go straight to bed. You're that tired and when it's really cold, you're that cold, all your thermals, you leave them on and get into bed and it'll be an hour before you start feeling warm. When it's really cold, when it's minus ten, minus twelve, and you finish at one o'clock in the morning, that's tough.'

Buskers have to find ways of keeping their hands warm. 'With the busking there are places where we play where we can find shelter but we tend to just stop. If it's really cold I do an hour and then someone else will take over and then I just go to Starbucks, sit down, warm up. Sometimes I buy these handwarmers from Boots. You just crack it open and it keeps your hands warm for a few hours. They're really good. Some people use fingerless gloves but I can't seem to get a grip with the guitar.'

A young scaffolder, hauling on a rope, a fag hanging from his mouth. The ladder descends from the roof. 'Cold? You get used to it. You just keep working. Mind your head, darling.'

Even in this temperate climate, heat can also be a problem. I talked to a few people during a June heatwave. A thin bearded man, fortyish, sitting cross-legged on the pavement, was begging and reading a newspaper outside Tesco on Mortimer Street. On one of the hottest days of the year he was in full sun, trying to cover his head with his sweatshirt. Not surprisingly, he told me he'd fallen ill the previous day. 'I was looking for somewhere to sleep and started vomiting. One of the men on the building site asked if I wanted the medics, and it turned out I had heatstroke.'

On the same morning a bulky man unhappily squeezed into a dark uniform was riding a cleaning machine across the pavement of a private square. His cropped head was sweaty and his English basic. 'Yes, hot. Yes, need hat!' And Barry, whom I met later in his closed-in street cleaning machine in Covent Garden: 'Very, very, very, very hot.'

Others, of course, relish the heat. On a day forecast to be the hottest ever in England (39 degrees), two bare-chested tree surgeons were working inside the garden of Bedford Square, firing a catapult up into a giant tree, trying to gain purchase to remove something problematic (I didn't gather what). They were not from the council but a private company which happens to have the Bedford estate contract.

'Nice contract!' I commented.

'Yes, nice weather too!'

On the same day, there were complaints from a fruiterer, shaking his head – 'Too hot.' One of his colleagues said, 'Soon be winter, darling.'

Even Hossain, the shoe shiner, protected as he is in Marylebone station, feels the effect of the weather. 'Sometimes it's raining, snowing, we don't get any customer.' But winter is good, probably because his customers are wearing proper shoes rather than sandals. Strangely, the selling of flowers flourishes in bad weather. Apparently, people want to cheer themselves up.

Roofless

But of course it's those who are sleeping rough who suffer most. And when winter shelters close, the cold of the streets can be all the more painful. A man running a coffee stall told me about his journey into work: 'I come through Finsbury Park when I come down to here now. Under the station, the railway bridge. And the mess there, and they keep trying to . . . they had a guy on the accordion this morning. Another one was asleep under his duvet. And it's absolutely freezing and the water from the rain is still dripping down and you think, how do these people . . . you know, in this cold weather?'

Rough sleepers have developed various ploys to cope with the cold: sleeping over a hot air vent is a favourite. One man talked of walking the streets all night to keep himself warm, catching a bit of sleep by day in a library, if they would have him. Some people spend nights on tubes or buses. It's safer, especially for women. 'For £4 you can go round and round and some drivers don't chuck you off.'

Unseasonal weather can catch you out. In May I talked to Freddie, sitting on the ground near Trafalgar Square, his back against a wall, with a little cloth in front of him on which were a couple of pairs of shoes and a few other bits and pieces for sale. Freddie is thirty-four. 'As long as I've got a roof over my head, I don't care. It's too cold out here. I was out on Christmas Day, nice people come round and give us presents and that but it was freezing. This time of year, you wouldn't think it would be that cold and I read the paper today, and they say it's going to be minus three. Snow could fall. Snow could fall? In May?'

'The worst thing?' asks one long-term rough sleeper. 'I don't know, I've never found anything worse. It's really cold at night, when you can't get warm. Once my feet were so frozen, last year, that they kept me awake all night, the pain was awful. So this time I make sure I've got two sleeping bags.'

Mayhew writes about homeless children running about barefoot. That's not something we see now, except for one girl whose shoes had been stolen. She said she was nineteen, but looked a good five years younger: a small girl sitting on the ground at the bottom of Charing Cross Road, in front of her the mandatory styrofoam cup and cardboard inscribed with a message about needing money for a hostel. Scratches on her nose. And curled-up tiny bare toes. 'Someone stole me shoes,' she says. I have no idea if her story was true or not, but the bare feet on the first coldish day of the autumn moved me to give her some money.

'I've got a self-clean body'

Many of those working outside – security staff, stallholders, chuggers – have to stand. All day. Inside some construction sites can be seen a random office chair or a makeshift bench to relieve aching legs, and in general, large sites have Portakabins to relieve other needs. But, apart from the sites of big developments and highway maintenance, there are few public conveniences, and workers and homeless people are dependent for 'comfort breaks' on kindly publicans, café owners or shopkeepers who will let them come in and use the facilities. Not surprisingly, in areas where homeless people congregate, like the back streets near St Giles-in-the-Fields, north of Seven Dials, and in the south-west corner of Cavendish Square behind Oxford Street, there's a smell of urine.

Race has come to terms with the problem: 'Toilet, washing? I'm lucky in that respect. I've got my tent, I always make sure I don't need to go in the night and if I do there's a bush there, just for a penny. Anything more, I – er – I go to Charing Cross station, there's a free toilet there, so it's good. Wash – I don't need to panic too much, because I've got a self-clean body, I don't give off odour. I don't have to worry about that too much. It's quite helpful. I don't stink or anything. I'm good.'

In the fresh air

There is much disinformation about people 'choosing' to live on the streets. A former director of an East End charity, who had worked for decades with homeless people, told me he had only ever met two who had really made a free choice to live on the streets. Otherwise, the 'choices' are not ones we would wish to make. Between the streets and an abusive home. Those who 'choose' to live on the streets rather than in a hostel often have good reasons, when their experience, or that of their companions, is that hostels can be dangerous places, where their few possessions are stolen, or they are threatened by those addicted to alcohol or drugs.

However, for those not living on the streets but working there, some do indeed make it their choice, and have found a contented life they have not previously experienced, either taking up a different activity or taking an existing activity out to the streets. It was a commonplace in our interviews to hear of the pleasure of working outside – 'I couldn't work in an office.' Many have had previous indoor jobs in a hotel or kitchen.

Safiya is a florist, working out of a stand-alone permanent stall in Tottenham Court Road.

'I love being outside. I've worked in shops as well but I love being outside, watching the world go by. I'm thirty, so I've done it for about fifteen years. No, I didn't ever imagine doing it. My dad was a butcher, and he used to have a shop in Hackney Market and my brother used to go and help. I never imagined myself working on a stall, to be honest, but I wouldn't change it. I could never go and sit in an office now. I like that every day is different, you get to watch the world go past. What else do I like about it? I mean, just standing here now anything could happen. Anything is possible. That's what I like about it.'

Dave, selling printers' blocks in Piccadilly Market, in the forecourt of St James's Church, says: 'The best thing? Bein' out in the fresh air. I've always worked in the fresh air, even when I was in Libya I was always outside. So to think I would be in like an office or shop for six, seven hours a day – I just couldn't do it. I mean some people, my friends, my mates say you're mad, it's pouring down with rain, why don't you go 'ome, but it just makes you feel better, bein' out in the open.'

A man working for Thames Water agrees. 'Yeah, I prefer to be outside than sitting in the office all day long. Doing the same day in day out. I prefer it out here doing stuff. Keep in the fresh air, keeps your mind going a little bit better. Everything's different every day, so it's better than rocking up to the office, doing the same things, sitting in the same chair.'

Zack, a young man outside Westminster Abbey handing out leaflets for a bus company: 'I love going outdoors, don't like really staying at home because I like to socialise with people, usually with strangers at times, just like getting to know people. That's one of the things. I mean I was brought up in a very small social circle, so I've always wanted to go out and see more of the world. And so I think when you go outside, you get a great opportunity to interact with other cultures, other people. And also get to see the life in the city. It makes you feel more alive.'

4

'People make mess'

Hassene is an Algerian street sweeper. Just after Christmas the roads are quiet; few people are back at work, and his work is easier. I commented on how quiet it was.

'Yes, few people. People make mess.' And people like him have to clean it up.

Hassene is a big man with a ruddy face, a smallish beard and a gentle voice. We pass each other often and have been trying to find a time to talk for some weeks. The first time I asked, he said: 'Oh, not now. Look at my eyes. See how tired I am. We do it next week. Yes mornings. I only work mornings, six till two. Yes, an early start, but we get used to it.' He has his own perspective on the weather. 'Rain? I wish it would; it would clear away all of this.'

We finally find a time when he's free. Hassene parks his cleaning trolley, shovel and brush, and we sit on a doorstep in a quiet residential street near Oxford Circus, just along from the doorway where he habitually sits during his breaks, checking his phone. Normally, when I pass, he says, barely looking up and without a breath: 'Goodmorninghowareyou?'

'My name is El Hassene Yettou. I've been living in this country about sixteen years, so I feel like a Londoner now. I work as a street cleaner. I've been doing that job for almost five, four and a half years, something like that, and I'm happy to do that. To be honest, I've been doing many jobs; I was working in the hotel for eight years, and as soon as I started working with this one, I was working with the agency, I feel much better, honestly. The reason I chose this is peace of mind. No pressure. I've worked in a hotel, I know what pressure is – do this, come here, do that. I have no one I'm working for.

'Lonely? No, I have a supervisor, support, and sometimes in our breaks we talk. And I have a phone. I like the peace of mind. And I like to do cleaning. I think it's something special to do for the community here. Cleaning is something very special, honestly. I like it. I'm a cleaner, trying to clear all the debris that people are doing.

'The public? Some of them, they are good, very polite. A few of them are very rude, honestly. A few of them, not all of them. But most of them – I'm talking about here in central London – most of them are very polite, they are very educated, but a few people, they are not polite – nah, they just chuck the rubbish on the floor, especially the people – I don't want to say it, but I have to, the people that work in construction, they're not really polite. They just smoke and throw the ashes on the floor in front of you and I don't want to, I can't talk to them. It's all about manners, you know.

'The worst, especially when it's night-time at the weekend – I'm talking about Friday night and Saturday night, so you have many people in the pub. It's going to be worse because all of them are smoking and drinking, and throwing the bottles on the floor, cigarettes on the floor, so the day after when you come in the morning it's going to be a nightmare. And you have to clear it.

'I do only mornings. It's very very hard to get up in the morning, very very hard. You have to go to bed very early, honestly it's not easy. Especially on wintertime, it's not easy to wake up, even if you go up early, it's really cold. I live in north London, Wood Green. I start work at six o'clock, so I have to wake up an hour and a half before, so waking up early in the morning, getting myself ready. It's not that busy in the morning so it takes me about forty minutes by bus but when I finish it takes me about an hour, something like that.

'When we start in the morning, we have to go to the depot, we get changed, we sign our sheet so we see our manager and he tell us what to do especially for today. Because we work with the council and they spread us – we've got eighteen beats, so everyone has his beat, and he's got a map so we have to do it, as soon as we get out, we have to go straight away to our beat and start to sweep the street and clean the bins, and sometimes when it's busy we have to take the glass from the street as well, especially when it's very dangerous. We also have to pick up the bags. And we have two breaks: we have a tea break from a quarter to to nine o'clock and we have another break from eleven to eleven thirty, which is OK.

'My beat is big, it's really big, because it's close to Oxford Circus, so it's busy, as you can see. I've got a lot of buildings here, I've got a lot of jobs here, restaurants, it's really really big, honestly, I have to be updated all the time so what can I do. And I have to work too much as well. No, I don't get paid properly. Just above the minimum wage, just a bit' – and he holds his thumb and forefinger very close together. 'To be honest, living in London, you know how difficult living in London is, very expensive, we don't get paid so much. The wages we get, nah. I'm comparing because we work for Veolia, you know? That's the French company, they've taken over, but we work for Westminster Council, so different. I think we are not getting that much, we should get more, I dunno.

'I was born in Algeria, and brought up over there and I had the chance to go to France, so I went to France, and then I came to here and I fell in love with this country. This is a life. You're in your country, and you can't find a job and there is no prospect over there, so you have to leave, you have to find that somewhere else. So when I come here, I find it very good. It's not easy, for a start when you come here, you don't know the language, you don't know people, so after that it's getting OK.

'I don't like France. Yes, we do speak French because we learn it in the school in Algeria, it's the second language. We didn't learn English, we learn it in secondary school, but just a few hours. But I'm very happy, because I speak English now when I come here, because this is the most spoken language in the world, isn't it? So wherever you go, you can speak English. I'm very happy with it.

'To be honest with you, when I finish, I'm very tired, so I have to go home because I wake up very early. So when I go home, I take a shower and I need to have a nap, at least one hour. And when I finish, I go out and see a friend, do something. And I do sports as well, so yes, sometimes I go to the gym, play football on the weekend, try to find something interesting. And I like to travel as well, especially here in England. When I have time I like to go to the countryside because you know London is very stressful.

'No, no family here, back home. Every three to four months I have to go there and see them. The future? I'll be honest with you, it's really hard here. It's nice but it's really hard. London is nice if you get a good job then you get paid very well so it's OK for you, but if you do the kind of job like I'm doing, minimum wage, it's really hard. I'll have to find something else, honestly. And nobody knows the future. For the moment, I want to stay here. Maybe in another ten years, I dunno. No, no problem with papers, I'm legal, I don't have a problem with that. Not any more, because if you're illegal you can't work.

'Yes, I'm happy, very happy. Of course.'

I ask how old he is.

'How old do you think I am?'

I'm puzzled, not wanting to offend. Forty?

'Forty-four. I'm old!'

What a mess!

In Mayhew's day, the mess on the street was of a different order: mud, horse dung and refuse. Three cartloads a day of dirt were swept up between Oxford Circus and Piccadilly Circus alone, four-fifths of which consisted of horse and cattle droppings. Street sweepers were either employed by the parish, or paupers from the workhouse were made to do it.

Of the different forms of pauper work, street-sweeping is, I am inclined to believe, the most unpopular of all among the poor.

The scavaging is generally done in the workhouse dress, and that to all, except the hardened paupers, and sometimes even to them, is highly distasteful. Neither have such labourers, as I have said, the incentive of that hope of the reward which, however diminutive, still tends to sweeten the most repulsive labour.

One man thus employed gave me the following account. 'Street-sweeping,' he said, 'degrades a man, and if a man's poor he hasn't no call to be degraded. Why can't they set the thieves and pickpockets to sweep? they could be watched easy enough; there's always idle fellers as reckons theirselves real gents, as can be got for watching and sitch easy jobs, for they gets as much for them, as three men's paid for hard work in a week. I never was in a prison, but I've heerd that people there is better fed and better cared for than in workusses ... No, I don't want to be kept and do nothink. I want *proper* work.

Like today, the streets were swept every day, sometimes by recently introduced machines with revolving brooms and spraying water. Almost like the man who drives a little machine that washes the patio of Broadcasting House every day. And Barry, from Sierra Leone, working in Covent Garden.

When we meet, on a scorching hot summer's day, he's driving a closed-in street cleaning machine in Covent Garden Market, then gets out to hose down the street. He turns off his intercom before the interview. He is employed by the private company Capco. He needs frequent prompting to say anything.

'My name is Barry. I'm working in Covent Garden. I'm a cleaner, and I live ... ' He gives his address near London Bridge. 'I've been doing it seven years. It's my job; it's what I love to do. I do enjoy it; it's something I've been doing for quite a long time so it's not new any more. I love it. I love being around people, there's a lot of people round here.

'What I don't like? Sitting in that for long, long hours. It's very hot inside there, yeah, definitely. But at least I manage. I have no choice. I wish I had a choice, but there's no choice.' He laughs uproariously. 'I'd rather not. I don't have no choice, so I have to live at the minute.

'What would I like to be doing? Reading books, travelling abroad. I used to be a security officer, used to be a trafficman, bounceman. I loved them, I loved all of them as well. I'm a man of challenge. I love different things. So I don't mind. I studied physics, chemistry and I studied a lot of environmental stuff. I'm always using them, but first thing come first. Everything that I'm using is part of what I've studied. So I didn't do something that I didn't like or didn't study. Anything that I am doing is part of what belongs to my career so this is what I love doing. In five years' time I like to be travelling with the family. Go back home. Have a . . . because I'm agricultural as well, do some farming, so that's the plan, yeah.'

He turns the hose back on. 'Mind out, don't get wet from the shower!'

Reminding us of the poignant story of little Jo in Dickens's *Bleak House*, Mayhew writes about the particular group of manual cleaners who swept crossings:

> That portion of the London street-folk who earn a scanty living by sweeping crossings constitute a large class of the Metropolitan poor. We can scarcely walk along a street of any extent, or pass through a square of the least pretensions to 'gentility,' without meeting one or more of these private scavengers. Crossing-sweeping seems to be one of those occupations which are resorted to as an excuse for begging; and, indeed, as many expressed it to me, 'it was the last chance left of obtaining an honest crust.'

These days, street sweepers are employed by local authorities, and it is a cleaning, not a scavenging job. In central London, they are almost ubiquitous, and most come from other countries.

October. A tall man in a hi-vis jacket sweeps up the piles of leaves in Cavendish Square as we talk. We've spoken many times but I don't know his name or where he comes from, just that he's a refugee. Autumn is not a good time for street sweepers.

'Oh, the worst time. And yesterday there was wind and rain. And someone complained to my manager that I do nothing. He came yesterday in a machine and said the machine don't sweep up the leaves. I asked an old woman – she knows me – to tell the manager how I work.'

'And the pay?'

He shrugs. 'Not much.'

'Enough to live on?'

He nods. 'Yes. And when I see the homeless' – he gestures to the pavement – 'and the disabled, I don't complain. I like it. If I don't like it, I do something else. I don't complain.'

Jimmy, however, is English. He's a bent, elderly man in the usual hi-vis jacket, picking his way through a sprawl of some thirty bags of rubbish, trying to clean the pavement in between.

'Goodness, what a mess.'

'Yes, there's only so much I can get in my cart. I've complained to my manager.'

'Well, thank you for what you do.'

'Bless you, darling. Have a good day.'

Another day, at the top of Charlotte Place. Jimmy declines an interview. 'No, better not. They tell us not to talk to press or anyone. Still, I retire in a year and a half, then I'm out. I might still work but not here. This is the border between Camden and Westminster,' drawing a line along the rubbish bags on the ground, 'and sometimes it gets left. Yes, just here. Yes, I'm Westminster.' His teeth nearly fall out as we talk, and he turns away to put them back.

We meet again, a few weeks later. He's very willing to talk but not to be recorded. A shy man with a roll-up between his lips. 'Born and brought up in London. Scots parents, both in the army. Married once, no children. She wanted to go back to Portsmouth and I wanted to stay here with my family. She was a lot older than me.' He complains again about the dirt and says he's ashamed. 'Tourists come and they see this and they go elsewhere and it's all clean. Yes, I retire on March 21st 2021.' He counts the exact date on his fingers. 'Pension, yes, first year taxed. Not enough to live on, but I'll manage. Do things. Hope I've got a good few years yet. No one's done a film about a road sweeper. We see all sorts here. The things people get up to.' He shakes his head. 'Haven't always done this. Worked in a meat factory for four years, oak-smoked ham. I work six a.m. till two p.m. I live in Stoke Newington, about an hour, but only thirty minutes in the early morning. But I leave about two a.m. Like to get things here sorted.'

He tries to take his dirty green glove off to shake hands. He refuses to shake hands with a dirty glove, so we do a fist bump: 'That's what they do these days, isn't it? Any details you want me to clear up, just ask. I'm always here, on this beat.'

The parks too have to be kept clean. Gerry, who works as a maintenance man as well as a gardener, gave me a graphic description of some of his work. 'This park here, because the gates ain't tall enough, you get a lot of people jumping over in the middle of the night, and they sit here drinking and smoking weed, and they leave rubbish everywhere. My other park, the fences are too big, no one can get in there, so you come in in the morning, and it's just how you left it the night before. But when you come here in the morning, it's as if you have to start all over again. Every day it's a losing battle, but the duties are mainly keeping the parks tidy, getting rid of graffiti, erm, any faeces, any needles, bottles. We do a lot of recycling here with the leaves; we turn them into mulch, so that's another good thing we do.'

Near Goodge Street station, just outside the American Church, which houses a homeless project, is an open space with benches and greenery. A very disgruntled cleaner is picking a lot of rubbish out of the bushes with a pick-up stick. He's much less positive than Gerry. 'This place is a dinosaur – they're trying to demolish it. It's worse in the summer. You get poo and all sorts from the homeless' – gesturing with his chin towards the church.

'Dirt? I'm immune'

Contending with the volume of refuse that householders churn out each week, not to mention the commercial waste poured out by builders, restaurants and other businesses, is a huge job. In Mayhew's day, 'dustmen' were exactly that, men who collected vast quantities of dust from dwellings, most of it the residue from fossil fuel heating. He says:

> There are in London upwards of 300,000 inhabited houses, and each house furnishes a certain quota of dust to the general stock. I have ascertained that an average-sized house will produce, in the course of a year, about three cart-loads of dust, while each cart holds about 40 bushels (baskets) – what the dustmen call a chaldron . . . It follows that the gross quantity collected through-out the metropolis will be about 900,000 chaldrons per annum.
>
> The dust thus collected is used for two purposes, (1) as a manure for land of a peculiar quality; and (2) for making bricks.

Nowadays, taking away refuse is the responsibility of local authorities, and it's a complex task. Most primarily residential areas have weekly collections, with separate bins for general refuse, recycling (of various kinds), kitchen waste and, in some cases, garden waste. In the West End, some areas have no bins, just bags to be put out at specific times (an injunction rarely observed). There are multiple collections daily, and still the streets are full of bags, which people put out all day long. I mentioned seeing a crow pecking at rubbish and throwing things out at random. A friend said, 'A true Londoner, then.'

Bulky objects are particularly problematic. With few having access to a car, people have to make arrangements with the council for the disposal of large items, though some authorities will remove fridges for free. Even for people who do have cars, rubbish dumps are few and far between. Hackney and Westminster have no rubbish tips; people living in Hammersmith and Kensington & Chelsea have to go to Wandsworth.

Dustmen are now more formally called 'refuse collectors' or more colloquially, bin men (and they are largely men), who collect the vast volume of assorted rubbish thrown out by households and businesses. According to the government website, London's homes, public buildings and businesses produce seven million tonnes each year. 'Of this, only 52 per cent is currently recycled and ... the capacity of landfills accepting London's waste is expected to run out by 2026.'

I caught up with one bin man – let's call him Gary – when he was doing his rounds. We jogged along the street behind the lorry. Gary has been a bin man for forty years. When I asked why he went into it, he was another who said he couldn't bear being inside.

'Left school at sixteen, worked in a bakery for a few days, not enough dough – gettit? – and hated being inside, then sweeping the streets for a couple of weeks, then they put me on this, and I've been doing it ever since. Love it. Because I get to be outside, out and about, meeting nice people like you.'

'But you don't have the time.'

'I make time. Of course not all are nice. Some go on and on. You have to zip your mouth' – he gestured doing so – 'you can't use swear words. Oh, they complain that their bin was missed, or the mess.'

'Don't you mind the dirt?'

'Nah, I'm immune! It was different in the old days when we had bins of hot ashes that we had to carry on our backs. When you'd added cold water to cool it down, it weighed a ton.'

According to the national careers service, the starting salary is a modest £15,000 rising to a maximum of £25,000, so I asked Gary if he was paid enough. He nodded seriously, not wanting to say much, then with a grin said, 'The wife helps – it's what it [marriage]'s for, innit?'

Gary was cheerful, happy to talk. It would have been good to spend longer with him, but he swung up into the lorry, gave me a thumbs-up and smiled, 'See ya!'

A couple of bin men in Islington were less happy. It was a snatched conversation as they went about their work: two burly thirty-ish men, one Eastern European, the other a Caribbean Londoner who did most of the talking. They start their day, he said, at 5 a.m. by hosing down vans in Holloway Road recycling centre, hoping to finish by eleven so he can do two jobs in one day – he wouldn't say what else he did.

They used to have more operatives, he explains; now there are just four per van: driver, two men on the van and a supervisor, who oversees the emptying process, checks with bosses if there's a problem with a bin and instructs his team what to do. The supervisor is reluctant to do much reporting, he says, as it then requires follow-up paperwork.

Apparently there's an ongoing problem with 'human fluids' – vomit from late-night passers-by – and also with the little bags of dog poo that people drop into the bins after their walks in Highbury Fields. The men are not issued protective clothing so they won't touch those bins. They don't replace lids, either, as it's not in their contracts. The supervisor reports to the bosses, who ignore his reports or say there's no money.

He talked about senior bin men who earn above living wage and get a mobile, saying there were too many bosses who have no idea what they are talking about.

Both men have been doing it for years, hanging on in the hopes of promotion to work in the recycling centre. They now have to cover approximately 20 per cent more streets, so are constantly rushing. They're all union men and feel that is their only safeguard against redundancy, but union power has been reduced, he says, so they can't fight all the extra work the bosses put on them. There's good camaraderie among the men, but they consider most people are dirty and it's a filthy job and there's no respect.

People make mess.

5

Good morning London

The life of the streets is constantly shifting, night and day.

6.30 a.m. A Monday in November. The dark streets of central London are illuminated by street lamps and in some places by the twinkling of premature Christmas fairy lights. High above it all, the top of the BT Tower – which, from its inception in 1964 until 1980 was, at 191 metres (627 feet), the tallest building in the United Kingdom – rotates, bearing the message: GOOD MORNING LONDON. Greeting those waking up to the day, or walking to work or to catch a bus or tube. In the street, people are putting out tables outside cafés, polishing brass, delivering beer to the pub, fetching laundry from the hotel. A street cleaner walks along in the road with his trolley, using his pick-up stick to gather litter from the gutter.

But for some, the day started many hours before, and for those working at night, this may mark the end of a working 'day'. Security men doing twelve-hour shifts, going home to sleep. In the early hours there's an overlap between those coming in from a good night out, and those going out to start their working shift. At 5.30 a.m. traffic is not as heavy as it will be at 7 or 8 a.m.; many of those who are on the road make the most of this by driving fast. There are still some night buses as the day timetable begins. Much of the traffic is made up of delivery drivers and people going to work, very few taxis or Ubers. The City wakes up early, although at this time it's mostly those working in construction and the service economy, rather than people in suits. By 7 a.m. there is twice as much traffic – people and cars – as an hour before. Many people walk at speed along the pavement, carrying cups of takeaway coffee or looking at their phones.

At 8.30 a.m., parents are taking their children to school; office workers are on their way, maybe dropping in to a local shop, market stall or café as they go. It's rush hour – people are travelling to work on crowded buses, trains and tubes. At 10 a.m., Covent Garden, largely a tourist destination, is still empty. At eleven, food sellers are preparing for the lunchtime trade. And so the day begins. London has its rhythms.

One fruiterer told me of his first customer that day.

'Tell the truth, our first customer was at four thirty.'

'Where was she coming from – off a night shift?'

'Off the rut, more like! We were at the van, and she passed by, and said, "Would you sell me a satsuma?" One satsuma. But she's still a customer, innit?'

Days are further lengthened for people on low incomes who cannot afford to live in the centre of London. Unlike Mayhew's era, when there was little affordable public transport and no possibility of work unless people lived near by, people now live on the outskirts of London, and it takes a long time to travel in. So for thousands the morning began long ago, as they drove in from homes in the suburbs to beat the traffic, or to avoid parking restrictions or the congestion charge, which in central London kicks in at 7 a.m. Piles of newspapers, tied with string, or crates of food or milk left outside shop entrances, bear witness to early-morning deliveries.

Some travel in on the night bus. Mac is seventy-seven, and has been window cleaning for over fifty years. He lives out in Kent now, near Sevenoaks, and leaves home in the early hours of the morning.

'I come to London every morning, well five days a week. I leave home at one thirty and I catch the night bus. Yeah, in the morning. And if you wants material for a book, Jennifer, you should get on that night bus. Have you ever been on a night bus? It's an education. Sometimes it's funny, sometimes it's not funny, but it's an education. I get into London three thirty. And the only good thing about it is when you get older, they give you a free bus pass! So you don't have to pay your fare.' We both laugh.

'I've got a little office just off Piccadilly, and I've got cleaning jobs, window cleaner jobs, caretaker jobs, anything to earn a shilling. Yeah, anything to earn a few bob. Yeah, I start work at three thirty and I'll be finished by eleven thirty, hopefully.

'Since I was widowed, every minute I'm thinking, is [the dog] all right? The first thing I do when I get home is take him out for a walk, get his dinner, about three o'clock, then I get myself a bit of dinner, about five o'clock, and I go to bed about six o'clock.' He laughs. 'It's a sad life, Jennifer! It's like being a monk in a monastery. It's not really, because I like doing what I do. You only go round once, don't you? Whatever you end up doing you've got to turn it into a situation where you don't dislike it, isn't it? You know, if you *hate* going to work, it must be awful.'

Mayhew describes the 'ordinary hours of employment' as 6 a.m. to 6 p.m.; some people in his day would have travelled from home along dimly lit and unpaved streets. Not that much has changed, even at the upper end of the trade. The organic butcher at Broadway Market, who lives in Wiltshire, describes his demanding schedule:

'My story on a Saturday is I wake up at two o'clock, full of enthusiasm! It does take a bit of getting used to and I don't think even after a year and a half I have got used to it. It's always difficult trying to get yourself to go to sleep at eight o'clock on a Friday night. I get up at two, go to our unit and I load up with the frozen goods and the ice that we take to market to help keep the products cool on the table. On my way to Broadway I go to Purton, which is a lovely little village near Swindon, and from there I pick up some dairy products that we sell at market. It's mainly milk, so we get raw milk that we distribute for them as well. I get there at four o'clock and the cows are full of energy and noise that early! ... I hit my first delivery at Acton at quarter to six, all being well. And I have to get to market at seven thirty. I struggle to get into my spot if I'm too early and I definitely won't get into it if I'm too late, so it's fairly time-crucial, but I do drop to about a dozen places on the way there as well. Luckily there's not too many people up at that time in the morning. It's amazing how much difference an hour can make coming into London.

'So I arrive at Broadway at seven thirty. Market finishes at five, which is when we start packing down. It takes about half an hour for us all to get the canopy and the tables away, load up the van. All being well, I usually get out of market at about six p.m., depending on who is there and where they're located. Then I stay with some lovely friends down Chatsworth Road [in Hackney]. I usually try to stay up and be social with them but nine times out of ten I go and hit the hay nice and early. Then I'm up at eight o'clock for Chatsworth Road.

'The market at Chatsworth closes at four o'clock and then I go straight to Wiltshire. I tend to get back home between seven and eight o'clock depending on how it is on the M25 and the M4. So I get back there, I unload the refrigerated goods back into the unit and then we sort out any returns the next day. I sleep very well on Sunday night.'

A young man with wispy stubble sells fruit at a solitary stall at Goode Street.

'Rain? It hasn't stopped for six weeks.'

'At least you've got an umbrella.'

'Yes, but it's the putting it up at three thirty in the morning. We have lots of orders. Have to get that done. The two vans, getting set up here before they start coming out of there,' pointing to the tube station. 'I get up at two thirty. I go to bed – well, seven p.m.'s a late night for me. Yeah, tell my girlfriend! I should've concentrated at school. It's fine in the summer – it's light, I quite like it. It'll be worse later when I have to go to the markets at eleven p.m. Yeah, I'll have to do that eventually.'

Ben, delivering meat: 'The driving? That's Monday to Friday, aye. You start at four in the morning, and you finish when you finish. So the quicker you are, the quicker you get home, basically. You've got a certain number of deliveries to do, all the restaurants, and what else. When you get it done, you can go home. It's round about six, seven hours' work. It's in central London. Central London and west London, You've got all of W1, WC1, WC2, SW1, you deliver to all the restaurants, hotels, top-end restaurants like Claridge's, yeah.'

London at night

London is proud of its image as a round-the-clock city. As the ad for Transport for London pronounces: 'Being in a city that never sleeps matters. You're 24/7. So are we.' Some people just keep working. I saw a group of men refurbishing a shop at 8 a.m.; they were still there at 8.30 p.m. Taxi and bus drivers keep driving. Shops, restaurants and cafés stay open late – some shops even advertise proudly that they are open twenty-four hours a day, seven days a week. They are catering for people working all hours, and for people on a night out. Making the most of London's vibrant social life.

The street at night is a very different place. As daytime activities come to a close, so new venues open: bars, clubs and casinos. Night-time activity can be big business. A council report reveals 'a perception that a strong and well-managed Evening and Night-time Economy can contribute to the broad "liveability" and wellbeing of cities'. 'Camden's evening and night-time economy', it says, is 'one of the largest in the country, with a turnover of £955.9m.'

Sound engineer Peter sees the night-time scene from the perspective of music in the clubs. Asked if he felt the music scene has died a little bit, he said:

'The trouble is over the years all the small venues have been shut down. It was a huge number because all that happens is that someone builds a luxury flat above a nightclub or opposite it and they can apply to have this nightclub shut, which is madness. You know, the nightclub was there first, but that's how it works.

'They've now realised that nightclubs are a massively important thing to London. It's a huge plus to our economy. That's why highly talented interesting people wanna live here and work here. They want to increase the number of small clubs so they've hired this nightclub tsar to increase the number of clubs. As a small nightclub you just don't make as much money as some big multinational chain and it's very difficult to compete with them.

'We managed to crowdfund a survival thing. One hundred and fifty grand, which is fucking insane. Took about a month, I think. It seems crazy. It did definitely help because we've got some well-known musicians: Chemical Brothers, Four Tet, Fatboy Slim as well. They played and donated the proceeds of their gigs to us, which is obviously a lot of money. I know tons of people who put fifty, a hundred quid in. There are a bunch of regulars. It's a place you can go and meet a few people you know and have a chat. That's really important.

'Because property became so valuable and it shut so many things down and that sort of spreads over, I mean you look at places like Hackney . . . they still have nightclubs and things but even I bet a lot of those get shut down because property becomes so valuable and gets redeveloped. It's just reduced the number of places that can do live music and that means there's less opportunities for new musicians and has a knock-on effect . . .'

Despite his name, Pixie is a mountain of a man. His bulk made him a natural for working as a bouncer.

'I started off 1978, I think. I was about seventeen. Rock Against Racism had just started and I'd moved back from being in care out in Essex into London, and I joined the east London Rock Against Racism. Obviously, I was quite big, and my job often became doing the door. All the London groups, especially the bigger gigs, you'd need quite a lot of security and stage managers, you know. We used to do the whole thing. So we would go all the way over to Southall and do the Southall gigs and the north London ones and the south London ones and they'd come to us.'

For some years in the late 1990s, Pixie worked at Brixton Academy, mostly during the day.

'I'd get to work at six thirty in the morning. Worked through till doors came open at six thirty, seven o'clock. Then I'd go up to the circle and supervise, unless it was a trouble gig. If it was a trouble gig . . . at the beginning of the nineties, I'm gonna be totally honest about it, ninety-five per cent of the trouble gigs were the reggae and rap gigs. It was mainly people steaming the doors, there was whole gangs coming and they weren't gonna pay. So I would have to work front door for those gigs.

'And I used to work the front door at other gigs because they wanted me to confiscate drugs. You know, a little indie gig, I'm not taking some little seventeen-year-old girl's little bit of puff off them at the front door. I wouldn't do it. And I used to get shit for that. But I also said to the boss, I will come when you need me there. You can get any muppet to be a twat, you can get anyone to do that but you want someone who will stand when there's a crew of thirty coming screaming at you, you want someone who's not gonna run away. I will do that. I'll die for you but I'm not gonna steal drugs off people.'

Elsewhere it was night work, and he'd be part of the scene.

'Brady's was madness. If you got kicked out of every other bar in Brixton you could go to Brady's and I was a doorman there. It was anything goes, that place. I was totally gutted when that place closed. It was before twenty-four-hour drinking but the place was always open all hours. The police never used to give it any trouble. It was really messy in there but people were having a lot of fun so the Old Bill just used to let us get on with it. There was a camera down the side street so the police could see that this pub was open for twenty-four hours, but they never got called there so they never bothered. And it's like they knew that all the people that they didn't want . . . we're not talking about rapists and murderers and whatever, we're talking about dealers and loud lairy people. They're just party people, people just wanna go out. We just partied there.'

At raves he'd work all night. 'Yeah. I worked there till six, seven, eight, ten in the morning, then I'd finish, stop doing the door, but then quite often the party would go on anyway so I'd just go join in the party. Then I'd get all my money, so I'd got a pocket full of money, about a hundred quid, some of the parties I would have been selling pills and stuff on the door so I would then have made another pack of money and we'd go out to spend it all. We'd go out, sit there drinking double Jack Daniel's and Coke, snorting coke and fucking party for another twenty-four, forty-eight hours.'

How he dealt with troublemakers depended on where he was. At the Academy, 'If you've got a hard case to deal with then you go up to the next supervisor above or you go up to someone else. If you're doing like squat parties and gigs like that, it was my door, so I just treated every case on instinct, you know, dealing with the person in front of me and the particular problem they were causing. I would deal with that person on instinct rather than a set guideline or from some sort of rulebook. That's what made me good at the job. I'm good at reading people and I'm good at doing what needs to be done in that moment.'

A businessman who is running a shelter for homeless women sleeps on the streets in solidarity. When asked what the worst thing about being on the streets is, he gave a very dark picture of night-time London.

'The sex offenders, the perverts, night life in London – people who live in London don't even know what goes on. Darkness, ten, eleven, twelve o'clock, and it lasts all night. It's Armageddon. The police do their very very best. I never criticise the services, I never criticise the hostels and I don't criticise the outreach and the street workers. You can only do what you can on the day. You're instantaneous, you're on the spot, you have to have the aptitude to be adaptable and adjust to the situation. It's very dangerous. The stabbings, the threats, the death threats, every night.

'I don't feel in danger because, luckily, I have a cross and I say if you're willing to take this cross on then go ahead and stab me. And they've tried. They have. They come on bicycles, young children, who are paid £25 and are smoking joints of spice. That is their wages for going to stab somebody. And there are stabbings every night. And they're not reported, because they say if you report me, we stab you or we rape you. And we'll come back and do it again afterwards. We'll get other people to do it as well, so *nobody* says anything. Nobody makes any police complaints or reports, nobody challenges them. The serial sex offenders who go round raping and punching women, spiking their joints.'

Night on the streets

For those sleeping on the streets, day and night can seem pretty fluid. Mo, an Irishman sleeping rough, says, 'Usually I stay up all night anyway. I sleep in the daytime, if it's a Saturday up in the block [of flats].' The acute discomfort of sleeping on the pavement, even padded by cardboard, is often too much, and sometimes it's simply too cold to sleep.

Some people, like thirty-three-year-old Darren, a homeless *Big Issue* seller, are fearful and only fall asleep when daylight comes. 'I sleep two hours a night if I'm lucky. I don't like sleep. Yes, get people threatening me all the time. But the dog looks after me, nothing happens now she's with me. Had Indy since she was eight weeks old, she's four and a half now.'

Seeing him a few months later, in December, I asked how he was. 'I've just woken up.' It was 5.30 p.m. 'I'm cold. I wake up cold.'

But many homeless people have a clearer demarcation between nights spent in a tent, under an arch or in a park, and going to a more central spot to beg, or possibly to a day centre for a wash. At 9.30 p.m. on Euston Road, between Warren Street and Great Portland Street, there's a line of about a dozen homeless people bedding down. And at 10 p.m. there are no beggars along Tottenham Court Road. Some have found a place in a night shelter, but most homeless people have gone elsewhere, out of sight, to sleep.

Freddie, on his daytime pitch outside St Martin-in-the-Fields, told me that 'at night-time my mate sleeps down by, you know Waterstones? The bookshop? He's sleeping there, and I'm sleeping on the Embankment stairs – under the bridge, the Millennium Bridge, the wobbly bridge? I'm literally under the stairs, all like cardboard, it's all nice and kitted out, see. I don't cause no drama or nothing. I keep myself to myself, but it's hard, really hard.'

6

'And then some are rich'

My earnest hope is that the book may serve
to give the rich a more intimate knowledge
of the sufferings, and the frequent heroism
under those sufferings, of the poor – that it
may teach those who are beyond temptation to
look with charity on the frailties of their less
fortunate brethren – and cause those who are
in 'high places,' and those of whom much is
expected, to bestir themselves to improve the
condition of a class of people whose misery,
ignorance, and vice, amidst all the immense
wealth and great knowledge of 'the first city in
the world,' is, to say the very least, a national
disgrace to us.

Fitzrovia is an area famed for its beautiful eighteenth- and nineteenth-century houses, and is a favourite area for filming period dramas. At 8.30 a.m. I noticed a forty-ish black man standing in the rain in his hi-vis hooded jacket, leaning against one of the bollards opposite, scrolling on his phone. At midday, many showers later, he was still there. Turns out he works as a security man for a company filming round the corner. He has to watch that cars (of which there are very few in this back street) don't go down the road or park in the way. He is bored, doesn't like being outside. He'd rather be inside, but he has to put food on the table for his family. He used to work in a factory, at £9 something an hour. Now, it's £10. 'Not much, and then' – glancing up at the beautiful Georgian house opposite, which was on the market a few years ago for £8 million – 'some are rich, but what can you do?'

'Is all security work paid the same?'

'No, some of it is worse.'

He was still there at 3.30 but at 4 p.m. he was gone. Eight hours in the rain, just standing there.

Fitzroy Place, built in 2016 on the site of the old Middlesex Hospital, is billed as the first new garden square in London W1 for over a century. A largely paved private residential and retail estate on the borders of Camden and Westminster, it's a pleasant, publicly accessible place for residents and workers to sit or play. Bounding the square are nearly three hundred luxury flats. In early 2020, a two-bed flat was advertised for rent for £1625 per week; a three-bed flat was for sale at £12.5 million. It has its own management team and security guards.

Private security is a growth industry. Apart from CEOs and street wardens, employed by the council, companies hire security personnel to guard individual buildings and squares. So there are a lot of job opportunities – on the whole for long hours and little pay.

Next to Fitzroy Place, her purple tent hard up against the railings, is Carrie. She finds the presence of the security guards reassuring. Earlier in the day I met her and the man she shares with, and made a time to talk. In the event, she was there on her own. She arrived on a bike just as I got there. I was touched when she invited me into her tent – brightly and prettily furnished with different-coloured cushions. A spray cleaner just inside. On the consent form she gave her aunt's address.

'My name's Carrie. I'm thirty-six. I've been homeless for about twenty-one years. I've been in and out of prison, I've used drugs. The story of my life, really. I grew up in London, back in 1983. I had a really good upbringing like until the end. My dad was violent towards my mum, so my mum split up from my dad when I was about ten and I just started rebelling against everything she used to say. I didn't see my dad after that, and I was too much to handle and I got put in care, and from there I went to the West End and was introduced to new exciting people, and I was taking drugs, and I just got involved in it. I was in care from fourteen up until sixteen, when I just left. So, yeah, I was homeless from then on. Never had a job.

'I want to get clean, I don't want this life no more. But it's a bit hard at the minute, you know what I mean? Not having anywhere stable to live. I've had this tent for about two months, because the council keep confiscating my tent. They give you notice to leave and because you've got nowhere to go, when you come back, it's all gone. They say if I don't engage with the drugs team then they can't help me, basically, because I'm not showing I'm willing.

'I do want to, but my life is chaotic at the minute, I don't know what's going to happen from one day to the next. No, he's not my partner, we're just sharing the tent. Only recently because his tent got confiscated by the council, so I told him he could come in here. I've known him for about eight years. We help each other. I mean he's out there begging now. Yeah, that's how I make a living: begging, that's it really.

'A job? You see, I've got itchy feet, I like to do anything and everything. I don't want to be having just one job. I want to be doing loads of different things.

'How do I feel? What, about this life? It's suicidal, at the minute.' She starts crying and I turn off the machine. We continue talking for a little without the recording.

'I move all over the place. I've been here before. I went away, and they took my tent and everything. A woman up the road bought me another tent. My aunt? No, she's got enough on her plate.' I see some books, and tell her about the mobile library for homeless people. She's pleased and plans to go. As I leave, she gives me a hug.

'I wish I could offer you a cup of tea. It's been good talking to you. I'm sorry I cried.'

The next time I passed, I saw a furry toy dog attached to the outside of the tent. Then the following day, someone who was presumably a council official, with clipboard, talking to a man (a different man, it seemed) through a slit at the top of the tent flap, hiding the interior. I wondered if they would be moved on.

A couple of days later, her tent flap was half open.

'Hi Carrie. You all right?'

'Not really. Someone stole my things.'

'Oh no! While you were out?'

'No, while I was asleep.'

She didn't seem inclined to talk further, so I gave her a little wave, wished her well, and left.

Two days later the tent and its inhabitants were gone. She had moved on, or, more likely, had been moved on.

As the epidemiologist authors of *The Spirit Level* so clearly demonstrate, deep inequalities within a country lead to most of the generally recognised indicators of deprivation, from suicide to teenage pregnancy, knife crime to drug abuse. Like many areas of the UK – and indeed the world – London is a place of deep inequality, where the wealthy and the poor live side by side. According to the Trust for London poverty profile, the cost of housing is the main factor in London's high level of poverty. Private rents in London are more than twice the average for England. Every borough has areas where the level of poverty is above the average in the rest of England. And many boroughs have people living in considerable affluence. Here are three particularly extreme examples.

Tower Hamlets is home both to Canary Wharf, one of the most important business districts in the UK and the world, and to some of the poorest wards in Britain. According to an evidence pack produced by the local council, 'Almost eighteen per cent of households [are] living on less than £15,000, while in 2011, the average gross annual earnings of those working in the borough was over £78,000.' For hundreds of years and thousands of refugees, the East End of London has been the arrival point in the country, and many live in poor conditions. When I arrived to start a community centre there in the late nineties, I was shocked at the overcrowded and damp conditions; one woman was so poor she couldn't afford to mend a window broken by vandals.

Westminster, home to Parliament, is another of the richest boroughs in London. It also has the highest population of homeless people.

The deep inequality of the city is nowhere so visible as in the Royal Borough of Kensington & Chelsea. According to the *Guardian* in 2017, the parliamentary constituency of Kensington is the wealthiest in England, while other parts of the borough are ranked among the most deprived in the country. The average terraced house sold for £4.3 million in 2016, yet the borough is also home to the twenty-four-storey Grenfell Tower, the block of flats in North Kensington where, on 14 June 2017, a fire broke out killing seventy-two people in a building later to be judged substandard. A group of local residents had for some time been complaining to the council about grossly inadequate local housing. The former MP for the area, Emma Dent Coad, wrote in the *After Grenfell* inequality report, 'It is a place where inequality has become a gross spectacle. Where childhood poverty, overcrowding and homelessness live cheek by jowl with opulent second homes, palatial apartments for the mega-rich and vast outflows of rent to corporate landlords.'

The inequality spills over into the world of work. Gone, on the whole, is the realm of domestic servants, but the service industry is alive and well; though, as always in the UK, rather despised. Office or residential meals in the City and Mayfair are delivered on foot or by bike to those who can afford to pay to be waited on, sometimes by people in a smart uniform.

Burlington Arcade, off Piccadilly, was built in 1818 to the order of George Cavendish, 1st Earl of Burlington. It is one of London's earliest covered shopping arcades and from the outset, it positioned itself as an elegant and exclusive upmarket shopping venue, with shops offering luxury goods. It retains that profile into the present day, with shoes selling for £400 or even £900;

jewellery is unpriced, with the implication that if you have to ask, you can't afford it.

In these elegant and beautiful surroundings, there works a shoe shiner. On a cold November morning, he was just setting up at 11 a.m., and showed me with pride the electric heater fixed to the wall above the chair. Round the chair were compartments with an array of brushes, creams, polishes and laces of different colours. He told me that the shoe-shining business is his own, and he lives off the £7 fees he charges. He founded his business in 2006 and works seven days a week. I commented that it was cold.

'I wish the bank could tell me I don't need to work in the winter.'

Passing a few days later, I saw him hard at work, polishing the shoes of a man on his phone and paying no attention to someone who, as in Victorian illustrations of boys kneeling at the feet of those they served, is indeed a servant.

Where people on low wages work for prestigious establishments, they often take pride in the association. Burlington Arcade is patrolled by the smallest and oldest police force in the world, dressed in traditional uniforms including top hats and frockcoats. They are called 'beadles'. The original beadles, created in 1819, were all former members of Lord George Cavendish's regiment, the 10th Royal Hussars. The arcade maintains Regency decorum by banning singing, humming, hurrying, and 'behaving boisterously'.

Charles, a Ghanaian in his forties, is an imposing figure in his top hat and cloak. He talks rapidly in accented English and lowers his voice, so it's not always easy to hear. 'I'm Charles, I'm one of the beadles in the Burlington Arcade. I've been working here for about eleven years. Eleven years, yes, yes, yes. My journey started in August 2008. That has been a smooth journey till today. Working in the Burlington Arcade, I've seen quite a bit of changes in the specialist shops. Shops come, shop goes.

'It's a nice place to work, I mean working in a place which is classed as the number one arcade in the world, I mean it's an opportunity. When you're given such an opportunity then yeah ... You need to physically have the Security Industrial Authority licence.

Which is issued to you by the Home Office, so those are some of the prerequisite requirements in order to do this. Quite apart from that, you should be someone whose relationship with the members of the public is spot on. On this job, you gotta have people who might come in and not be nice, but then you should be able to have the temperament to be able to manage and control it. Sometimes we get people whose actions go a bit overboard. But I mean it's part of what I call the occupational hazard. Me personally, I have really met some nice lovely people.

'I was born in Ghana and quite apart from this I have a degree in law, a master's in law, so part of the legal background, I have legal qualifications, so yeah. I came to the UK to have a bit of life, a change of life. That was twenty-eight years ago' – I think he meant he was twenty-eight when he came – 'and I'm forty-two now. I used to be a teacher, and I taught in this country as well.

'Absolutely I enjoy it. I've met nice people. I've seen people I've never met, I've had my picture taken by a lot of people, I'm happy to work here.'

'Do you like being outside?'

'Erm . . . yes, I'd probably say yes, but not for that long. I mean if there are breaks in between then that's fine. This one, for instance, you do it for two hours then half an hour, so I'm happy with that. We are paid hourly.'

'Can you tell me what that is?'

'Oh, I need not to make complications with my employers, I need to keep that between me and my employers, yeah.'

'Do you like your uniform?'

He laughs. 'Oh yes. When people say, Oh I've never seen that before. Oh, that looks smart, it makes my day.

'My duties here is to enforce law and order in the Burlington Arcade. From there to there is about two hundred yards. And once you're here, you have to make sure that the set of rules are adhered to, so there's no running, no whistling, no cycling, no skating, no alcohol, no hooking umbrellas, and stuff like that, I don't allow anyone to do any of that. There are eight of us, so we run a rota basis.

Today for instance, five of us, so other people are away. So tomorrow for instance I'm not coming in but other people come in, yes.'

'So there's a sense of community?'

'Yes, that's right. Mark Lord' – the head beadle – 'has worked here possibly seventeen, eighteen years, and I'm the second oldest, and I've worked here eleven, twelve years.'

The Langham Hotel is also a luxury establishment – a five-star hotel. I talked to Daniel, one of the doormen, also dressed in traditional uniform, with a fresh flower at his buttonhole. 'Myself? Well, I'm a Londoner, I'm an ex-cultural intellectual history student, so I'm very familiar with the history of London. I like biographies as well, I read a biography about Blake, which is very London-centred; Peter Ackroyd is a terrific writer about London, highly recommended. I've been in this industry for er thirty-odd years, a long time now, since I was eighteen. My father was in the business as well, the concierge's department, same as myself, worked at the Berkeley, the Savoy, the Connaught. I worked at the Savoy with my father for some time, which was quite amusing. In the banqueting department. The majority of the time I've been working outdoors as a doorman.

'I love it. I love it. I love it, even in the winter. It's the engagement with the people. Erm, to a degree it's autonomous – as a doorman in a five-star hotel, you're out front and you're not directly overseen by anybody, so you kinda run your own show to a certain extent, yeah.

'I went into the business because of my father. I was originally a luggage porter. No, I withdraw that. I originally worked in a bar – I worked at Playboy, that was my first job, back in the day, when they owned the casinos, the Claremont Club, which was an extraordinary place: amazing building, amazing people used to come there. Used to get people coming up from Annabel's, we used to get the likes of Elizabeth Taylor, Omar Sharif, and I served Björn Borg and McEnroe after the 1981 Wimbledon final, one of their classic finals. But thereafter, from 1985 onwards, I worked as a luggage porter until 1994, and then I was a doorman.'

'And is that how you see your future?'

'Oh, yes, another ten or fifteen years before retirement, hopefully. I'm fifty-six. So yeah, ten to fifteen years, hopefully. Keep going. If they keep putting the retirement up, it'll probably be another twenty years.' He laughs. 'It's good. It keeps you fit, keeps you healthy, you're interacting with the public, you're outside and you know, you're engaged with people all the time. Twelve-hour shifts, yeah. It's hard on your feet. My record is twenty-four kilometres in a day. Walked, according to the steps on my phone. Twenty-four kilometres, it's quite something to do on your shift.

'Nobody ever goes into doorman straight away, off the street, even if they were qualified with a full catering degree. You have to work your way up to that type of job. Typically, you'd start as a page boy, then you progress to luggage porter, then you progress to a doorman. So usually four or five years' experience in hotels before you'd even be considered for that kind of role, because you're such an ambassador for the hotel.'

'What about uniform?'

'We've got the winter uniform – you wear your fleece and your thermals and your double socks and all that stuff, and then you have your beautiful coat, a individually made coat by a specialist company, which is properly lined, thermally lined, it's very very good. And gloves. It's like a greatcoat, really. It's more or less like a military coat they wore in the First World War. An officer, that kind of coat. Double-breasted. We've got a hat, which is not a bowler, it's a derby, don't ask me the difference, I don't know.' Another laugh. 'I think it's a little bit flatter on the top. Derby goes back I think to the hansom cab times. Some wore top hats, but some wore derbies. Hats come in handy for hailing cabs. They see you waving a hat from half a mile away, they assume it's a doorman, you know. So, er, yeah, we've got a very very good uniform, everything supplied, shoes etc. Trousers etc.'

'Any downsides?'

'You get strange members of the public, you get to deal with odds and ends, drunk people, occasionally violent people, very occasionally you get people who are aggressive. That's part and parcel of being on the streets. Working on the streets, everybody has that to a certain extent. There's no real downsides.

'We do a shift pattern, we either do six to six or we do nine to nine or we work twelve to twelve. And occasionally you stay later than that till one o'clock in the morning. There are eight doormen. Typically on any day there will be four doormen working, but given that there's cover, and people have to, have to, have holidays, when holidays, time off are accounted for, sometimes it can be three on a shift. In the main, we get on very well.

'I don't think you could do this job without a sense of humour. I think it's a main criteria, having a good sense of humour; you've got to have a certain amount of charm, otherwise it's not going to work.'

'Aren't you shattered at the end of the day?'

'Yeah, a bit tired. Some days are worse. When I'm on twelve to twelve, when I get home I just go straight to bed. You're that tired.

'It's still worth it. Keeps you fit and makes you strong. But if you see, most people who work in an office have a very structured existence, not a lot of diversity, don't meet different people every day. I still find a virtue in this kind of work. And I think this is the best hotel in London. It's an incredible place. An incredible history. If you think that *The Sign of Four* was commissioned over lunch here, *The Picture of Dorian Grey* was commissioned over lunch here, Dickens stayed here, and Dickens wrote about it in his American Travellers' Guides, so there's still that affinity with the place.'

A man meticulously scraping down the railings that encircle the large private garden (1.8 acres) of Bedford Square, works not for the council but for an Islington company in Brewery Road. He gets his pride and satisfaction from the status of the job. 'This is *listed*. When they told me I'd got this, I went, Woah! Top job, this is, lady. Never done anything like this before. Love it, especially the preparing – eighty per cent preparation, twenty per cent painting. Too much for one person, but another three turned up today, so that's OK. Listed, this is. English Heritage, isn't it?'

One day I stopped to admire gold being painted on the details of a lamp post in St Martin's Lane. Smiling with pride, the painter said: 'You can see the ones I've done further down the road.'

Another workman came up the road: 'Don't listen to him. He's got three wives already. He's always trying it on.' London banter.

7

Community

It's a cliché that London is a collection of villages. Even if a village feel is more apparent in the suburbs of Greater London, it is also true of inner London, including the less residential districts. Shopkeepers know each other, as do long-term residents. As I walk around my local streets, I wave or exchange greetings with the man from the dry cleaners, the Turkish restaurateur who has just returned to the area after some years away, the publican next door, and the *Big Issue* seller round the corner.

Madeleine talks about her adopted home, where she walks her dog twice a day.

'Brixton is my home. I fell in love with Brixton before I moved here, which is twenty-seven years ago. I thought it was the best place ever and I've lived in a lot of different places. North London, west, east. Anyway, I came here and I've never left. It's got the best community in that people say hello to you in the street. I love it. It's vibrant but I'd say if anything when I've taken myself away from here, one of the best things I like about it is coming back and people recognising me and the non-judgemental atmosphere that pervades the whole place. At the end of the day people don't judge you. They do go, Oh, your hair looks bad today, or something, but they don't make you feel like a piece of shit. We all know what that's like, Na, don't we?' She says this affectionately to her dog, who seems to be listening to every word she says.

'I don't want to talk about my disappointments here much but I think when domestic squatting was made illegal it completely changed the character of my road. It's becoming gentrified without a doubt. For a while I felt like running away but now I'm happy here and there are still people here – they haven't all gone – that have been around for ages, there are still families. I feel part of the whole general family of Brixton, the community of Brixton, if you like. I was attracted to Brixton in the first place because of being quite displaced and this place took me in and I loved it. It gave me a home and acceptance and the love and I don't think that's gone.'

But community is built up of even smaller patches. Homeless people value the support of others down the road; those selling hot food in the same street look out for each other and help with dismantling each other's stalls. London Underground staff keep an eye on the woman running the fruit stall outside the station, taking over when she needs a break.

A young Thai woman, new to the business of selling Thai food, appreciated the help she got from a nearby stallholder when a man tried to trick her. 'Ah, someone come to try to complain my food, yes, he try to complain like that. He say diarrhoea? Yes, diarrhoea. But he lie, because he go over there' – gesturing to the next stall – 'and he try to complain, but the owner say, "I didn't come here last week. Why you diarrhoea from my food?" He came by my pitch and complained that. But they call the police and they take him away. I don't know. If [the other stall keeper] didn't tell me, I have to pay him. Yeah.'

Paul H, a trader selling 'tat', as he puts it, at Brick Lane, said: 'The thing about the camaraderie, people will look out for each other. And once you've been next to someone for two or three weeks running, the friendship develops quite quickly because there's kind of a Wild West spirit there in the sense that a lot of people don't have full-time jobs, have never wanted full-time jobs. They've been trading twenty, thirty, forty, fifty, sixty years.'

And a Covent Garden busker: 'Yeah, we do look out for each

other. With other musicians, if the shops are shut and I've got a spare string, I'll help someone out. It's a community, we have a laugh.'

Robin Smith, of Soho Dairy in Berwick Street, says it's 'much harder than working out of a warehouse on an estate, so that's a challenge, but everyone shares the same challenge, so it's quite a good sense of camaraderie, or what's better than that, community on the street. Everybody covers each other's back. You have, you know, thieves and unpleasant, quite abusive people sometimes coming through to you on the street, you're exposed on four sides, you can't have sets of eyes, but you rely on everybody else to watch out for you.'

Most people selling on the streets rely on faithful customers, a community built up over many years. Akim, with his coffee stall near Oxford Street, Hossain the shoe shiner at Marylebone station. And Robin Smith again: 'We have clients, so we have about fifty regular accounts and then we have local customers as well.

'Then we've got our oldest customer, ninety-three-year-old Rino Nintongo, born and bred in Soho, coming in with her family. She's been here all her life. She's amazing. She can buy some milk of course, but she comes here for a chat, more than a chat, I'd say, and we are very much the social epicentre, because we're on the street. It would be more difficult if we were stuck in an office somewhere, it would be less interesting. Our life on the street is what really makes it magical, even though most people don't know there's a community alive and well in Soho.'

Even buskers, who rely on passing trade, do find people returning to see them. Jeremy, the Covent Garden magician, said: 'If you work regularly on one spot, you can get fans, sort of groupies, people who will come back and enjoy watching the show over and over again, not because there's any surprise left in what the tricks are, but because they enjoy the presentation. And then they have friends come and visit, and if they know when you're working, they bring their friends and see you, because part of coming to London was, oh, we have to go and see Jeremy. He's got this great trick that I want you to see. So it's really, it's really fun just to be able to do that.'

There's also a sense of community with his fellow buskers: 'There's a lot of camaraderie among the guys who work on this corner. There's probably about ten people who work here regularly, so on a Saturday in the summer, in the height of the busking season, there can be seven or eight guys here. Everyone has half an hour.'

Syd's Coffee Stall in Shoreditch is a local landmark and a focus for the community. Jane, whose family have run the stall for generations, says: 'People could park up and have a bit of food, have a bit of a chat with their friends and with you and the other customers. It was a community and it still is. Obviously most of those customers have retired, passed on, whatever, but it was a real good community, whether it be taxi drivers, bus drivers, workers, people driving lorries and parking up on their route through London or whatever. It was all kinds of people, which was the good thing about it. I can't understand why people go into these places where they wouldn't get any of that. Everyone just sits in their own bubble. How sad is that?'

The sense of community at established markets goes deep. Community not only with other traders or regular customers, but with the entire group of buyers and sellers, customers and traders: a sense of a shared history. When I asked a man selling plants at Chapel Market in Islington why he still continued to trade after thirty years and with declining custom, he waved his arm around and said, 'Well, this is family, isn't it?'

Bouncer Pixie made the same analogy. 'This is my family – the people ... that I've known and worked with and for. There are people here I've known for twenty-five, thirty years. They've seen me as a glowing knight in shining armour, a really lovely total hippy, and they've seen me be an utter piece of shit. They've been through the journey with me and they're still my mates. They've seen it when I decided at the age of fifty to be a crackhead, ended up losing my mates and they're still my mates afterwards. They gave me loads of shit for it, they didn't let me off, they didn't say, Oh, it's all fine, but they're still my friends. D'you know what I mean? It's family, isn't it? You know, we meet up. We used to live in each other's pockets but then we were younger and there was a lot more going on for us.'

And, of course, rough sleepers. The sense of community on the streets is a vital factor in their survival. And a much derided one.

George, who has been selling the *Big Issue* for many years and lives in a hostel, reflected on his early experiences: 'Many people who sleep rough, you feel part of a bigger thing, there's actually a kinda social network, and you know things, experiences that can make you feel very isolated you can share because there's many other people in that network who have had those experiences – the disappointment, the sleeping rough and walking about at night and not having any money, you know, having holes in your shoes, getting soaking and not being able to get dry, drying socks in McDonald's under the hand dryer in the toilet, you know and these kind of things that, that can seem very isolating if you only know today's society and everyday life. And so the network, if you like, and *Big Issue* land and the street, allows sharing of experiences, and these things are less isolating.'

Irishman Mo says: 'I got a lot of street mates, we look after each other. If I've got a little money I help them out. A lot of them are on the crack, you know. I was too, but I got off it.'

The reason why newly housed people sometimes can't cope is not only the unfamiliarity of being inside, or the difficulty of coping with bills for the first time – both of which are real – but the loneliness. They miss their companions.

Even Safiya, operating out of a solitary brick-built, permanent stall at the bottom of Tottenham Court Road, felt part of the community around her. Although she was on her own, she was in a good position to watch what was taking place on the streets. As a florist she was surrounded by a beautiful display of roses, lilies, pot plants and a variety of other flowers, the scent colouring the street around her. When asked what the worst thing about her job was, she referred to how someone else was treated.

'I don't like, for example, there's a lot of homeless people around here, and I got really upset the other day because there was a guy who sits here all the time. He's harmless. And *five* police officers and two community – I think they're something to do with Camden

Council – came to move him. I personally don't think you need six [*sic*] people to move someone.

'And I thought, for God's sake, leave the poor guy alone. I mean what a waste of taxpayers' money, as well, having so many people. I felt like he felt a little bit intimidated as well. Everybody's got their own story and they're fighting their own battles. I try to be nice to people. But I hate seeing people being horrible to other people.'

She gave me a couple of stems of lilies and eucalyptus and, as I left, said: 'One more thing. I think it's important that stalls like this remain – they help the community.'

8

All in the family

Syd's Coffee Stall has been in Calvert Avenue next to Shoreditch Church for over a hundred years. It is a cart from the horse-drawn era that has been adapted, added to and strengthened over the years, and has an awning that lifts up when the stall is open for business. A catering company called Hillary's Catering was also set up by the same family. Now the stall is about to close, and Jane, the last of the line, agreed to talk about its unique history.

'Tell us a bit about yourself and this famous Syd's Coffee Stall. Have you done this all your life?'

'No, no. As a family, friends, family, neighbours have always helped with our catering business but as far as the stall goes, my dad took it over when they brought him home from a secret mission in the war. 'Cause my grandad had a pension from the First World War and he was gassed in the war as well. So he wasn't a well person. But when he married my nan, my nan used to work there as well, and they used to have other men helping, you know, 'cause it was open more or less twenty-four hours. But when my nan got injured, it was when a bomb dropped just down Boundary Street . . . think it was '42, something like that, and it came down so quick after the siren they didn't have time to get down into the bank [their air raid shelter] and as she was going across the pavement, a piece of shrapnel hit her in the leg. I can always remember me and my brother finding it a bit amusing that she had a big dent in her calf, at the back of her leg. That was well before I was born.

'My mum was a Hackney girl and her family and then my dad's family, my grandad and that ... he used to live in Woolwich Arsenal across the river. But then when he came out the war he came over here and he saw there were ... not wagons really but stalls, they used to have all the way down Shoreditch High Street. This was in the twenties. Just after the First World War. This stall is from 1919. All original, that's why it's getting a bit delicate.

'They wanted the stall to stay open during the Blitz. Because even though it was lights out and that sort of stuff ... it was quite subtle with the lights 'cause they didn't have electric lights. Well, that' – pointing – 'was a gas lamp ... But when it was converted to electricity in, I think, I don't know, probably late thirties or something, because they thought so much of my grandad, they wired him up from the lamp post to have electric at the stall.

'There were all the open stalls down Shoreditch High Street here, when my grandfather came over from Woolwich Arsenal and liked it over here, liked what he saw, he wanted to go bigger and better so that's why he decided to use his war pension to pay to have this specifically made, so it was made as a horse-drawn wagon, say seventy-five per cent, and then this side of it with the counter and everything so that it could be used as he wanted it. It was more upmarket, shall we say, than just standing out in the cold.

'So because Nan wasn't well, the mayor of Shoreditch, the vicar of Shoreditch Church, the environmental health or whatever they were called in those days, and the War Office got in touch with him because as they said we must have the stall open for Simon, the policemen, the ARP ...

'My dad wasn't like Corporal Jones,' she says with a laugh. 'I would say he was like Captain Mainwaring, in fact. He knew what he wanted. So ... because Grandad couldn't help and my nan was injured, they all got together and got the War Office to bring my dad home from the Middle East. He was on a secret mission with the RAF, but they brought him home to run the stall.'

'Right. They thought it was important for morale in London?'

'Exactly, yes. Marvellous isn't it, really. So he came back, took over the stall, that was like up till about late forties, early fifties – 1952, I think it was. Plus his sisters ... my grandad also had cafés around here, so one used to run one café and one used to run the other. It was all family orientated. It was marvellous. So when my dad was here, in the old days they used to do the old people's dinners for Shoreditch, which was like two or three hundred people. In Shoreditch Town Hall.

'The kitchen was in the basement and for that amount of people it was all hands on deck. I don't know whether my brother used to do it, he was a bit younger than me, but I can remember being in the kitchens down there. They didn't have a lift to go from the kitchen up to the rooms where they were doing the dinners. They had a little ... what do they call it? A dumb waiter, which was only about a yard square, you know, so you couldn't get much on there, but I can remember doing that and it was all hands on deck and other people running the stuff upstairs.

'So you know the name "Hillary"? He wanted a name for the catering company 'cause he said he wanted to do weddings and things like that. "Syd's" wasn't really upmarket enough even in those days. You know, my dad was a go-getter. Because Sir Edmund Hillary had just conquered Everest in '53, he decided to call it Hillary Caterers. This is always Syd's stall, but a lot of people know us from Hillary Caterers because we've done so many functions around here, as well as all over London.'

'The people that use the stall, you must know a lot of them personally. The taxi drivers, people working around here, people working on the streets?'

'Oh yes, anybody and everybody. Yes, because we used to open up at half past five in the morning. Till about half past five in the afternoon.

'When I was leaving school my dad said, "What are you gonna do?" And I said, "Well, I haven't really thought about it but the only thing I know is catering." So he said, "Well, if you're gonna do catering, you're gonna go to college and do it properly." Yes, City and Guilds, and I went to ... it was called ... Ealing. Four years.

'Dad wanted me to have the proper background even though it wasn't fancy catering as, you know, it can be today. You still have to learn the trade, know all the background for the catering business. And then I started to take over the store. Must have been over thirty years ago.

'Dad was still doing too much anyway because not only was he working at the stall, he was doing all the outside catering at the weekends. My mum was coping on her own most of the time and obviously doing all the cooking and the preparation for the outside catering, so it gave Daddy a bit of a break to be more at home and be able to organise more for the outside catering, which all the family still helped with. It was a real big family enterprise, everybody together.

'The stall was five days a week. It's always been five days a week 'cause the council ... I don't think, for some reason, decided not to give Grandad a seven-day-a-week thing. It was just during the week, which was fine because then Daddy was doing the outside catering.

'Very rarely on a Sunday, but obviously Saturdays were a big deal. The fact that we were really busy and used to have really big queues round the bank into Shoreditch High Street warranted in those days always two people, usually three, and at times four people. Everybody was sitting with their elbows closed in ... everybody had their own little job. One was up the tea end ... Doubling up. So it was real good days. Lovely, usually ladies when I first started. That would have been the eighties and nineties. It was marvellous.'

'And was it already becoming famous as a sort of proper old-fashioned coffee stall?'

'I don't know the bigger picture but the food and the drinks were proper. Good value for money. It was a magnet to workers in the area, whether they worked in the shops on the street or they were just passing through, and it was a good place to stop because you could park in those days. And we had all the facilities around us, like public loos and a newspaper shop and the bank. What else could you ask for?

'And there was still the manufacturing, although it's still going on today, is not as much as it used to be, is it? So it's unfortunate that Shoreditch is not the stall's area now because ... you know, with all these fancy restaurants and coffee shops and so on. People are earning more money than is sensible to my mind and even though we're still reasonably priced, freshly cooked, a nice bit of banter across the counter, they would prefer to just go into a coffee shop or whatever, order what's there – look at their laptop, or they come away and there's no interaction, which is what we love.

'People say I talk too much but you have to be like that to run our sort of business, always has been. 'Cause my dad was always a good talker.' She laughs. 'Somebody told me, God, do you ever stop talking? I said, Oh, no because there's always something to talk about, especially about the stall because of the current situation. People like to hear about it.

'So I took over the running of the stall in I'm not sure whether it was '86 or '87ish ... most days it would be jump out of bed about four thirty in the morning 'cause I had a flat down the end of the avenue. That was really convenient. So half past four I used to be up, and along there before five o'clock. We would open up and we would still have customers waiting. And we stayed open until about five in the afternoon. Because we had all the facilities for our customers around us, it was ideal.'

'And do you remember when you first started doing the stall in the eighties, there was quite a lot of homelessness in London in those days. Did you have homeless people and people on the streets sometimes?'

'There was a few sort of regulars, I mean we've still got a couple of regulars. You saw John, who just came with his dog and his artwork. Yes, we still have and obviously in the old days it was more. Although it's going up again now, from what you read.'

'Where are these folk going to go when the stall closes then, Jane?'

'I have no idea, because I don't think anybody else would entertain them. Particularly because they're on the street they wouldn't let them in their premises. So we're the only people there and have been for a long time that could offer them that. Where do people go? Places are few and far between these days. I don't know anywhere that does unless you're in the market and they're actually serving off a stall. The markets are dying off now. They're not what they were. It's very sad, 'cause I'm a real market fan.'

'Have you ever had any difficult customers?'

'Oh, well, there's always a few. We have a few at the moment! Characters, this is what makes it so interesting anyway. You put on your best customer service face, of course, never changes.

'But the stall's getting so fragile now and has been for a while. To have reached a hundred years is a feat in itself but it's always going to be very hard. Even if we run it for a few more years it's not gonna last forever because of being out in all weathers for a hundred years. You can't mollycoddle it because you can't do that with a stall. It's our family business and when I go . . .'

'It's going to go . . . into the Museum of London, in fact.'

'Yes, exactly. What's not to like? That's fantastic. We absolutely think that's marvellous. And again have all the history there because that's what we always display at the stall. People come up and say different things. The other day this lady came up and said that it was her grandad that built Grandad's stall, because she saw us on the TV. She was talking about it with her family and saying, "Grandad used to do that". She even gave the address, 280 Hackney Road, and I said, "Yeah, that's it, G. W. Richards," and she said, "Yeah, that was my grandad, George William Richards." He actually made horse-drawn wagons.

'I picked a little piece out of the paper or magazine somewhere recently and it was a picture of a 1919 horse-drawn wagon and I thought, oh my God. It didn't give me any more information than that. That was Grandad's day.

'We are closing on the twentieth of December. That would be our normal closing day for Christmas, but obviously we won't be coming back. That's the plan. I'm dreading it. I know it's gonna be a marvellous day, because past things with the TV crew and stuff and everybody's seen it all over the country. It's gonna be a marvellous day, but it's also gonna be a very sad day and that makes me quite emotional. Family come up to support us, my brother … people from the old days will be there.'

'It's forty years at least that you've been on the stall and it's been a part of your life, hasn't it? From when you were a little girl?'

'Of course, always. When Mum and Dad were off doing other things that we weren't old enough to do, my mum's mum and dad would look after us. I can remember those first few days working at the stall, and he'd come out in the dark every morning … it was different times. In those days you didn't worry about horrible people but obviously in latter years I'd worry about Cheryl [her assistant] opening up on her own like I used to do. There's some horrible people about and I've had the misfortune of being involved a few times. People stealing my handbag and just not being very nice. You take the few with the many good times. Because you're exposed.

'But if Grandad had ever envisaged that it would be going to this day … Once we go I don't think there's anybody else around … apart from the church, that's older than us really! Oranges and lemons! As I say, life won't be the same. But I'm sure I shall be thinking about it every day because it's been part of my life every day for the last thirty-odd years. It's gonna be a big wrench.'

The story made news, on the BBC and in numerous newspaper articles. The 'gentle author' wrote in *Spitalfields Life*:

Syd's Coffee Stall is a piece of our social history that does not draw attention to itself, yet deserves to be celebrated … By a miracle of fortune, and thanks to the hard work of the Tothill family we enjoyed London's oldest Coffee Stall here in our neighbourhood for a hundred years. We cherish it now because the story of Syd's Coffee Stall teaches us that there is a point at which serving a humble cup of tea transcends catering and approaches heroism.

The story of Syd's Coffee Stall is a remarkable one. We might think it anachronistic in twenty-first-century London, but in the world of market trading, family businesses are still a powerful force. When one fruitseller told me: 'But it's a family business, I was expected to do it,' he was speaking for many.

An elderly man at Chapel Market was unpacking vegetables round the back of the stall when his assistant called out: 'How long have you been running this stall?'

'A hundred years.' The young man grinned. 'Not as long as that, but it's been in the family for a long time.'

In the world of trading, the family business is alive and well. More surprisingly, even when there is no family business to support, particular kinds of work are still handed on from father to son. I asked Ray why he had chosen to work for one of London's water companies.

'It's gone through the family, the generations. My dad's done it, my grandad did it. So I thought I could do it. It's better and easier when you're brought up into it. You sort of know the job before you turn up to do it, so that's the way I did it.' The young man sitting next to him turned out to be his nephew. 'Yeah, he wants to come in the trade, so I've taken him on, and I'm showing him the ropes at the moment, see if he likes it or not. If he doesn't then he can try something else. He's eighteen. I've trained probably about ten people in my lifetime, and they're all still doing it, higher up in the trade, doing their own thing now. My brother's been trained up, two or three of my friends and some other people I've trained up as well. My brother still works here in central London. Yeah, it feels like family. All my uncles are in the trade, so it's quite a family little thing . . .'

I asked him about how things would have been in his grandfather's day.

'They're called Victorian water mains. They're still in the ground. So there's two parts, there's R&M, that's water maintenance, and VMR, that's Victorian water mains repair. So still trying to do it from there, it's an ongoing struggle and battle.'

As he talked about his grandfather, and working on the Victorian water mains, one could almost imagine a direct line going back to Mayhew's time, when the Waterworks Clauses Act stipulated that constant piped water had to be available to all dwellings in London. But it only meant that mains had to pass by the dwellings; connecting them to individual houses was up to the residents. And water companies did not abide by the insistence on a 'constant' supply.

Family can be felt both as an incentive and a pressure.

Fadi, selling food: 'The best part of what I do is feeding my family, looking after my family, looking after my son. Yes, I make enough for me to survive and live here.'

Bike courier: 'I love it. If it wasn't for the fact that I wanted a family and to buy a house and a normal life, I think I'd be able to do it for the rest of my life.'

Laura, a dog walker and car boot vendor: 'I was a dancer – ballet, tap – but had to give that up at seventeen because my mother was ill and I had to earn some money. I didn't finish my degree, in performing arts. So went to work for an estate agent, mostly clerical, admin. But I had ants in my pants, anything to get out of the office.'

Mac is still cleaning windows at the age of seventy-seven. 'The guiding light is the struggle my mum and dad 'ad during the war and just after the war, to feed a family of six children, and they kept a smile on their face, and it must have been an awful struggle. So,' he says with emotion, 'I think to meself compared with what they managed done, it's like Christmas every day for us, isn't it? And I think of me poor old mother. I've got four kids, but they're all over the country, children now go to university. There's one in

Liverpool, one in Chester, St Albans; the only one who's near me
is my daughter, Nancy, she's the youngest. The struggle they had
on their face is always there' – he points to his head – 'so I won't
moan about anything, really. No I won't moan about anything.
There we are.'

And when family expectation is not met, it can lead to a sense
of failure. A homeless man told me: 'I failed with the marriage, I
failed with my family, I failed … Even if I called somebody they
would be like, oh he's fucked up again. He should have gone into
the military or he should have gone to university.'

Family is often mentioned as a support and an enabler. Many people
on low incomes can only survive because of their partner's income,
like the motorbike courier, Duncan. 'No, no family. I've just got a
wife, a house and a dog.' We laugh. 'I'm lucky because my wife has
a good job.'

Or because they live with their parents or other family member.
Tashomi, in his thirties, is living his dream as a sax player. 'I live
with my mum in Catford,' he says. 'Not for much longer, I hope.'
The shoe shiner, Hossain, originally from Bangladesh, and street
cleaner, Barry, both came to London to study, stayed on, and live
with their families.

Covent Garden magician Jeremy also relies on his family. 'I had
some health problems, and it sort of put some pressure on the family
relationships, so er well, everyone agreed I should come to England
and recuperate a little bit, so I stayed with my brother for the best
part of a year.'

Zack, giving out leaflets outside Westminster Abbey, has to
live with his parents. 'But I still have to pay rent, because we are
a family with a very low amount of funds.' He holds his thumb
and first finger very close together. 'And rent prices in London, as
you know, are going higher and higher all the time, and there's
nothing much people who are renting can do about it. Yeah, that's
life, I'm afraid.'

Some rely on parents for childcare. Romanian *Big Issue* seller Livia has three children, aged four, three and one. 'I've been here more than eight years, selling the *Big Issue* since 2011. I'm coming when I have eighteen. I have kids, you know, babies. I'm selling, I buy everything for my kids. I'm working for my kids because even if I have a proper job my boss worries me any time but here any time my mum call me, me leave and go home for my babies.'

'So your mother looks after the children?'

'Yeah, yeah. I live Woolwich, Plumstead, yes. I work here long time because Plumstead . . .' The noise of a motor bike obliterates what she says. 'Not every day, my mum is sick, is bad, one year ago, and then I am not coming every day. Two, three times a week, not every day. Morning nine o'clock till two or three o'clock. No longer because my babies cry.'

As one of the vagrants' statements from *London Labour and the London Poor* shows, family can be an incentive to give up a life of crime:

My mother came out to the garden in front of the house, after my father had gone to his work, and spoke to me. She wished me to reform my character. I could not make any rash promises then. I had but very little to say to her. I felt myself at that same time, for the very first time in my life, that I was doing wrong. I thought, if I could hurt my mother so, it must be wrong to go on as I did. I had never had such thoughts before. My father's harsh words always drove such thoughts out of my head; but when I saw my mother's tears, it was more than I could stand . . . After that I stopped knocking about the country, sleeping in unions, up to November. I came to London again, and remained up to this time. Since I have been in town I have sought for work at the floor-cloth and carpet manufactory in the Borough, and they wouldn't even look at me in my present state. I am heartily tired of my life now altogether, and would like to get out of it if I could. I hope at least I have given up my love of drink, and I am sure, if I could once again lay my hand on some work, I should be quite a reformed character.

The same is true for Freddie, currently sleeping rough: 'Criminal life? Yeah, I'm done wiv all that. I promised my mother I'm never going back. My brother's doing eighteen years inside. He's been in since 2012. Yeah, I visit now and then, because it's so far up the country, Long Larton he's in, it's right up the top and my mother's ill, as well. She's in a bad way, she faints a lot, and like I promised her I'd never go back. She needs me. My mum and dad, they're getting on, and I'm worried, like, because my brother gets out in 2030, I'm thinking whether my mum and dad will make it when it's time for him to get out, because my mum's sixty, my dad's sixty-five, sixty-six.'

A painful childhood or lack of family is still keenly felt. McGinlay, who has been diagnosed with PTSD, said, 'My mother is, unfortunately, a violent alcoholic. So for my own safety I went into foster care and then my relationship with my father deteriorated after my parents got divorced when I was ten.'

A man dealing drugs said: 'My dad was my best mate. We were really close but he died when I was fourteen.'

Anthony, drawing caricatures in Trafalgar Square, was also missing his family. 'I ain't got no kids myself, but I have sisters and brothers. My mum and dad's dead now. They died in Jamaica. They lived in England for forty or fifty years, then they went to Jamaica and then they died.'

On the other hand, *Big Issue* seller Darren dismisses the whole idea of family.

'My mum, she's an alcoholic, so she just couldn't handle looking after me and my sisters. Don't do family. Brought myself up, can be done.' He laughs. 'I got eight sisters but I don't see none of them, they all got adopted. They got their lives. Yeah, I've got five children. Same partner, together ten years. No, not together now, No, no, it's better. Prefer being on my own. All the children in care.'

II

Market Traders

9

Billingsgate then and now

To see this market in its busiest costermonger time, the visitor should be there about seven o'clock on a Friday morning. The market opens at four, but for the first two or three hours, it is attended solely by the regular fishmongers and 'bummarees' who have the pick of the best there. As soon as these are gone, the costers' sale begins.

The morning air is filled with a kind of seaweedy odour, reminding one of the sea-shore; and on entering the market, the smell of fish, of whelks, red herrings, sprats, and a hundred others, is almost overpowering.

The wooden barn-looking square where the fish is sold, is soon after six o'clock crowded with shiny cord jackets and greasy caps. Everybody comes to Billingsgate in his worst clothes, and no one knows the length of time a coat can be worn until they have been to a fish sale. Through the bright opening at the end are seen the tangled rigging of the oyster-boats and the red worsted caps of the sailors. Over the hum of voices is heard the shouts of the salesmen, who, with their white aprons, peering above the heads of the mob, stand on their tables, roaring out their prices.

In the darkness of the shed, the white bellies of the turbots, strung up bow-fashion, shine like

mother-of-pearl, while the lobsters, lying upon
them, look intensely scarlet, from the contrast.
Brown baskets piled up on one another, and
with the herring-scales glittering like spangles
all over them, block up the narrow paths. Men
in coarse canvas jackets, and bending under
huge hampers, push past, shouting 'Move on!
move on, there!' and women, with the long limp
tails of cod-fish dangling from their aprons,
elbow their way through the crowd. Round the
auction-tables stand groups of men turning over
the piles of soles, and throwing them down till
they slide about in their slime; some are smelling
them, while others are counting the lots.

'Ha-a-ansome cod! best in the market! All
alive! alive! alive O!' 'Ye-o-o! Ye-o-o! here's your
fine Yarmouth bloaters! Who's the buyer?' 'Here
you are, governor, splendid whiting! some of
the right sort!' 'Turbot! turbot! all alive! turbot!'
'Glass of nice peppermint! this cold morning
a ha'penny a glass!' 'Here you are at your own
price! Fine soles, O!' 'Oy! oy! oy! Now's your
time! fine grizzling sprats! all large and no small!'
'Hullo! hullo here! beautiful lobsters! good and
cheap! fine cock crabs all alive O!' 'Five brill and
one turbot – have that lot for a pound! Come
and look at 'em, governor; you wont see a better
sample in the market.' 'Here, this way! this way
for splendid skate! skate O! skate O!' 'Had –
had – had – had – haddick! all fresh and good!'

Everybody was soon busy laying out their
stock. The wrinkled dull-eyed cod was freshened
up, the red-headed gurnet placed in rows, the
eels prevented from writhing over the basket
sides by cabbage-leaves, and the soles paired
off like gloves. Then the little trucks began to
leave, crawling, as it were, between the legs of
the horses in the vans crowding Thames-street,

and plunging in between huge waggons, but
still appearing safely on the other side; and the
4,000 costers who visit Billingsgate on the Friday
morning were shortly scattered throughout the
metropolis.

Along with the fruit and veg market of New Spitalfields and
Smithfield, which sells meat, Billingsgate is one of London's three
major wholesale markets. It is the country's largest inland fish
market, with nearly a hundred stalls, thirty shops, a café and an
array of cold rooms and freezers spread over a thirteen-acre site at
West Poplar, in the shadow of the Canary Wharf skyscrapers. It
serves as a wholesale market for fishmongers and restaurant owners,
but it is also open to the public. The market is free to access, open
from 4 a.m. to 8 a.m., Tuesday to Saturday (it often stays open an
extra hour on Saturday, which has become the most popular day
with the public).

Billingsgate Market was set up at its original site in what is now
the area between Tower Bridge and London Bridge by an Act of
Parliament in 1699. Fish were sold on the riverside from shacks and
stalls on one of the first wharfs built along the Thames. Despite
moving twice, the market has always been an iconic site in London,
and its next proposed move, along with Smithfield and New
Spitalfields, to a purpose-built site at Barking Reach in Dagenham
Docks at the end of 2020 is causing concern amongst people who
fear that the market will become a casualty of the capital's compul-
sion to modernise blindly at the expense of its history.

Billingsgate's first move came in 1850 when, in response to burgeoning trade, the market relocated to a purpose-built site on nearby
Lower Thames Street. Over the following century, the market
continued to grow, forcing another move in 1982, this time to its
current site at Poplar Docks. At the time of the move the docklands,
which had been obliterated by incessant bombing during the war,
offered cheap real estate.

Questions as to the suitability of a wholesale fish market at the heart of the world's premier banking district were raised at the same speed as its burgeoning skyline. Nobody could have imagined, however, when the London Docklands Development Corporation (LDDC) was set up to redevelop the area in 1981, that Billingsgate would end up in the middle of one of the world's most expensive business hubs.

The market is a strange place to visit, especially at 4 a.m., when most people are asleep. It's difficult to find your way in, with a lack of signs to direct you towards the several sets of narrow brick steps cut out of the wall to the front. But everyone else seems to know the drill. Customers stride purposefully, shoulders down against the wind, towards a functional edifice dominated by its quirky iconic yellow roof. The blue capital letters that exclaim BILLINGSGATE MARKET are emblazoned on a rim sitting beneath a series of bright yellow tubes which jut brashly skyward in a series of adjoining pyramids. Set against the grey uniformity of the office buildings that tower above it, the roof is like a playful kid who has accidentally stumbled into his dad's solemn corporate boardroom meeting.

But that's where playful ends. It's a market, so of course there is the usual banter, but this is primarily wholesale trade. Buyers and vendors are focused and busy, especially for the first hour between four and five, when you'll find the professional big buyers sourcing the highest quality produce.

While your mind may be struggling to process the feeling that you've accidentally wondered into the back entrance of a factory on the docks, you suddenly find yourself in the hustle and bustle of the main hall. Beautiful it is not, but it is most certainly stunning, and on a multi-sensory level.

It's fish, and there's a lot of it, so the first thing that hits you, even before you enter the main hall, is the powerful smell. Once inside, it can feel pretty claustrophobic, with no effort to sanitise the experience for retail customers who aren't used to the cold, the noise, the wet floor, that smell and the myriad types of fish, which are truly a sight to behold. It's a sensory overload on so many levels, but the stars of the show are the fish. For me, at least, they're as good to look at as they're as bad to smell. Rows of square white units are packed with a fascinating variety of marine life in a multitude of different colours, shapes and sizes. Sea bass for a tenner a box, prawns at twenty-seven quid a kilo, salmon, I'm guessing of the wild variety, for £18 each. The fish are like glorious sculptures, some of nature's most beautiful work. There's one huge specimen that looks as if it's made up for a Kiss concert, while another creature (to call it a fish would be a stretch) bears a disturbing resemblance to the star of Ridley Scott's *Alien*.

Their wet, multicoloured scales blink rapidly in the light, which in turn is reflected by the glistening lake of water on the concrete floor. The result is a beautiful lightshow that adds to the strange intensity of the experience. Juxtaposed against this shimmering light is the incessant crashing of an industrial market chorus, led by the booming voices of stallholders and supported by the rattling pallet trucks and trolleys. Customers hand over grubby notes for fish either pre-packed in boxes or unceremoniously stuffed into black plastic bags. The process of exchange is accompanied by the effortless banter of vendors and buyers well practised in the art of the verbal exchanges that grease these transactions.

It became easier to appreciate the rhythm and rituals of Billingsgate as the professional buyers started to leave around 6 a.m. The market calms down after that and there are bargains to be had after seven, with some stallholders already packing up. As the crowd thins out the retail customers begin to appear, the odd savvy customer pitching up at 7 a.m. to hunt down potential bargains. Jim, who comes to the market three times a week, said, 'You can get some right bargains around this time. It has to go, you see, so if you know what you're doing you can get some great deals.'

As things wound down, I chatted to a few stallholders and market staff about their work and the impending move to Dagenham.

Shak, who has worked at the market for twenty years, said, 'I think it's going to be better, because all three markets will be in the same place. So we might get more customers. People aren't really talking about the move much. The original market was in Tower Bridge, so nobody is concerned with the tradition of this site. Really this isn't the right place for a fish market.'

Jo Neville, a stallholder, said, 'Some people are moaning about the move but I can't see it. As long as the transport links are all right out there. For me getting there will be a lot easier 'cause the Blackwall Tunnel can be a nightmare. Transport should be better. At the end of the day this place has only been here thirty-five years and wasn't designed as a market. This was an old warehouse. When it moved, there was nothing else here except for 1 Canada Square. I love the idea of the new place, it's a great concept. One worry is that Tesco and Morrisons want to put a stand in there – you get a lot of people who come down here and they go, Oh, you can get this and that at a supermarket for a lot less, but a lot of that stuff isn't fresh. It's frozen. Obviously we get it fresh, straight from the coast, but still I don't know how the supermarkets even do the prices they do.'

With hindsight, Billingsgate was on a collision course with its neighbours from the very beginning. The market's latest move is being lamented by those who see it as one the last vestiges of old London, but the writing has been on the wall for the traditional ways of the market since the system of using 'fish porters' there was revoked in 2012.

10

Selling on the street

Each salesman tries his utmost to sell his wares,
tempting the passers-by with his bargains. The
boy with his stock of herbs offers 'a double
'andful of fine parsley for a penny;' the man with
the donkey-cart filled with turnips has three
lads to shout for him to their utmost, with their
'Ho! ho! hi-i-i! What do you think of this here?
A penny a bunch – hurrah for free trade! *Here's*
your turnips!' Until it is seen and heard, we
have no sense of the scramble that is going on
throughout London for a living. The same scene
takes place at the Brill – the same in Leather-
lane – the same in Tottenham-court-road – the
same in Whitecross-street; go to whatever
corner of the metropolis you please, either on a
Saturday night or a Sunday morning, and there
is the same shouting and the same struggling
to get the penny profit out of the poor man's
Sunday's dinner.

'STRAWBERRIES, BEST STRAWBERRIES, TWO FOR
A POUND!' A huge voice soaring over the noise of traffic in
Tottenham Court Road. A fair-haired young woman with a broad
and friendly smile, made stocky by a puffa jacket worn against the
January cold.

'That's quite some voice.'

'Thank you.'

'Do you sing?'

'No. I sound like a strangled cat. STRAWBERRIES, COME AND GET THEM HERE. ONLY TWO FOR A POUND!'

Unlike the traders shouting over each other in Mayhew's market scene, Julie is on her own. She works on a solitary fruit stall opposite Goodge Street station, open on weekdays, mainly to serve office workers in the area. We stand at the stall, and from time she breaks off to serve a customer or greet a passer-by.

'I was working at a flower stall in Finchley. Got into it through an aunt, then they needed someone here – no, not family, they're friends of friends. I've been here about fourteen months. I was meant to be here for a day, and I stayed.

'Yes, I'm here every day, Monday to Friday, one till seven. It's my work. I love it. You get all sorts here – Hong Kong, America, all over. Bad experiences? I've had a couple. Rude customers, I've had things thrown at me, I've had people threatening to fight me – it happens. Just because they don't get their own way. And you get some . . . Well, Arab men, they're very anti-women so when I don't back down to what they're saying, they call me all the names under the sun . . . No skin off my nose, water off a duck's back. I tell them to come back and see my dad. They go, What? And I say yes, you'll have to take it up with him. And they never come back.'

She stops to direct someone. 'Yes, fifth turning on the left.' Turning back to me, 'Obviously I look like a fucking info post. And there was a black cab strike, and they were all lined up here, and people asking me, What are they doing? What are they doing? Don't get me started.

'Oh, we get all sorts here, we do. Every afternoon we get the trombonist that goes along, and then the Hare Krishnas coming past. Sometimes they meet in the middle, which is oh God! When the station closes, that's always hilarious. I get on really well with all of them in the station. Because I'm out here by myself for a lot of the day, they'll keep their eye on me. If I need to go anywhere, they'll come out here and serve for me while I run off. And when they close it, the way people speak to them, I don't know how they do it. And they get people screaming and shouting at them.

'One of them comes and hides behind the stall when she needs a cigarette, she comes out here and we both hide from whatever we're hiding from. And there's a customer, she comes here nearly every day, and when she comes, one of the blokes is normally here as well, so I can kind of run away from her. I don't want to serve her, she's been literally chasing me round the stall. I'm going, I don't want to serve you, go away, and she says, I want to be served by my friend, and I go, we're not friends, I'm running away from you, I'm trying to hide. She's just really hard work. So when it's four for a pound she says, I'll take five. And I say, no you won't. If you don't do it in Tesco's, you don't do it here.

'Hello, my love, what you got there?' And she goes off to serve someone else.

Napoleon (and Adam Smith) famously called England a nation of shopkeepers. They might have called London a city of market traders, or, as Mayhew would have called them, costermongers. (Though 'costermonger' referred literally to people who bought fruit and vegetables wholesale and sold them retail, it was applied more generally.) He estimated that there were thirty thousand costermongers in London, about fourteen stalls to the mile, selling fruit or fish on the main thoroughfares. Market traders are at the heart of *London Labour and the London Poor*. Hundreds, maybe thousands of pages are devoted to the selling of almost anything people might need, from watercress to dog collars, from shellfish to stationery, from second-hand clothes to dolls, boot laces and rat poison. And devoted to those who sold them – men, women and children; their habits, education, lodging, and the way they talked.

There is not so much variety, nor quite so many traders, today, but still a considerable number of people try to make their living by selling on the streets. Many of them are in small groups of stalls or individually, often in purpose-built stand-alone cubicles. Newspaper stalls are often to be found outside stations, as are people selling luggage, bags and hats and gloves. Solitary fruit and veg stalls can be found outside a number of tube stations. On Tottenham Court Road is a permanent cubicle catering for mobile phones, and Alan, who has just started selling flowers there. He finds being on a solitary stall isolating. 'I wouldn't recommend it.'

One of the more informal groups of stalls can be found at Peckham Rye. A windy September day, leaves and rubbish blowing along the street. A grubby station, with a few stalls scattered along a road smelling of fish and a breath of spice. The shops sell Afro cosmetics and wigs and a wide variety of fruit, veg, fish and meat, sometimes all in one store. The stalls too have an African flavour. One sells dresses made in Thailand but with African designs. Prices are low: three vests for £4. Hats too. Another stall across the road sells similar items, but scarves rather than hats. Behind them, there's a colourful vegetable stall catering for a largely African clientele, but also for more recent white middle-class incomers. Lots of peppers in stainless-steel bowls, aubergines, okra, ginger, limes, apples, bananas. All pick your own. Eight peppers for £1. Five crooked cucumbers. On the day I visited, there were no white customers.

But most outside trading in London is contained within established markets. Mayhew only lists thirty-seven, which specialised less than today, selling everything from vegetables to fish to fruit, depending on the season. Today, there are, apparently, 280 retail markets in London, a rise from the 163 mapped in 2010. Research for a report by the Mayor of London's office found that retail markets in London support 13,250 jobs.

London is renowned for its markets. Crowds from all over the world flock to the world-famous Covent Garden, Camden Lock, Petticoat Lane and Borough markets, to buy antiques, specialised food, and artefacts from pottery to jewellery, organic cotton baby clothes and handmade soaps and cosmetics.

As the report says, 'Markets ... are an expression of our communities and who we are. They help build a strong sense of local identity. And they are also a source of fresh and healthy food, as well as important meeting places where people from different backgrounds can come together. Markets are the original business incubators; as accessible open workspaces they offer a unique, low-risk opportunity for people to test business ideas and learn new skills.' A London Markets Board has been set up in recognition that 'while some markets are flourishing, others are facing challenges'.

As this report recognises, there are many kinds of market. The privately run farmers' markets are doing especially well. These are typically open once a week in venues all over London, from William Ellis School near Gospel Oak, to Bloomsbury, to King's Cross, and they tap into a trend towards healthy and organic food. Here the discerning foodie can find smoked salmon bagels at £4.50, home-made black pudding at £7 for a small one, £12 for a large; three macaroons for £5, or 250 grams of Somerset brie for £7. But I want to concentrate not on farmers' markets, nor on those named in the report as 'iconic', both of which cater largely for more affluent sectors of society and those coming from outside the area, but on the traditional street markets, reflecting the changing needs and nature of their local communities.

A special case needs to be made, perhaps, for Covent Garden: for centuries a central part of London life. In Mayhew's day, the costermongers were at its heart, selling a wide variety of fruit, vegetables and flowers. Few had fixed stalls, but with goods carried on their backs, heads or in barrows, thousands of traders wove their way through the market.

I have memories of visiting in the 1960s, sometimes when coming back from the opera, when the market traders were setting up for the day. Even then the wholesale flower market, on the site of what is now the transport museum, was England's premier flower market, with flowers coming in from all over the world. Covent Garden was a colourful, chaotic scene, with piles of fruit and vegetables, and barrows being pushed from one place to another. By the end of the 1960s, traffic congestion was causing problems, and in 1974 the market relocated to the New Covent Garden Market, about 3 miles (5 km) south-west at Nine Elms.

The old Covent Garden site today is a very different place, though the fine structure, stone pillars and metal arched roof are the same. It's much cleaner, more elegant, with no trace of the dirt or the piles of vegetables and fruit. Covent Garden today is a haven for tourists, with stalls selling everything from jewellery to T-shirts, organic toiletries to fine art prints, with cafés either under cover in both levels of the market itself or in the open air round the edges of the square. The only reminders of its past are the old-fashioned (but new) barrows, bearing flowers and directions and street maps for visitors, and some of the names. The Apple Hall is a reminder of the apple women of Mayhew's day:

> Then there are the apple merchants, with their fruit of all colours, from the pale green to the bright crimson and the baskets ranged in rows on the pavement before the little shops. Round these the customers stand, examining their stock and counting their money. Groups of apple women with straw pads on their crushed bonnets and coarse shawls crossing over their bosoms . . . chatting in Irish and smoking their short pipes.

It's a pleasing coincidence that the computer firm, Apple, should have a big shop in Covent Garden.

Traditional London street markets like Chapel Market in Islington, Roman Road in the East End, and others are under pressure, particularly from gentrification, changes in population, and competition from online retailing. The refrain most often heard from white, working-class Londoners is that 'fings ain't what they used to be'.

To run a market stall as a trader, you need either a temporary ('casual') or permanent licence from the local council. The fees and charges are based on agreements established in the London Local Authorities Act 1990, which manages how councils should regulate markets. Prices vary according to the council, the location, the day of the week and the type of stall. Fruit and vegetable stalls tend to be more expensive, because of the cost of managing the waste.

Apparently, managing fruit and vegetable waste accounts for half of the entire running cost of Hackney's markets.

At Ridley Road in Hackney, it costs £75 per week (or £69 in zone 3 of the market) on Monday to Saturday for most stalls, but for those selling fruit and vegetables it's £116 (or £108). Per day on Friday or Saturday it's £31 (£28). And in the various markets in Tower Hamlets, the cost of stalls is considerably more at weekends. The costs per day are:

> Chrisp Street: Monday to Friday, £7 for a normal stall, £8 for a
> large one; Saturday: £27 or £47
> Whitechapel: Monday to Friday, £7; Saturday £30
> Columbia Road: Sundays only, £47
> Petticoat Lane: £7; Saturday n/a, Sunday £34.

Aisha, who sells mattresses in Whitechapel Market, told me: 'We have to pay for the pitch every day. That's another way we are surviving, because we only pay for a day. So if I don't come tomorrow, I don't have to pay.' Mattresses need a very big pitch: 'Yes, we pay two, three times, we pay double, we pay extra.'

But costs are not altogether straightforward. People have to pay for extras, like storage and parking. Referring to Berwick Street, Robin told me, 'The cost of the stall is quite difficult to calculate, technically the cost of the stall is not very much – the pitch, rather, not the stall. The reason the pitch price is not very much, you may consider, is because there's no services or infrastructure in Soho. So you have to store for yourself, you have to drive in for yourself, drive out for yourself, there's no wash towel facilities, there's no toilet facilities, you have to get those for yourself. There's *nothing* here, it's all been sold off.'

Paul H, the trader selling 'tat' at Brick Lane, likes the lack of bureaucracy there: 'One good thing about Brick Lane – you don't have to jump through any hoops. You turn up at five. If you're not a regular you probably get half a table, share with another non-regular. So you don't have to deal with Tower Hamlets, you don't have to provide a DNA sample or any of that bollocks. Islington for example – I believe – you have to have your ancestry traced about five hundred years back. Bermondsey I think you can sort of set up, but you need to talk to Mike who runs Spitalfields as well.'

As in Mayhew's day, markets offer a wide range of goods and services: from clothes to jewellery, from pet food to luggage. Stalls selling dairy products are quite unusual, but Robin Smith's at Berwick Street Market is one.

Berwick Street runs south from Oxford Circus, with the market on a pedestrianised patch at the southern end. Robin is a shortish man in his fifties, with greying stubble and glasses. He was too busy and stressed on two previous attempts to interview him, and on this occasion he again said he would be stressed. It seems to be his permanent state. In the event, against the noise of a development behind us, he talked for a long time, rapidly, fluently and with passion, hardly pausing to draw breath. On a humid July day, we sheltered from the rain under the awning of his stall. In the half hour we were together, just two customers came, and one fellow stallholder. The price of his milk, surprisingly, is comparable with that of supermarkets: £1 for a two-pint bottle, 50p for a pint. They are still using plastic, but hope to get into glass.

'We sell the highest welfare produce we can source commercially, so that's not to say it's all the highest. If it were all the highest, it would be four times the price and not sustainable in that we could buy it every day.

'I picked dairy because it was the hardest thing I could imagine doing on the street. If you go into any modern supermarket or modern food outlet and you can't find milk, you're probably not going to shop there. My ambition is to bring the street back to life, and so unless you can do things like milk, vegetables, there's very little reason to see you other than as a visitor attraction, and that's not what the street's about. It's very much a wholesale–retail street with people supplying to businesses around and businesses buy back to the street. So the reason people have invested in us, it's not money, it's trust.

'Without Berwick Street, there's no Soho, really: it's the heart of it. There's a couple of beating hearts in Soho, there's the gay community and creative industries, and so on, but this is one of the beating hearts and without it Soho would be at least a third poorer, if not more. So that's important. And, just as importantly, we're supplying some of the people who used to buy from the market as well as the new players, and that fills us with confidence, that we're able to talk to both sides.

'But the greatest thing about doing dairy, despite the challenge, is that we're able to walk into kitchens every day, and share stories and collect stories, so we've got conversation going around daily. How's that going? How are you? Which is remarkably fulfilling and so useful, in as much as I say, what's going on here, and what we can do about it to ensure that the Soho we leave is better than the one that we found. And that's why I do it.'

On the corner of Warren Street and Conway Street is a reminder of the past in the name and history of The Old Dairy café, which used to be a dairy, and kept cows. But otherwise it's a far cry from the sale of milk in Mayhew's day:

> The principal sale of milk from the cow is in St. James's Park ... The milk-sellers obtain leave from the Home Secretary, to ply their trade in the park. There are eight stands in the summer, and as many cows, but in the winter there are only four cows. The milk-vendors sell upon an average, in the summer, from eighteen to twenty quarts per day; in the winter, not more than a third of that quantity. The chief customers are infants, and adults, and others, of a delicate constitution, who have been recommended to take new milk. Soldiers are occasional customers.

Local markets

But, traditionally, it is fruit and vegetables that have been the mainstay of local markets. It is easy to suppose that Victorian London had access to fewer varieties of fruit and vegetables. Not so. Most fruit and vegetables available now could also be found in Mayhew's day. It was during the Second World War that many varieties of fruit and veg became difficult to obtain. True, in Victorian England there were no avocados or kiwi fruit, but the first recorded sale of bananas in England, though they were expensive until the end of the nineteenth century, was in 1633. Peaches too were rare and expensive until the twentieth century. But in the nineteenth century, pineapples became cheaper, and were first canned towards the end of the century. Bunches of watercress, such an important foodstuff in Mayhew's time, are rarely to be found in markets now. Just packaged in larger supermarkets.

Goods such as potatoes or meat were sometimes weighed in Mayhew's time (though there were often arguments about weight) and sometimes sold by the sieve or other container. Modern markets have moved away from weighing – there were arguments about rigged scales in the 1970s too – and the cheaper markets usually sell bowls of anything from aubergines to plums for £1. Haggling, so much a feature of Victorian markets, is rare but still to be found in London, especially in markets like Roman Road and Ridley Road, which cater for local residents from communities for whom haggling is the norm.

Ridley Road Market in Dalston, Hackney, has been a London institution since the late 1880s, encapsulating the area's rich history of immigration and cultural diversity. At various times in its existence, the 150-stall market has been taken over by the Jewish, Caribbean and Turkish communities. A friend who lived near by in the 1980s said that at that time the customers were mainly Caribbean, the food for sale reflecting their presence. Now, she thought, it was more African, as well as attracting a fringe of middle-class residents who have moved into the area.

The market stretches the length of a street spreading out immediately opposite the entrance to Dalston Kingsland station. It's a traditional market, full of all sorts of products: fish, children's shoes, pig's trotters, bras, incense, fruit and vegetables, yams, fabrics, herbal remedies, belts, carpets, bags, hats. There's a notice on

a fruit stall saying 'No tasting pl'; at another stall, someone giving back massages. The stalls run down the middle of the street, with small shops set into the fabric of the buildings on either side, and one or two scruffy little cafés with a couple of tables and chairs. It was bustling on a Friday morning, the customers mostly Afro-Caribbean, the stallholders of a variety of ethnicities. I bought a pair of 'handmade' earrings from a woman at a stall outside her hairdresser's shop. She told me that the shops were separate from the stalls, and were owned by 'a Jewish man', whereas the stalls were council. She pays £900 a month for her shop, and agreed it was a lot, but said she had been there for many years.

Some stallholders are distant figures presiding over a giant fruit and vegetable stall, banked to make the most of the higher cost of the pitch. Other stalls are smaller and more intimate; many of their customers have been coming for decades. Stallholders call out, 'Come and have a look. Come and have a look.' 'Bananas, two bowls for a pound.'

'You see those shops?' one trader said. 'Know what they were? They were stables. In those days, there were no cars, everything was horse and cart, so that was where people put their horses when they were running stalls. The man on the next stall, he's dead now, he had a horse and he kept him there.'

The market has an ancient history, but doubt has recently been cast upon its future after traders within the covered section of the market were served eviction notices. The evictions were cancelled after a petition by traders and local residents gained more than nine thousand signatures, but its future is still uncertain.

Lower Marsh Market, near Waterloo station, is one of London's most ancient. According to its website, the first references to Lower Marsh date from 1332 when the name of the road was first given as Lambeth Marsh. In 1889, with the introduction of the new Borough of Lambeth, the road's name was changed to Upper and Lower Marsh. At that time, the market ran from Blackfriars to Vauxhall.

On a day when the then Mayor of London, Boris Johnson, walked down the street with Prince Charles, one of the vendors was heard to murmur, 'That'll be the end of Lower Marsh Market.' And certainly, despite the hype, it has changed beyond all recognition. When I worked near by in the 1970s, it was a scruffy, lively street, full of quirky shops and market stalls selling a whole range of produce and crafts. Now street food has taken over.

Shepherd's Bush Market runs down a long road from Shepherd's Bush Market station to Goldhawk Road station. A long-term resident of the area told me that as a result of the hike in oil prices in the 1970s, many people from the Middle East came to the area, and it became known as the only market in London where haggling was permissible. The local people running the stalls learnt some Arabic to deal with it. Since then the stallholders have apparently shifted from predominantly Cockney to Sikh.

The resident pointed out that the area is now divided by a wall: there's a barrier between the Westfield shopping centre which caters for more affluent shoppers from the outside, and Shepherd's Bush Market for locals. Parallel worlds, divided by a wall. The division is indicated by the difference in the stations. Shepherd's Bush Market and Goldhawk Road stations are shabby, with long flights of stairs – often used by elderly people with sticks and crutches, finding it hard to cope. Wood Lane, the station for Westfield, however, is noticeably smart. A short distance to the north is Latimer Road, with the appalling sight of the burnt remains of Grenfell Tower, now shrouded in white plastic; a notice at the top bears the message 'Grenfell, forever in our hearts', and the picture of a heart.

Tower Hamlets in the East End of London is exceptionally rich in markets. Unsurprisingly for a borough with its history of migration, its markets – Roman Road, Chrisp Street and, above all, Whitechapel – reflect the diverse population.

My memories of Whitechapel Market from the late 1990s are of emerging from the tube station on to the main road to be greeted by a fragrant waft of spice. In 2019 there's no such smell, no spice stall – although this is a weekday morning in the summer holidays. Maybe Saturdays are different.

But still the array of stalls that stretch along the north side of Whitechapel Road – selling anything from lengths of cloth to golden costume jewellery, bowls or mountains of fruit and vegetables, with Asian specialities predominating towards the eastern end – is a rich one. Fish, shoes, Indian dresses, and tops from £5. Prices are low, the clientele still mostly Bangladeshi, as are many of the stallholders, though the fishmonger is from Italy and sadly, my Italian doesn't quite stretch to the necessary vocabulary. Men and women pass by, dressed variously in flowing robes and Western attire.

The big dark-skinned man selling drinks with a straw straight from green coconuts says that trade is good. As they do the importing themselves, and sell 'about four thousand a week', he finds it fine. I watch him hack off the end of the fruit, pierce it and insert the straw. It's a traditional Bangladeshi street drink and, at £3 a time, it's evidently popular, especially on hot days, though I considered his estimate of numbers a little extravagant.

The man cutting keys has little English, but pointed me towards Aisha, the woman selling mattresses, who, he says, has been at the market for twenty-five years. He does say that there used to be lots of people but now hardly anyone passes by. As seems to be the case, but I had put it down to the time of year. It's 7 p.m., closing time, stallholders are dismantling their stalls, wheeling equipment and produce up the streets in trolleys.

At the eastern end is a very large pitch, with wooden slatted bases and plastic crates, from which the stallholder's son is removing the mattresses and starting to store them in a van. Prices vary from £225 to £245 for a double mattress, £275 to £295 for the whole bed; a single is £55 or £75. Aisha, a tall strong-looking older woman, goes to move the other van. With a background of traffic and sirens, we sit on a slatted base and talk.

Aisha starts by telling me about a very hard worker whom she misses, but who was a drug user and always had his mind on money for drugs. 'He sold a mattress and stole a hundred pounds. I don't know where he is now. Maybe in prison, but I'd like him back. He's a very good worker.

'I live in this area all my life. I sort of grow up here, and am getting old here as well.' She laughs. 'I'm nearly seventy. I've been selling mattresses here for the last five, six years. Because we didn't have the money. My husband died at a very young age. So we lost it all; things weren't going very well. He left a very big debt. My husband overdraft, so we didn't have the money, the children were small – very young children. So they grow up, and we end up here. Mattress? Because there was a guy here before. We knew him for all our life, really, yeah, he was telling me and we didn't have anything, and he was just living close to us, and he was gone, so there was an opportunity. There was no one else selling mattresses.

'Money? It's OK, not really like a rich one, but coping. How many we sell? I haven't got a clue. Sometimes we don't sell any, sometimes we sell five. It doesn't know every day what will happen tomorrow, nobody knows.

'We get them here, in England. Before, we had this fashion business when my husband was alive. We used to have a wholesale business. When I was younger I used to make these garments. He left everything like that. My son he was only six year old. So it's very hard when you have this business. Couldn't cope for very long, they were running round all the time, yes, it's very hard when the children are small and you are working; it's terrible. Thirty year ago, 1999. All that time.'

Pause. 'I enjoy it because ...' She laughs again. 'When I had visitors I used to think everyone selfish, but since we are here you always meet good and bad, who don't have sense, mad people, young people, you meet them all. But you always get a feeling, you always learn how to cope, how to live with the people. Yeah, I really enjoy being out here, because I've been here all my life, nearly everybody know me. My son help me, full time. One or two women come before, but they come and gone, maybe they had a husband, maybe they couldn't cope. But because I don't have any other income, I had to cope. We had to do it, isn't it?

'Before I started market I applied for the jobs, I was fifty at that time, I was a machinist, I was a driver, I apply for everything, but no one came for the job for two months. Because when people go for jobs, they always look for young people, innit? So then I gave up. And I ended up here. Tough, very tough. The market. Yes, the last three years I do get tired. When I was younger I never used to get tired. Oh, people keep telling me I should retire in a year, or something like that. I can afford to now, because they are grown up now, my children are grown up.'

As I leave, most of the stalls have been dismantled. Plastic bags blow across the street, and the Clean Team move in: white vans discharge an army of men in hi-vis jackets with brooms. A well-drilled operation.

*

Roman Road Market, in the heart of the East End, started in 1843, when it was illegal but withstood several attempts to close it down. It was first recorded as a market in 1887 by Charles Booth, who toured the area and reported that Roman Road was one of the great market streets in London. 'Going down the Roman' became a phrase that passed into common usage.

In the space of a generation the market has changed from selling the widest variety of goods, fruit and veg, flowers, clothes and so on; now it's almost exclusively clothes. On a recent visit not even one fruit and veg stall could be found, while until a couple of years ago there were at least four or five. There is a flower stall at the junction with St Stephen's Road, and the stallholder there lamented: 'It's changed beyond all recognition since I've been doin' my stall. The atmosphere, the community here, it just ain't what it was. I still come, what else am I gonna do? But some days it's barely worth it.'

Mary Portas visited the market for her Channel 4 series *Mary Queen of Shops*, which attempted to revive the fortunes of Britain's high streets. But many market people did not take kindly to her suggestions. She wanted to introduce crafts, artisan bread and pastry stalls, and designer coffee, but although 'The Roman' is only a few bus stops from Bethnal Green and Hoxton, the heartland of cutting-edge digital and hipster culture and coffee shops, the stalls still persevering with her vision were not doing a roaring trade on the day of the visit. East Enders of all nationalities and cultures still shop in Roman Road, but they are demanding customers who only open their purses for bargain-priced items. The pound shop and the non-hipster coffee bars were doing a decent trade, and there was plenty of browsing of the various clothes stalls, mainly offering cheaper versions of the latest fashions: dresses, evening wear, track suits and bedding.

Chapel Market was around in Mayhew's day. 'The first handful of food shops and non-retail businesses opened in 1841, but the street remained predominantly residential. The first indication that market stallholders were moving in came during 1844. A man who was repairing the roof at number 26 mentioned a woman "who keeps a fruit stall opposite the house from which he fell".' Then in 1863, a doctor at number 19 complained of a butcher's stall set up daily opposite his house. By 1876 clothes sellers were setting up pitches. The market became a staple trading spot in Islington, so that in 1879 it was officially designated as an area for a street market. According to a survey of London markets, by 1893 the street was home to sixty-eight stalls: thirty for drapery, twenty-three for vegetables, twelve for meat or flowers and nine for fish.

On a bright cold Saturday morning in January, Islington is bustling with shoppers. The market runs from Penton Street to Liverpool Street. Painted on the road are the numbers of pitches, going up to 99, though they publicise room for 224. There's a chatty, friendly atmosphere. It's fairly busy, but not crowded. There is the usual selection of stalls selling fruit, vegetables, clothes, hats, luggage, jewellery, and one lonely stall away from the others selling Arsenal memorabilia. Unusually, there are no cooked food outlets except one sandwich stall. All the traders I speak to have been in business for many years. A huge plant stall, covering five pitches, is run by a large bare-headed man with whitening curly hair.

'Been here thirty years.'

'Is it worth it?'

'Yes, we have a lot of fun out here.'

'What kind of fun?'

'Socialising. If you don't have fun you might as well go home.'

I point out that everyone there seems to have been in the business a long time. 'Where are the newcomers?'

'They can't take it. They're not built like us.'

I come across a vegetable stall bearing the proud banner: 'Trader of the Year, 2019', where vegetables are weighed and priced per pound. I ask a young man: 'What does it take to be trader of the year?'

'You fill in all the forms, then customers vote.'

He's only been working there for a couple of years to make money while he does his studies.

'I'll move on to other things at the end of the year. But the stall has been here a long time.' He calls across to an older man busy at the back of the stall, but the older man disappears before I can ask what he feels it takes to be voted trader of the year.

Checking it out, I discover it is Islington's market trader of the year, in the non-street food category. That narrows it a bit! But on the Islington Council website, one of the people voting for him says: 'I have bought from Dave Jackson for over 32 years. He has the freshest fruit and veg on the market, and his demeanour and banter makes me go and buy there every week. I look forward to seeing him, and his daughter Katie. My five a day (and my son's) all come courtesy of Dave Jackson. Wouldn't go anywhere else!'

Thieving is a constant problem for those selling on the street. I was twice warned to look after my bag and Robin, in Berwick Street, told me a story. 'We have the strangest thing – at Christmas, there's an old couple who come by, and they distract you, one, the lady will distract you, the man will distract you, and before you know it, something's gone' – he laughs – 'and they catch you, twice now. Third time would be stupid, it won't happen again. Twice it's happened, and I go, how did I let that happen? But you need to smile. I think it's their Christmas outing.'

The appeal of markets

Why do people still shop at market stalls? With the greater ease and accessibility of supermarkets and shopping on the internet, what is the attraction?

Ellie, who works on the covered fruit and vegetable stall at Kentish Town station, says she can just fit me in before the school-children start coming out. I stand beside her and we pause from time to time as she serves customers, punctuated by the occasional loud noises of sirens and an engine revving.

She still weighs most of the fruit and vegetables that she sells. 'It's part of the attraction, isn't it? People live on their own, they want to buy fresh, so they can come and buy a couple of mushrooms, one carrot, one potato, and then come tomorrow and buy something else, not have to buy a whole packet of stuff that they have to eat for each day in a row before it goes off.'

'Do you think that's the reason people buy at markets and stalls like yours?'

'Well, it's various. There's the price, it's often cheaper – there's the fact that you can choose it, and just because it's in a packet doesn't necessarily mean it's good, you find when you get home that it's bad. Lots of people now say they don't like the packaging, and they don't like big supermarkets either, and they can say to me, How do you cook an artichoke? Whereas you can't say to anybody in Sainsbury's, How do you cook an artichoke? No idea at all. And you can't talk to anyone in Sainsbury's any more, can you? Even if you don't use the self-service checkout.'

As well as the attraction of lower prices, market goers enjoy the colour, the noise, the banter and the sense of bustling competition between the different stalls. The life on display is still a draw.

Decline

Nevertheless, even by the 1850s most costermongers told Mayhew that business had been better decades before. And so it is now. The GLA report posed a number of questions about the future of London's markets. Do privately run markets reflect the needs of local communities? Are markets that concentrate only on street food sustainable over the longer term? These are questions that the traders themselves are asking. The view of many long-term stall-holders is that markets are in decline. Long-established markets are close to the heart of their local area and community. When a market goes, it's a loss to individuals and to the family. Some have already gone. The fruit and veg market in Inverness Street, Camden Town, was for over a hundred years a traditional street market, with stalls selling fruit and vegetables. Rents became unsupportably high, and in 2013 the last food stall closed. Kensington Market, an indoor market that from the 1960s to the end of the 1990s catered to various subcultures of modern music and fashion, was closed in early 2000, and I learned while writing this book that the market at the Elephant & Castle shopping centre was to be closed in July 2020. And other markets are under threat.

When I was a child my mother used to take me from time to time to Berwick Street Market to buy fruit and vegetables when we visited Soho to buy sheets of ravioli from Fratelli Camisa. Now the market is a shadow of its former self. In 2016 the *Guardian* reported that Westminster City Council wanted to 'privatise' the market by bringing in a commercial operator as the stallholders' landlord. The traders responded by launching a campaign to 'keep Berwick Street Market independent'; they fear that as rents go up, the market – which dates back to the eighteenth century, and in its 1920s heyday was home to one hundred and fifty stalls – will be transformed, and the street will lose its distinctive identity as longstanding independent businesses are replaced by coffee bars and retail chains.

Robin Smith chairs a newly formed Berwick Street Traders Society, and is leading fundraising efforts to have the market listed by Westminster Council as an asset of community value. He believes that if the plans are not halted, 'we're heading for a grotesque, departure-lounge retail scenario'. In line with other traditional street markets, Berwick Street's decline is long term. Whereas twenty years ago there were two rows of up to fifty stalls selling fish, meat, fruit and vegetables, plus assorted household goods and clothing, today there are as few as a dozen on a quiet day.

'I've worked in Soho for about thirty years,' Robin says. 'It's about three hundred and fifty years old – no one knows its true beginnings but it seems to be a licence granted by James II, 1686. But it came under threat through the development of Soho, which has become extraordinarily massive over the last five years, and particularly with demolition after demolition, it's been relentless. I set up the dairy in October 2015 to try and do something for the market and hold its place and then developed a street petition of 27,000 signatories to support our attempt to stop the market being sold off as part of the redevelopment, which we won on 21 March 2017. And then we had another battle to save street traders by making sure that people who had committed to the street had the protection of current licences as traders, which they are due under law. On 31 March 2017, we won that battle.

'So now we are in a holding position where we are waiting for the developments to finish. We've been five years into the one behind us' – he turns to check the number – '90 to 104 Berwick Street, which was a Co-op. Some regular street stores, like a hardware store, organic store, Fairtrade shop, things like that, they've all gone. They'll be quite expensive stores when they come back on; you can imagine they'll be quite fashionable, high-fashion businesses – they'll change the character of this street, and present another challenge, I imagine, to the street market. There'll be expensive windows.' He laughs. 'They won't want stallholders in the way. On top of that – literally on top of that – there's a hotel and some des res, so that too could present a challenge. Hopefully there's a positive solution in it but it's very hard to see that such a major development is going to take kindly to street traders.'

Chrisp Street has also fought back. A large East End market, open from Monday to Saturday, it's edged by shops which include a halal butcher, a pie shop and a couple of bakers, as well as pubs, cafés and flats. Many of the eighty market stalls, run predominantly by people of Bangladeshi origin, are under cover. Among the kitchen equipment, ironmongery and textiles and a newish fish stall, is an array of extremely cheap exotic fruit and vegetables, many of which would be hard to find elsewhere. In 2016, local residents supported the traders to fight off a bid to redevelop the site – a victory that might not have been possible a few years ago.

The future of Queen's Crescent Market in Camden is also in question since the council took it over from the local community association, and, say locals, have run it into the ground.

A loquacious man selling pub signs at the 'Christmas by the river' pop-up market on the South Bank usually sells his products online, but does this for fun. 'Markets are dying. You can get anything on the internet. People come to London and would go to Portobello Road, Borough Markets – but the rest ... Think of the South of France. All the locals flock there.'

A friend who worked at a market in the 1970s, blames the councils who are doing nothing to encourage new traders. Obviously, the growth of supermarkets is a factor, along with the general trend of retail. 'You can try clothes on in a shop – you can't at a stall, and there's no guarantee they'll take it back.' A decline in business leads some to reduce the quality of what they sell, buying cheap, with the result that the goods may not even last the journey home.

The decline of markets was passionately expressed by a disgruntled man selling trinkets outside the British Museum. He refused to be recorded but was nonetheless forthcoming with his comments, pouring out a tirade against market owners – 'Israeli Mafia' – and how they are shutting out the poor. 'I'm all right. I speak languages and have the right to remain.' He has an English wife, pays his council tax and is against benefits. 'Good people don't want benefits.' He worked in markets for thirty years and now feels forced out. 'Vendors have no rights – we can be pushed out. The customer is always right. What about us?' He complained about escalating costs, and the impetus towards selling only food. 'That's all [councils] want, because they can charge more.'

The fruit and vegetable stall at Kentish Town station has been there for over twenty years. Stallholder Ellie says, 'At one point I think there were seven of us working here. Not all full time but two people setting up in the morning, they'd come and close, and two other girls and me serving.'

She explains why she thinks business has declined: 'We didn't have any competition, really, apart from the Co-op, because there was no Lidl, there was no Sainsbury's, and the online delivery business, and the fact that people don't know what to do with a raw vegetable any longer. They bring children from the schools, and the teachers say, "What is this?" and some of them can't even identify a tomato! Because they only see it cut up in a burger or something. They really just don't know. And I suppose they can't be bothered to peel – you know, have you got any bags of pre-peeled carrots? or something, and no we don't, it's not the sort of thing we go in for. So, despite all these cooking programmes, there are few dedicated cookers, and lots of people who just couldn't. They don't want to spend the time, they can't be bothered and they just plain don't know.'

The local markets that survive and thrive are maybe those whose clientele still does cook, and which sell fruit and vegetables that are not so easily available in supermarkets. Markets like East Street in Walworth and Ridley Road in Dalston are sustained mainly by their local customers on low incomes, for whom they cater much more responsively than supermarkets can. Brixton too is thriving, mainly because it seems to have come to terms with irresistible change. Madeleine, who has lived in Brixton for many years, portrays it well, in all its complexity. When asked what she thought of the market, she replied: 'Do you mean the old bit or the new bit?'

'All of it, I guess.'

'I think change and commerce keeps everything going at the end of the day. I mean a lot of the eateries I can't afford, but basically it's nice to see not just the same old nail shops. It's nice to see change. I'm never going to say no to progress and commerce as long as it's not completely run over by it, you know. As long as it doesn't become a shopping mall in the sense of Bluewater or something like that, I'm OK with that. When I moved here, I always thought this place has got something, got potential. I'm not completely sure I'm completely happy of how it's ended up in my lifetime but I've always thought I love this place. It's the energy.'

Brick Lane in Bethnal Green is open on Sundays, and, unlike most markets, permits the sale of second-hand goods. In the 1980s, the stalls there were mostly of the flea market or car boot sale variety. After that, as the East End opened up, Brick Lane became known as a trendy market for clothes, records and collectables at about the same time as second-hand became known as 'vintage', sometime in the 1990s. It still has that edgy feel, with lots of street

art, visible urban decay and echoes of the history everywhere, but there are many more trendy designer shops. These are most obvious in Columbia Road and Broadway markets, but Brick Lane seems to straddle both worlds.

Paul H's stall is at the poorer end of Brick Lane, the bit that most closely resembles a flea market. He is, as he says, 'a bloke in his sixties', selling his 'tat' to supplement his other income. His stall has lots of silver, watches and bric-a-brac, collectables. Being at the market for him is 'just an occasional thing really. I don't make a lot of money down there. Some Sundays are better than others obviously. It's shed clearing, getting stuff out of the flat. When I'm back in full-time work, which is working for charities, I'll have more money to buy more tat – sorry, stock.

'I don't like new tat, I like the old tat. And if you do buy a lot of stuff you suddenly find yourself being a hoarder or a collector, and then if you move that on at a small profit, then you're an entrepreneur, so the transition I find to be poetic and possibly psychologically healing.

'I think it's always been in me. When I was about nine or ten in the halcyon days of jumble sales and charity shops, I used to run errands for an antiques guy in Bournemouth. I think from my Irish background there were traders and a gypsy or two, so it's a very romantic myth to say I therefore can't help it because it's nature not nurture. But I always liked swapping pens at school. Chatting to other traders, there seems to be I think a common crew psychological line drawing of them, a kind of profile, if you like. I think there's a bit of glue that keeps buyers and sellers. Sort of self-governing units in a way.

'I think the main downside is ... like being a musician, you rehearse, turn up to do a gig and there's no one there. You turn up and you have a really bad day, you don't even cover your costs. But even on a bad day ... you might make forty quid if you're lucky, but you've bought forty quid's worth of good stock for the following week.

'I don't think you have to be a salesman to be good on the market, you need to have good stuff but be able to chat to people. 'Cause if you've got the stuff that buyers want, it'll sell itself. But then ... there's the thing about repeat business. And I love a bit of banter with some of the customers. It's like, nah, mate, I can't do less than twenty, and then it goes backwards and forwards. I'll haggle with people when I buy stuff. I don't even wanna buy it, I just like to haggle.

'Like walking into a shop. If there's a cold, frosty reception, it's like, hang on a sec. You know? But if you're just looking around and someone's on you already explaining the history of the object, it's like, leave it out. I think with the stuff at Brick Lane, Spitalfields, Bermondsey and the other markets before they turned into luxury flats is that it is old tat, it's fascinating objects that seem to have a history. I imagine they were handmade. I'm not very keen on the twenty-first-century sense of design and how society's moving and all that stuff but I haven't got ten hours to go into that. The thing of maybe chasing a bit of idealised history, objects found in one's childhood ...

'I was chatting to a couple of traders. I said, "Does your flat look like your stall?" And he said, "Yeah, it does a bit." I said, "It's weird 'cause if someone keeps poking round on my stall I'm like oi, oi, oi! Don't chuck it down, mate, all right?" Yeah, my stall looks like ... you know, plump up the cushions before you go.

'I'm very into thinking about and sometimes writing short stories and the trading life is incredible for a portmanteau of stories. Each stall is a different chapter, and yet there's the common thread. We're talking about going back centuries, before capitalism managed to encourage people to buy. People have always bartered, haven't they? There's always been an exchange in order to survive. And also, of course, a gathering space where people have a chinwag. All the things that I believe this society would be keen to crush ... put up a luxury shopping mall ... Shopping malls are very much like ghost towns, aren't they? Without the tumbleweed. Such lonely, dreadful fucking places. So Brick Lane for me is a sort of nostalgic hark back.'

What is clear is that markets matter. At the end of his interview about Berwick Street, Robin spoke of their importance. In a quiet voice, he said: 'The street is very important. So many people depend on this street; it's not just here for social reasons. The street's kept people alive, all through history. I think this street has not just fantastic history but fantastic culture. The spirit still lives in the ground and the acid test of that is if you put something on it that's relevant and see if it works. And it does, it comes to life.

'We are, this is, a working business. It's doing well, under the circumstances. It could be doing great. Every day you're having to deal with issues which you shouldn't have to deal with, like dust and dirt and demolition and all the rest of it, but that aside, I think there is a great opportunity for the street. Personally I hope it's not all street food, but, hey, it's still people with lives and livelihoods and families and they're doing their thing, so maybe it's going to be part of it for ever. Maybe not, who knows. But, as long as people are going to Berwick Street, and saying I like the sound of that and it works, there can be a market here.'

Reuse, recycle

The trade in second-hand apparel is one of the most ancient of callings, and is known in almost every country, but anything like the Old Clothes Exchange of the Jewish quarter of London, in the extent and order of its business, is unequalled in the world. There is indeed no other such place, and it is rather remarkable that a business occupying so many persons, and requiring such facilities for examination and arrangement, should not until the year 1843 have had its regulated proceedings.

When my children were young, I remember garage sales and car boot sales as events held at home for individuals to get rid of a few excess objects – books, kitchen equipment and so on – and make a little money. Now, they have become public affairs, listed on TripAdvisor, with fields and car parks opened up for hundreds of vans and cars to bring a variety of objects to sell. They have become an enjoyable way of spending a Saturday or Sunday afternoon, with the possibility of finding a bargain or unusual curio; but they are also for many a way of acquiring necessary clothes and household equipment more cheaply. For the people selling, sales can equally be an occasional sideshow, or a means of bringing their income up to an acceptable level.

Car boot sales are not markets. One of the most established sales, held at St Augustine's Church in Kilburn on Saturdays, has been going for over twenty years, and makes the distinction clear: PLEASE NOTE THAT WE ARE NOT A MARKET AND OUR CAR BOOT SALES ARE STRICTLY FOR SECOND HAND GOODS ONLY. In practice, as Brick Lane demonstrates, the dividing line between the two is not always clear, except that car boot sales tend to sell lower-cost items and food is not included. It's full of people trying on shoes, picking over clothes

and knick-knacks, household items. For both the seller and the customer, it is a lower-cost level of market: making or saving just a bit to make ends meet.

To enter Kilburn as a customer, it costs £5 before 11 a.m., then £1. The first time I went, it was in November, the day of the rugby World Cup final, and it was raining. There were a few bedraggled people in the car park outside; no doubt there were more inside. Some bigger displays of second-hand clothes, footwear and bric-a-brac were held under cover at the edge of the car park – a privileged spot, no doubt.

The first person I approached was a man selling electric bits and pieces from a couple of tables and a plastic cover, which he was shaking to remove the rain. I mentioned the subject of the book. 'Working or living outside? That's us. Sometimes I sleep in the van,' he said, but even on my return he was too busy to be interviewed.

A woman standing alone in the middle of the car park had a few things on a tarpaulin at her feet. She told me that it cost £20 for her pitch. 'No,' she said, 'I don't come often. A few times at this time of year to help pay for the heating. Fuel poverty,' she said, laughing. Then a customer arrived.

It was here that I met former dancer Laura, a young dark-haired woman standing under the shelter of her car boot lid. Everything was 50p. It turned out that she rarely comes into central London, but she was keen to do an interview, so we agreed to do it on the phone.

When we connected, she said, 'Just as well we didn't do it at the market. There're thieves, can't take your eyes off it. I only do a couple of car boot sales a year. Mostly I'm a dog walker. And look after children. Basically an au pair. I look after eighteen families, mostly Greenwich, Dulwich, but up and down the country. The market? Just to get rid of stuff from the house. People give me things and I get fed up. Whenever I see a friend struggling, I come up with ways to deal with it. I love embracing cultures. There's more to life than what's on your doorstep.'

It rained again when I went back to the car boot sale a few weeks later. Even so, at 9 a.m. there were many more sellers than the previous time, some with little tables, some with goods spread out on the ground. Several women refused to be interviewed – either suspicious, or wanting more money for an interview. One, under the overhang shelter, selling shoes and clothes on the ground, said, 'It's not a good life. My life is sad. I'm not going to talk about it.' Another, referred to, and deferred to, as 'the boss', had a more extensive collection of articles, including some good-quality glasses. When I found her at the end of the row, she said she had been coming for three years. When I asked, 'Once a week?' she replied as if to say, you'd better believe it, 'Oh YES.'

In Mayhew's time, second-hand articles had value. Petticoat Lane was an entire district devoted to second-hand clothes, and people reused not only clothing but material, unpicking, remaking and selling on. Car boot sales are one of the few places in modern London where the reused, the second hand, is valued: a throwback to a time before disposability, a time when 'make do and mend' was part of the culture.

In markets there are still a few stalls selling or offering services to mend. Some stand-alone stalls scattered throughout the capital offer services for mobile phones. There's a key cutter at Whitechapel Market, and at Chapel Market a small man wearing a hat with ear flaps offers a service cutting keys and sharpening knives and scissors. He has been there for forty years. There's a steady trickle of customers, he says, though all markets have declined, including the high street. Only the services survive, because they haven't (yet) managed to do those on the internet. Broadway Market in the East End, now very much a foodie destination, had until 2018 a bike parts stall where repairs and adjustments were carried out on market day, but the stallholder has moved on, as has the musical instrument maker and repairer, probably because the rent went up.

Otherwise people rely on the internet, or throw things away. Pablo, a cycle courier and former squatter, offered an interesting perspective on recycling:

'That's something that I think in the big cities, not about making a profit out of it, but like many things you can reuse like people used to do before, like all these things that you find on the skip. We used to do a lot when I was a squatter. Now I still do, if I find something that might be useful, yeah, I will take it and try to fix it. Like an electronic appliance or anything else you might need. I learned about fixing things because of being in the squat and then just trying things on your own, trial and error.

'Uh, it's the same idea with bicycles. You might find that here because they steal so many bicycles, they will take the wheels and then the owner will come and they'll save the lock and just leave the frame. So you know, this can be good for some of us that know how to fix things, even if it's just to recycle a couple of parts ... some people here they live just from that, these people carrying a big trolley and people like that. Like somebody's rubbish is somebody else's treasure. For some people something is worth nothing and to someone else it's like wow, I was looking for that for ages. Or I used to have that thing in my childhood and now I would love to have something like that.'

11

Food to go

Market traders deplore the trend towards providing prepared meals rather than food to cook, and it's true that the burgeoning of street food has taken over much of the space and changed the ethos of traditional markets. One customer at a solitary fruit stall in the West End said: 'Anyone would think we never ate before. Leather Lane' – 'I used to love Leather Lane', interjected the fruitseller – 'it used to be all market stalls, now it's all food.' Even Berwick Street has been infiltrated by chicken and meatballs, paella and falafel.

On the day that I visited Lower Marsh Market in south London, on a Monday lunchtime, it was a pleasantly quiet scene, with office workers sitting at scattered tables eating street food supplied by the various stalls – offering a variety, from chicken and chips to Goan, Nigerian and Thai cuisine, costing something in the range of £5 to £10. But where were the market stalls? There was only one stall actually selling something other than cooked food.

Hoxton Market, close to the City and Old Street tech corridor, seems to have embraced its new identity as a site for takeaway and 'street food' businesses. Here you will find everything from falafel wraps to kebabs, jerk chicken to Thai and other curries and stir fries, as well as plenty of veggie and vegan options. There are still one or two fruit and vegetable stalls, and shops with large fruit and veg displays. There are even a few tool stalls on Saturdays, but market clients seem mainly to be workers from local offices coming down at lunchtime for a bit of fresh air and a bite to eat. Roman Road, with fewer offices in its catchment area, has not been able to embrace this new trend.

An Islington resident who grew up in the borough appreciates some of the changes. The quality of the cooked food, she says, is better than it used to be. She remembered the apple fritters at Chapel Market. 'They didn't change the oil from one month to the next, and the smell was terrible.'

Street food provides welcome sustenance for office workers while giving swathes of skilled cooks from all over the world an opportunity to work. Few things reflect better the diversity of modern London than the street food cooked by a range of nationalities to suit the tastes not so much of the local residents as those of its cosmopolitan working population. This is largely a lunchtime trade. Some workers are too busy – or lazy – to provide their own lunch, and cooked food provides a hot and tasty alternative to the supermarket sandwich, and without the expense and time it takes to sit down at a restaurant or café.

Market traders understandably complain that cooked food is taking over. However, though it lacked the sophistication and variety of today's offerings, the provision of cooked food on the streets is nothing new. In Mayhew's day, few people had cooking facilities and it was cheaper to buy something out than eat in.

> Men and women, and most especially boys, purchase their meals day after day in the streets. The coffee-stall provides a warm breakfast; shellfish of many kinds tempt to a luncheon; hot-eels or pea soup, flanked by a potato 'all hot' serve for a dinner; and cakes and tarts, or nuts and oranges, with many varieties of pastry, confectionery and fruit, woo to indulgence in a dessert; while for supper there is a sandwich, a meat pudding or a 'trotter'.

At the upper end of the price range, 'smarter' markets, such as Borough in south London and Broadway in the East End, provide a more sophisticated range at more sophisticated prices: Broadway

Market sells everything from pulled pork sandwiches and fresh pasta, noodles, curries and wraps to Scotch eggs, juices, oysters and coffee.

But it's not just in markets that food stalls can be found. Some are on sites specifically for cooked food in places where there's a need to supply it. All over London, on the South Bank and smaller sites like Goodge Place, Old Street and Tottenham Court Road, can be found a variety of cooked food stalls.

The South Bank is a vibrant cultural and tourist centre, and in the summer it's one of the richest sources of street food. On a sunny June day, I wandered west from Blackfriars Bridge to Waterloo Bridge, along the Thames Path from the Globe Theatre past Tate Modern to the cultural centres of the National Theatre, Festival Hall and Hayward Gallery. Just beyond the National Film Theatre, the path opened out into a wide area full of a couple of dozen food stalls – from ice cream and burgers to German sausages and doner kebabs. Piped music blasted from a BBQ drinks van. From their pizza stall, two young women called, 'Hello, try this.'

It was very different on a cold February weekday afternoon, when there was a solitary van selling Mexican food. A local shopkeeper told me that the food stalls were only there for the Christmas festival, and sometimes in the summer.

The open space near Goodge Street station offers a respite from the shops and is a nice place to sit in the summer. Beside it, and outside the American Church, is a little village of stalls selling lunchtime food during the week – very popular with local office workers as well as shoppers. The food on offer ranges from falafel to halal to Indian to vegan, and, unusually, one stall sells grilled fish, including salmon and sea bass. It turns out that the staff come from the fish and chip shop round the corner. They get the fish from Billingsgate, delivered at about 2 a.m. by a company that have keys and let themselves in. The stallholders used to go to Billingsgate themselves but no longer have the time. They run the stall from about 11 a.m. to 2.30 p.m., then go back to serve in the shop.

Round the side of the American Church, among stalls selling

burgers and sausages, is a little enclave serving South American cuisine – Mexican, Peruvian and Argentinian. When I asked why, the woman at the Peruvian stall shrugged. 'Don't know, but we've been here a long time, about four years. It's popular, so if it sells . . . '

Outside Shoreditch fire station on Monday to Friday lunchtimes are three stalls selling vegetarian food (falafel, houmous and halloumi), Thai street food, and kebabs and wraps. They've been there since about early 2019 and seem to be thriving. Prices, at £4 to £6, are very reasonable. At midday on the Friday that I visited, by far the longest queue was at the vegetarian stall – a sign of the times and the neighbourhood, primarily of young office workers.

Fadi has a van selling food, one of a few in a small mews off Mortimer Street in the West End. It's a basic site, with no toilets, water or electricity, parking or canopies. He's a tall, handsome, bearded man with a warm smile and dark engaging eyes. We met when he warned me about some broken glass and we arranged to speak later in the day. I interviewed him as he cleared up from his day's work, with other stallholders also busy loading up their vans. Fadi lives in west London, near Queen's Park. He's married, with one four-year-old child.

'I'm originally from Lebanon. I came to London in 2000, so I've been here for the last nineteen years. So now I consider myself as a Londoner. I came to find a different adventure for my life to live and see the other walks of life. I used to be a student. This work, first I used to work with someone on the street, doing Lebanese food – falafels – and then it became one of my interests.

'I used to always love the food from my mum when she used to cook, so I came up with this idea, and I make it as my business. My idea is, when we used to be kids, my mum she used to cook a chicken not like traditionally, we do it on the pan, like pan fried or pan grilled. The chicken with the halloumi cheese, that's the idea, like to make something like my ethnic background, and cooking on the streets of London. Not specific training for this thing I'm doing but in general I used to work in food industry for the last fifteen years, working in the kitchen. I started as a kitchen porter and then I was assistant chef and then I became a chef myself, cooking for myself as well. I didn't study, it was like an experience.

'I love it. I love it because I can express myself. Myself, I like nice and tasty food, so I can cook nicely, and I taste it myself before I give it to the people. I have a big passion for it as well. I have lots of customers, and I have a special relationship with them, greeting them when they come. I often ask how they are, how was their weekend? Yeah, I try to build a good relation with my customers so I can – even if they don't buy from me – so we have this relation, like passing by me in the morning or afternoon, greeting me or greeting them. That's the way I deal with my customers.

'The worst part? Sometimes the pressure, the stress of making things good, satisfying the customers, being on the street in the bad weather. When you're stuck in traffic. You know London is a busy city. You have to be on time, you have to do things good and stuff – lots of pressure. Customers? I can always handle the customers. There are no bad customers. Because of the pressure of the life you find that some people are stressed a little bit. But I do understand it, because I am one of them. I live in this city, and I know the stress of it. I can understand the frustrations sometimes of the people; I can always deal with them in a way to satisfy them or calm them down.

'On a normal day, I wake up around seven o'clock, go out from home around half seven, quarter to eight, turn on my van, go to the market. Buy the chicken, buy the veg, come to the market and start to do my usual routine preparation, cutting the salad, cooking the chicken, cutting the cheese and cooking the cheese, and start selling the food. By half eleven I'm ready. Serving the food until around half two, as you see. By half two, three o'clock, I start again, packing up, cleaning, then packing up and going home again, and prepare for the next day.' He laughs. 'It's boring, yes, it becomes like a daily routine. Any routine is boring. You know, I try to socialise with my neighbours, with the customers, the people like you, lovely people. Yes, I do it on my own, these are colleagues, neighbours we call them.

'I'm not sure to answer whether I am happy or not happy to be here. Because I came here when I was like twenty years old, and then I live almost twenty years here, so half of my life was back home in Lebanon, and half of my mature life was here, so I think I kind of get used to here. Because when I grew up in Lebanon, in the early stage of teenager, I wasn't that mature enough to know how it was good or bad back home or here, but now I realise that here the life is a little bit difficult but I have to carry on, because I got responsibilities now. I have a wife, I have a son I have to look after, and I kind of get used to the city here.

'When I go back home like for a visit, it's really hard to see myself here or there. I don't know, I can't decide to stay here all the time or go there. If I go there, I miss here, I come here, I miss there. I'm kind of between. Family there, that's why I go and see my family often. You know back there we have a strong family relation, it's because I come from a village that we are more attached to family than the city, so I think the city life is a bit different from where I come from. That's why I don't know what to answer you. I'm between here and there.

'In the future, hopefully I'll grow my business, I'll be somewhere good. On this spot and expand a little bit. I might look for a restaurant or something like that to establish myself slowly, because it's really hard to be on the street all the life. Being on the street is not easy job, especially as you get involved in a lot of physical work. We have to load and unload, you see the van is full of stuff. Standing as well, yeah. I think in the future, after a while we're all going to get aged and get old. I cannot do this all my life, so I might be doing something which is, I can bring people in and manage something. Or I can manage here myself. With food, yes, of course.'

A couple of months later, seeing that the council was renovating the cobbles in their street, I stopped by to see if the traders would be able to continue. Yes, Fadi said, they would have to move out for six weeks, but the council was looking for alternative places for them all. At least they will not be deprived of their income.

On Rupert Street in Soho, alongside a large lorry emptying a stage set from the back of the Gielgud Theatre, four food stalls are setting up. It's about 10 a.m. on a Tuesday morning.

Chariya works there one morning a week, making and selling satay. She is a dark-haired petite woman, with patchy English. There's a board indicating the price – chicken satay with peanut sauce £7 – and a warning about allergies. Another young woman is chopping vegetables and putting them in pretty little wooden bowls. There are polystyrene boxes with bits of chicken in.

'My name is Chariya. I come from Thailand twelve years ago, because my husband here. He work here. He is a Thai like me. We want to live here.

'I started street food two months ago. I like it because I can work at home, prepare the food before I come to the field. At home I can play with my son. I have to look after my son all the time. But it is hard work. I have to look after him, take him to his play. I come here one day a week, every Tuesday. Actually, I want to stay at just one day a week because I think I say to my customers if you want to eat my food, you have to come every Tuesday, no other day.' She laughs. 'I think my customers not eat my food every day but once a week is good. Some ones come every week. They told me I like your sauce, I love your pickle. I am pleased with your food.

'In Thailand I did not cook. I work in the office. In Thailand I didn't need to cook because my mum, she really good cook, she always cook for me, and my husband he is a chef, and he always cook for me. And when I have a son, I start to cook and I learn from my husband about five year ago, and now I love it. My husband works as a chef in Thai restaurant in London. He works in Thai restaurant about nineteen years, nearly twenty years. I don't work there because I have to look after my son at three thirty when he finish at school. In restaurant finish very late, like five p.m., that is very late for my son.

'Not much money, because one day a week and I have to pay for the pitch. For Tuesday, it is £50. I want to make at least £200. That's it for me, because if I work I get about £10 for an hour, if I work in the restaurant, but I can work just four hours, because I have to look after my son. I work here from about nine, but before nine I prepare the food, I can look after my son. And I go back to clean everything, prepare the next week. I leave here at two thirty.

'Just one helper.' She gestures to the young woman chopping vegetables. 'Her name is Clim, Climmie.' We say hello. 'I come to set up the pitch. This one' – she gestures at the roof awning – 'I pay for someone to set it up for me and I chop the vegetables and half cook for the chicken. When the customers come, I have to finish cooking the chicken first and put in the box. I have to have a hygiene certificate by law. The full box it costs about £4. You can see the price on the card.

'Sometimes when it's rainy, today maybe no customers come to see me but it's OK. I hope next week it will be different. Yes, the raining I feel sad, but it's OK. No bad experiences not now, because I only start a few weeks.

'Customers are nice, really nice. Two weeks ago, I really busy, I had a queue.' She gestures round the corner of the stall and talks fondly, with a smile in her voice. 'The customers always smile at me. I say sorry, you can come to me next week, they say, it OK. Really nice. Enjoy. I enjoy meeting the people and other stallholders. And the money,' she adds with a laugh.

'How far away do you live?'

'Not far, about twenty minutes. Yes, really near, my house. Yes, I drive, and parking £20 for four hours. Very expensive round here. I don't like the parking. Some days I can't find a parking spot round here. I have to drive to my house and take the bus, and when I finish, I have to take a bus to my house with all my things. I don't like it. I hate it. I have to leave early to sell the food, not happy, really sad.

'I buy food from Sainsbury's and Booker – you know Booker? – wholesale, very good, very cheap. Once a week, every Sunday. Just one day per week, it's OK. But I'm looking for another day, maybe Friday, Thursday, two days a week. In five years? I want to have, like er two branch, just two or three. Two day a week or three day a week and different market, three market I think. Manage other people doing it. Because my friend, he is my mentor, he is very successful so he is my idol. So I want to do same.'

Some food stalls are peripatetic. The woman selling German sausages from a van at a one-day festival in South End Green, Hampstead Heath, had been in Henley-on-Thames the previous day, the hottest of the year. 'Lovely place, Henley, but they all lay around under the trees.'

'I guess it was too hot for people to want sausages.'

'About five o'clock they did.'

'Don't you get tired?'

'Sometimes. I'm getting on for sixty-two. I might take it a bit easier. In the winter, that is. Same with everything. It's OK when the weather's nice.'

Amando is a young man from Albania who sells caramelised peanuts on Tottenham Court Road. He charges £2 per cup (the cost to him is about 20p). He talks extremely fast.

'I'm Amando, and I sell peanuts, I'm twenty-five. Peanuts is something that it's easy to do, and the thing is, you know, it's movable, so if one location doesn't work, I'll go to somewhere else and try it there. Erm, it's easy, it's just peanuts, sugar, vanilla mixed together, so it's not something that's complicated to do. We make it from scratch. We buy the peanuts, 25kg, the bags which come on pallet of forty, the sugar which comes from the average Tesco's, cups from the pound store, we can get like a hundred for £1, you need for all the bits to come together, yes, that's it.

'The peanut trolley, we have to buy that. It usually costs, we've got one maker that does it for 250, or you can get smaller versions; there's two sizes, you can get the small one which is 200, the big one is 250. There's a lot of people, if you go to Russell Square there's another person, there's someone at Tottenham Court Road, Tower Bridge, Tower of London, Oxford Circus, so there's quite a few people. You've got, like you know, I'm Albanian, so you've got the Albanians, there's a Brazilian guy who does it as well.

'I remember, when I used to come out sightseeing when I was a little kid we saw people, but then they used to trade at Buckingham Palace as well ... then Dad sort of did it, and then Dad started doing something else, and then I did it now and then, but I have another company as well, I have a decorating company, so that only happens in the mornings. So, for instance, we have an event to sort, I wake up at six o'clock and go sort it, then I've got the rest of the day free so rather than being at home and doing nothing. I'm running two things at once. Sometimes I come Monday to Friday, sometimes I just come two days a week, it depends how flexible I am during the week.'

'Do you make a living?'

'Out of this it's not so much, not a living out of it, no. You can't because it's not a busy place, but you've got your little bills you can take care of, foodwise. And I'm a smoker so I can have smoking, travel, and then you've got a bit on the side, you know, not a great deal of it.

'It's worth doing only because it's either this or stay at home, and then I start spending money from the other business as well, and then it's not really ideal. The job I've got now, like I said I have to wake up six o'clock, fix the place, then it's that done, so I've got another six, seven hours during the day. What am I supposed to do then? So, I'm at home, I'm spending money rather than making. With this you're not making a great deal; however, it's better than nothing.

'I live in Ilford. It is a long way, but I drive, so Saturdays and Sundays, parking's free. I put this in the van, I take it home. It's a flexible thing, you're not required to leave here. I work for myself, so if I want to stay till six, I stay till six, if I want to stay till five, I stay till five, or twelve to twelve. If I want to do a twelve-hour shift, then I can stay. Like I said, it's not the best of ideas, at least it's an idea. Better something than nothing.

'I just got married. I have to support myself and my wife, and

I also have an autistic bruvver, and he requires more than me and my wife put together, because he needs for me to buy him toys and that sort of thing, special events and things like that, because he's not a kid that stays at home ... He's got a routine. He wakes up and goes to school. He's autistic but he knows his routines. He's about twelve. Twelve to thirteen. I'm really bad at ages.

'We moved here in 1998. In Albania you work all day and the most you can make in Albanian money is ten, in English money it would probably be seven pounds per day ... But, saying that, the bills here, you've got your electric, your gas, your rent. Put everything together, you're not making that much. I'd rather be here than there but in terms of making money and stuff like that, a lot of people think, you came from a different country, you're working, making a lot of money. They don't realise how hard it is here, but yeah.

'I go there once, maybe twice a year. Not a lot of people, mostly the old ones, Gran and Grandad, because I've got family members in America, family members in England, so they're all sort of scattered about. Every time I go on holiday, I remember when I was a little kid.'

'Do you like working outside?'

'During the winter,' he smiles, 'not so much. During the summer months it's OK. When you work for yourself, it's different ... you've got to be flexible. Because I worked in a hotel, in a pub, I was the assistant manager for a hotel, for about three years and a half. It went into liquidation so we all lost our jobs. But in that period, I picked up a lot of skills. Obviously, the business I've got now, it came from that. That, with this and the other one, they're not all the same. Out here is completely different from being inside. Being inside is easier than being outside in the winter. But there, again, you work for yourself, so I call the shots. When you work for yourself, it's the best thing you can do.

'You do have to have a licence to do this. I do not have a licence to do this. But obviously when the council do come, they will either give you a fine, or they will take the trolley and send you to court. It depends, because a lot of us used to work in Westminster, so over there it was mainly a fine and they take your trolley. It depends where you work as well, but as long as you respect the people around you, like at times there's a kiosk near here. And I know they're selling veg and I'm selling peanuts, but I know they pay for their licence, and I'm not going to damage their business, so I'll go to another place. I know I haven't got a licence, but I still try to behave like a decent person.

'You are going to get some people who say, you know, you haven't got a licence, you shouldn't be here. If I had a licence, I'd rather have a kiosk. A kiosk has more appeal, is more presentable. I'm not going to make a great deal, probably maximum £100 a day, where I am now. So no licence, but would you rather a young person going out stealing, selling drugs, misbehaving . . . I know it's not licensed, but I still pay my fines if I get a fine.'

From the beginning I was struck by the thoughtfulness of this young man. He asked when it would suit me to interview him, and whether I would prefer if he was anonymous or not. He told me that the previous day an American couple had come with a £10 note, wanting two cups. He had run out of change, so he gave them the peanuts free of charge.

Sameh sells fruit juice at the edge of Brixton Market. We shelter under the tented cover of his stall on a day of pouring rain, with the radio on in the background. He's self-conscious about his temporary teeth, so won't be recorded. As we talk, a couple of customers arrive. When they hear I'm interviewing him, one says, 'Good man.' I watch as he makes their juice, charging £2.50 a cup. Blue plastic gloves, a simple hand-operated squeezer on a table with a sink. Bags of oranges, grapefruit hanging up. Pouring the juice into a measuring jug, then into plastic cups, puts a straw into each. He makes an extra cup for me.

'I've been doing this for about eighteen months. It's very good although not that good on a day like this. I do orange, pomegranate, clementine and grapefruit juice. Next week, I hope to be doing carrot, beetroot, ginger. I have regular customers. Some of them come for a gallon. Many don't drink alcohol, so it's a treat for themselves.

'I was a night-shift engineer at No. 1 Hyde Park for eleven and a half years. I don't know how much you know about night shifts, but it was killing me. I like drinking pomegranate juice, but could never find it. My cousin in Palestine said why don't you sell it, and he went on nagging me till I did. I'm actually a fisherman, used to be a fisherman in Palestine. I came here and went to college and trained as a mechanic. I came here because I married an English girl – it didn't work out.

'This is a very rewarding experience, especially when people appreciate it. My partner works at British Airways, but occasionally helps out. At the end of the year I bugger off home for a month. I generally work six days a week – I come when I feel like it, but usually about nine thirty to set up for ten and stay until I get bored, which is about now.' (It's 4.15 p.m.) As he scrubs the table and sink, he continues: 'I have to keep it clean. That's why people keep coming back. How much fruit? It depends on the quality of the fruit. I try to get good quality fruit, usually from New Covent Garden or New Spitalfields, two or three times a week, between midnight and six a.m. One big pomegranate and two oranges make half a pint. Sometimes you can get five pomegranates and not enough juice.

'I make enough, but our life is not about money. I did PAYE, all that. Night shifts damage your immune system, make you ill. I'd rather earn less and be happy and healthy. Fishing? When I go back in January, February, I do it with my brother. It's a good time: there are lots of fish. We've done it for generations and maybe when I'm sixty or seventy I'll go back. My partner – half English – is not that happy here. I don't know what I'll do when I'm older.

'Ninety per cent of the people are nice, pleasant, cheerful, polite. The odd one is grumpy, got out of bed on the wrong side. If you treat people with respect, you'll get it back. It doesn't matter what your colour or your height is.

'I live in Brixton. I came here twenty-seven years ago and never left.'

Before I say goodbye, Sameh insists on mending a spoke on my umbrella with 'true fishing twine'.

Coffee

Coffee has become a fashion item. At any self-respecting café, on offer is a wide variety of different styles of coffee – flat white, espresso, decaf, Americano, and so on. And in specialist shops, there's a choice of beans from different countries. I saw one chalk board advertising 'New single-origin Peruvian organic decaf coffee'. Ticking all the boxes. Most coffee is drunk in cafés rather than on the street, but there has been a proliferation of stalls too. In Shoreditch, says one resident, you can't move for hipster coffee shops, with very good quality coffee at £2.50 to £2.80 a cup. On the parade on Hackney Road near where he lives, there was one tiny hipster coffee bar in 2010; there are now three on the same 100-yard parade, plus several more along the road, and a mobile coffee stall outside Hoxton station.

Coffee stalls were a feature of Mayhew's London – there's even a picture of one in *London Labour and the London Poor*.

> The coffee-stall usually consists of a spring-barrow, with two, and occasionally four, wheels. Some are made up of tables, and some have a tressel and board. On the top of this are placed two or three, and sometimes four, large tin cans, holding upon an average five gallons each. Beneath each of these cans is a small iron fire-pot, perforated like a rushlight shade, and here charcoal is continually burning, so as to keep the coffee or tea, with which the cans are filled, hot throughout the early part of the morning ... The coffee-stalls, generally, are lighted by candle-lamps.

And he too remarked on their proliferation:

> The trade, I am assured by all, is overstocked. They are half too many, they say. 'Two of us,' to use their own words, 'are

eating one man's bread.' The following is the statement of one of the class:

'I was, indeed, a labouring man. I could not get employment. I was for six months without any employment. I did not know which way to support my wife and child (I have only one child). Being so long out of employment, I saw no other means of getting a living but out of the streets. I was almost starving before I took to it – that I certainly was ... Many said they wouldn't do such a thing as keep a coffee-stall, but I said I'd do anything to get a bit of bread honestly ... I went to a tinman, and paid him 10s. 6d. (the last of my savings, after I'd been four or five months out of work) for a can, I didn't care how I got my living so long as I could turn an honest penny. Well; I went on, and knocked about, and couldn't get a pitch anywhere; but at last I heard that an old man, who had been in the habit of standing for many years at the entrance of one of the markets, had fell ill; so, what did I do, but I goes and pops into his pitch, and there I've done better than ever I did afore. I get 20s. now where I got 10s. one time; and if I only had such a thing as 5l. or 10l., I might get a good living for life. I cannot do half as much as the man that was there before me. He used to make his coffee down there, and had a can for hot water as well; but I have but one can to keep coffee and all in; and I have to borrow my barrow, and pay 1s. a week for it. If I sell my can out, I can't do any more. The struggle to get a living is so great, that, what with one and another in the coffee-trade, it's only those as can get good "pitches" that can get a crust at it.'

The first thing you notice on Akim's stall are the flowers. A tiny, tidy coffee stall outside a bike shop near Oxford Street in central London. And it's festooned with flowers – on the back of Akim's own bike, in pots round his coffee machine. Saddles for seats. It's all immaculate. He serves up all kinds of coffee, including flavoured ones. 'Have you got a window box? Here, I give you some coffee grounds. It helps the flowers grow.'

Like Mayhew's coffee-seller, Akim used to have another career.

'I've been here twenty-one years. Many experiences outside this bike shop. I used to work, I've been working, as a translator – for immigration, social services, different contexts. I was born in Algeria, brought up in Algeria, studied in Algeria, came to this country to get some experience – in languages, and in art. And actually in Italy as well. But in the UK for languages – I worked as an interpreter for a time, part time. I really enjoyed working part time, unfortunately it didn't work, because of the nature of the job, and on the other hand I've been doing art as well, painting. I really love art. So now I am trying the café, and trying to balance three jobs, which I enjoy. Very complicated to get enough money, but I sold a couple paintings, my first painting. A couple of years ago I used to copy, but now I have found my own style and am very confident to sell. Mostly to tell story through painting. Money from translating and coffee. Not a lot, but I don't spend much. I don't drink or smoke or anything, so I have a very good balance of budget, I live West Hampstead, don't go out every night. It's very important to eat well and to dress well, the rest . . .

'Yes, I enjoy working outdoor. I did a course, how to foam the milk. It's very enjoyable to do the coffee, to work outdoors, I've got used to – I have regular customers. Especially working outside the bike shop, they're a very good team, especially the director, I get on with him very well.

'When I come, there was already this coffee shop. It was very quiet to start. The first year, I was making about £25. But I'm very confident to build it up, I have regular customers and I make sure I've always the right coffee. I found it very difficult at the beginning, but now I'm relaxed.

'No, no problems here, in the area. Some . . . time . . . sometime – very rare. I enjoy working with the director, the customers – I see them every day, I get used to working in the same place, which is good. The customer, the team management, I like working outdoor and I like making coffee! Even in the cold I enjoy it. I get used to it. I enjoy working on my own, on my own initiative, self-employed. Favourite customers – I had my favourite political satirist, from the BBC, Rory Bremner, I had a good chat with him. He has very good skills. I used to imitate people as a kid, you know, how they talk.' He serves a customer. 'Sugar?

'BBC people, some politicians, Russell Crowe, he has been. I don't know how long I'll do it. At the moment I'm very happy to do this. Five years? I don't know, might stay here. Destiny. In UK? Dunno, hard decision, very hard to say if I stay. I have not decided yet. Have family in Algeria. I like to go home skiing, but the time is difficult.

'When I go home, I leave early. I work Monday to Friday between eight and half past four, five o'clock. Sometimes I go home early and try to do something, do some painting, some experimenting. I don't know. Making soap. I like to make soap, I enjoy it, but I don't have time. Only Saturdays and Sundays. I try to do this. I'm forty-nine. Young. I got energy, I don't mind.'

A few weeks later Akim tells me that one of his customers – pointing out the house over the road – is interested in commissioning him to do a mural for his house. He's sent fifteen suggested designs, and is obviously thrilled to be getting a commission. He's tired, though, and looking forward to his holiday.

III

What's Enough?

12

Working on the streets

There are, of course, only three modes of economising labour, or causing the same quantity of work to be done by a smaller number of hands.

1st. By causing the men to work *longer*.

2nd. By causing the men to work *quicker*, and so get through more work in the same time.

3rd. By *altering the mode* of work, or hiring, as in the 'large system of production,' where fewer hands are required; or the custom of temporary hirings, where the men are retained only so long as their services are needed, and discharged immediately afterwards.

We're not a society that likes to talk about money. And when someone is on a low income, pride will often prevent them from revealing exactly what it is they earn. Some people are vague about how much they get. Others are preoccupied with their exact hourly rate, and will move jobs, where they can, to earn an extra 50p an hour – that's £20 a week.

Delia, a Nigerian woman in her fifties, gives out free magazines and is studying law. She knows exactly what she gets, down to the last penny, from the different magazines. 'For the church, it's completely voluntary. The different magazines, no, they don't pay the same. *Time Out* doesn't pay much. *Balance* is on Mondays,

Time Out Tuesdays, *Independent* and *Standard* every day. Roughly, minimum wage, just above £8; but the addition is different. I think, I'm not so sure, because I'm paid weekly. The highest is the *Evening Standard*, which is £8.80, which is followed by *Balance* £8.30, and *Time Out*, which is £8.20. But they are all what they call minimum wage, what they pay like in McDonald's. There's no sick pay but holiday pay. But for that you have to be working! You work! If you haven't been working, you won't get holidays. You go on holiday, but you don't get paid.

'Pension? I hear that you have to get to a particular grade or something, but not like a merchandiser ... and I'm not yet there. We are really at the lowest level. I think if you become a supervisor or team leader or something like that ... We are still at entry level. I think it would take four or five years, at least. Some people will leave. In order not to be disappointed, they need to know that you are staying on. I don't know if I'll stay or say I'm off now!'

Susie, the apprentice gardener in Regent's Park, earns £8.21 an hour, and she's thirty-five. If she works forty hours, that's just £328 a week. £328, when the average rent is higher than that. Not to mention food, travel, living expenses, bills and, in some cases, child care. No one can survive on that, unless they live with parents or have an earning spouse, like Susie. Even she is better off than her agency colleagues who are on zero-hour contracts. If they are laid off, for whatever reason, they get no pay.

Jeremy, the magician in Covent Garden, was quite specific at the end of his show, when he invited donations: £5, £10, or 'make my day' – £20. He feels that what he does has given him a different attitude to money.

'You have some tangible sense of what your work is worth on a given day. Most people don't have that sense of, I worked today, and I was worth so much money, whereas for a busker you can come out and say today I worked and I was worth three hundred pounds because that's what I come home with. And a friend of mine who served as my mentor back in the States said when you start to busk, your whole relationship with cash changes. Because for most people, they have to wait for the pay cheque. Whereas for a busker it's like I'd like to go and have dinner but I don't have any money – so I'll do a show. I'll bang out forty pounds and go eat. So it's a little like having your own little cashpoint, ATM, here on the street.

'One of the challenges now is that of course fewer people are carrying cash, so I think that's also impacted on how much money people make. But card readers are now being more widely used, are more widely accepted, and most buskers, including myself' – he takes out a neat little white object – 'now have a card reader, so if someone doesn't have any cash, they can still make a contribution.'

As for the proffered donation in exchange for an interview, I found many differing attitudes. One stallholder at Ridley Road Market said, 'Don't offer us money. It's insulting.' The next asked, 'How much is it worth?' and at the end of the interview reminded me to pay it.

It's 9 a.m. A tall friendly Afro-Caribbean man from a security firm contracted to the BBC greets people as they go by.

'Yes,' he replies, 'paid per hour. Oh, we get well over the minimum wage – that's about £8, isn't it?'

'No, more than that.'

'Well, they put it all together now.'

'As long as you have enough.'

'What's enough? People want more and more. I work out the basics, then see what's left over. I don't always manage it, but at least I'm struggling in the shallow end, not struggling in the deep end.'

But it's not just about the hourly rate – and this is where many workers are vague. What about sick pay, holiday pay, pensions – rights to which all employed people are entitled? Many people have never even thought about that. Apart from being excluded from rights held by those in formal employment, workers can face hidden costs, for things like the equipment and specialised clothing that are required for some occupations. If these are not supplied, a meagre rate of pay is further diminished. What is 'enough' also depends on outgoings: the cost of housing, transport and child care in London is very high.

The gig economy

Although few people working on the streets have much choice in how they earn a living, the freedom of a lifestyle that is to some extent self-determining is a real draw – but it's one that can be exploited. The crucial question is about a worker's status. In the past, workers were either employed – with all the benefits and possible exploitation that can bring – or self-employed contractors with all the consequent freedom and insecurity. Government figures showing increased employment hide details of the quality of that employment – including zero-hour contracts and other unacceptable conditions.

And, as tribunals have established, there is a third type of worker, known as a limb (b) worker. A new union, the Independent Workers of Great Britain (IWGB), was set up in 2012 in order to fight for better pay, terms and conditions for workers in the gig economy and protect their rights. Key workers' rights, based on EU law, include minimum paid holiday, regulation of working hours, equal pay, protection against discrimination and consultation on redundancy plans. IWGB represents some five thousand workers, a thousand of whom are EU citizens, and relies upon these aspects of EU law in a number of workers' rights court cases. But these rights, recent though they are, are seriously threatened by Brexit.

According to the IWGB:

> The so-called 'gig economy', consisting of private hire drivers, couriers, and other low paid workers, is infamous for the companies bogusly classing these individuals as 'independent contractors' in order to deprive them of employment rights to which they are legally entitled. Whilst it's true that most private hire drivers and couriers are self-employed, what the tribunals have told us over and over again is that they are limb (b) workers,

a type of self-employed person who is entitled to rights like minimum wage, paid holidays, pensions, protection from discrimination, and more.

In the gig economy, rather than being salaried employees, independent contractors are paid by consumers for a specific job – a 'gig'. The companies in the middle, linking supply and demand and known as 'platforms', argue they do not employ staff but simply connect customers with people seeking to make money. Research by the Trades Union Congress (TUC) estimates that one in ten workers in the UK now regularly do 'platform work'.

The following conversations give the picture.

A bike courier: 'They don't pay you per hour but per job. The machine tells you how much per job. So, if it's half a mile from W1 to W1 you might get £3; if Kensington to Bethnal Green, it might be £10. I don't know how much the company gets paid, but they obviously take a cut. It used to be on paper, and people signed for it. Now it's all on the phone. The contact tells you where to go and what to pick up. So um, there's no, there's no security. You only get paid if you do a job. You don't get a pension or anything like that.'

A meter reader at Marble Arch, asked if he was willing to be interviewed: 'Sorry, I'd like to but I'm a contractor. If I don't work, I don't get paid.'

I asked Andrew, who has been working as a casual labourer: 'But when you're ill – you hurt your back the other week . . . '

'Oh no, you don't get paid then. But, that's fair. I mean if you're not on a salary, you're not going to get paid when you're ill.'

A man running a restoration company pays his workers well: 'Yeah, if you're a labourer, then probably' – he pauses – '£13 an hour; if you're a stonemason, probably £25 an hour. It's good money.'

But: 'Presumably there's no security, if you're not on a job?'

'No, not really. The guys that work for me, they're all self-employed.'

In the past, employees struggled to have their rights recognised; now workers struggle to be recognised as employees at all. But in many ways, the gig economy has simply created another version of the same issues of conditions and rights in the workplace. Many people in the gig economy make things run smoothly, oiling the wheels of our daily lives – and are largely invisible.

Minimum and living wage

Most people we spoke to had no idea of what the minimum wage was, or knew of its difference from, or even the existence of, the London Living Wage.

The notion of a minimum wage came as early as 1891, when in the papal encyclical *Rerum Novarum*, Pope Leo XIII proclaimed:

> Let the working man and the employer make free agreements, and in particular let them agree freely as to the wages; nevertheless, there underlies a dictate of natural justice more imperious and ancient than any bargain between man and man, namely, that wages ought not to be insufficient to support a frugal and well-behaved wage-earner. If through necessity or fear of a worse evil the workman accepts harder conditions because an employer or contractor will afford him no better, he is made the victim of force and injustice.

In 1998, the New Labour government introduced the first compulsory minimum wage in the UK. Employers fought against it and said it would lead to mass unemployment. It did not do so; instead it set a standard which all employers had to pay. The downside was that some employers saw it as 'all they had to pay' and some workers' wages were even reduced – and it was never enough for London, where the principle of a voluntary London weighting for public and private jobs had been established (initially for civil servants) since 1920.

In 2001, Citizens UK, a community organising group founded in London in 1996, built on that precedent and took the bold step of launching the first Campaign for a London Living Wage, setting their own level and organising large numbers of people to lobby to achieve it. This was despite initial resistance from those who felt that it was for employers and government to set levels, and from unions who felt it was their job to fight for it. The success of this campaign helped win the case for a London Living Wage and big corporations like Barclays, Aviva and HSBC actually encouraged the group to broaden the campaign to the rest of the UK, and thus to all their employees, in 2010. One of the first steps was to insist that all members of Citizens UK had to pay their employees the Real Living Wage.

In 2015, confusion was sown by the government renaming the minimum wage 'the National Living Wage'. The Real Living Wage has always been voluntary, set by using the cost of living. It applies to contract workers as well as in-house employees, and there are two figures: one for London and one for elsewhere. The government's so-called National Living Wage is compulsory, only applies to those over twenty-five, and is set at the same figure across the whole country, mainly by employers and unions sitting on the Low Pay Commission.

In April 2020, the government raised the National Living Wage for those aged twenty-five and over to £8.72. At the time of writing, the London Living Wage, based on the cost of living, is £10.75 per hour.

Outsourcing

In recent years councils and other employers have shifted the responsibility for some of their work to outside companies. It's a process known as 'outsourcing', which began in the 1970s and escalated to become the norm in the 1980s. As someone else has to get a cut, it is inevitable that outsourcing leads to lower wages. And it sometimes leads to a situation where staff no longer know who employs them. Along with its campaign 'for all members to receive at least the London Living Wage, contractual sick pay and other rights, dignified and safe conditions, and general respect', the United Voices of the World union says, 'We also challenge outsourcing itself, which creates two-tier workforces in order to slash wage bills and deny important rights.'

When transfers of employment occur, the pay and terms and conditions of public sector workers have been protected since 2006 by something known as TUPE (Transfer of Undertakings and Protection of Employment). Thus when staff are transferred, in theory their rights and pay are protected, but in practice conditions may not stay the same. One man spoke of his experience of having been TUPEd from the Metropolitan Police staff to a private company when the catering was outsourced. His pay stayed the same but the amount of work tripled to the point that he became ill and had to be signed off for stress.

And since TUPE does not apply to new staff, all new staff join on worse terms and conditions, so over time those terms come to apply to the majority of the workforce. When the UK leaves the EU, it is possible that TUPE itself may end.

Gerry, working in the gardens of some of Westminster's squares, is among those employed by a private contractor. 'Yeah, get paid per hour, get paid weekly. I make just over £370 a week. Last week I made £530, because I was doing extra overtime, so hopefully this week it'll be the same money. Five hundred and something pounds, yeah. £370 isn't really enough to live on. We in't on minimum wage at the moment. They have promised, by April next year, we will get £10.37 an hour, which is the national minimum wage. But at the moment we ain't getting that. We're getting £8.70, and if you drive, I think you get £10 an hour.'

'And there's no London weighting?'

'No, nothing. This, this Westminster, it's one of the richest boroughs in London, but they pay their workers the least money out of all of them. If you go to Camden Town, you'll get your £10.37, you go to any other borough, but here they don't give you the minimum wage. Continental Landscapes, they've got the contract, yeah. They pay Westminster, then they pay us.

'My girlfriend works, so that's quite handy; she's got a part-time job in Marks & Spencers. She works four days a week and we've only got a one-bedroom flat, it's quite expensive there at the moment. My rent comes £160 a week, so half my wages has gone straight away and then there's the food shopping, and my son needs this and that. Yeah, well, we're all in the same boat. We all get the same money.'

According to the Trades Union Congress, Britain's gig economy more than doubled in size between 2016 and 2019 and now includes some 4.7 million workers. One in six UK workers are in low-paid, insecure jobs, where employees can't afford to take sick days for fear of losing their wages.

Bella is a student chugger. I asked her, 'So if you can't work, if you're sick or something, you don't get paid?'

'You can. You have holiday pay, you can ask, take it out of my holiday pay. Basically, every two weeks, that accumulates as one day's holiday pay, so it's all right.'

'Obviously no pension or anything like that?'

'I dunno.'

Andrew's blithe agreement that 'if you're not on a salary you're not going to get paid when you're ill' is easy enough to say for a healthy young man with a secure roof over his head, but it's more serious when someone is dependent on the work to live, and when serious illness strikes. And lack of sick pay provision has become particularly serious since the coronavirus epidemic, when someone forced to self-isolate must either break the law or be without means of support.

Casual labour

'In no country in the world is there such an extent, and at the same time such a diversity, of casual labour as in Great Britain.' Mayhew felt passionately about the working poor, and held that casual work, which he called 'that vast national evil', was at the heart of it. The types of work may have changed but current conditions raise the same passions about unfair practices and inequality.

Casual, temporary work can be a godsend for young people needing to support themselves during study, or on the way to a more lucrative occupation. Working in a pub or on a market stall are just two options in a broad spectrum of money-making possibilities. Many people do casual work in their student days. There are fewer jobs now, and higher levels of student debt, but from Andrew's story it seems that, with ingenuity and an adventurous spirit, casual work of various kinds can still be found.

But flitting from one temp job to another can too easily become an ingrained way of life – a life begun in student days, perhaps, but continued well into adult life. A precarious life, albeit with a heady sense of freedom. Years of such work can leave someone unsuited for other employment, especially if few qualifications have been gathered on the way.

In recent years there has been a considerable shift in work practice from the concept of a 'career' to more flexible, less secure modes of employment. At the high end, where people have some choice, they can assemble what has become known as a portfolio career. At the low end, workers struggle with zero-hour contracts, poor conditions and minimal pay, taking on more than one job in order to meet their living expenses. The same was true in Mayhew's day. 'Most workers did not have a single job that sustained them, much less their family. Instead they patched together a series of jobs, either ones they held regularly, or seasonal work, to pay for basic sustenance and a room, or part of a room, to sleep in.' Patchwork jobs, then and now.

Patchwork jobs

Paul H has a multi-faceted life as a market trader, musician and photographer.

'I played a lot of gigs as a saxophonist, did a bit of busking, bit of recording, quite a lot of jazz courses. There were lots of gigs around, not only to play in but to go and see. Around '88 Shoreditch was getting the reputation of being a boho area. I was just one of the people involved. I haven't played for about four years now. I'm having a sabbatical.

'I was doing a lot. The most gigs I was doing was sort of jazz trio and then a quartet, and then a fusion set-up, tabla, sitar, tenor and soprano, sax and bass, and that was called Dah. That went really well but I was working full time for the first charity of three that I've worked for, and getting gigs, arranging rehearsals, it always seems to fall to one band member. I said to my boss, "Look, if there are gigs ..." "Not a problem, not a problem." I suppose I just got a bit tired ...

'I have every intention of playing again, I'll probably play quite a lot of finger percussion. The sort of set-up I'm thinking of would be humming bowls, tenor sax, finger percussion, thumb pianos, maybe cello or string bass, so acoustic stuff, maybe around Indian ragas.'

A *bit extra*
'Well, I've got a day job. It's a bit extra. These days you've got to have a bit extra, with this government.' This from the chatty blonde woman with a London accent in a van selling German sausages at a one-day festival.

And that's the story of so many people on the streets – making a bit extra to supplement a day job, inside or out, that doesn't pay enough.

Caval is in his twenties, trying to make money to go back to Romania to take up his studies in architecture. He is working as a living statue, but that does not pay the bills. 'I have other work in the country, at Amazon, on the nights. And in the day I am here for this. I need the money to pay the council tax, to pay the TV, I have to pay for everything.'

A young man is handing out leaflets for Uber Eats at Chapel Market. He's Italian, from Calabria, cheerful and friendly, but feeling the cold. 'No,' he says, 'I don't do this full time. I have another job, in a restaurant. Just do this for a bit extra – London is expensive. I am only here for six months, to improve my English. I speak good German – we have many Germans in Calabria, but I need to improve my English. Yes, we get paid per number of leaflets we give out.' He shrugs.

On a hot bank holiday weekend, I came across a young man laying tables at a Covent Garden café. It turned out he was a youth worker who needed to make some extra cash. Another young man was standing in Paddington station, promoting *The Economist* for a marketing company. He is a musician. A young woman has been busking in a market on Sunday mornings for months to supplement her office income, which doesn't cover much more than her rent. In the summer she and a friend can make enough to buy groceries for the week.

It was at the Kilburn car boot sale that I met Ben. He was standing in the pouring rain with an older-looking woman; like everyone else they were well wrapped up, in parkas, hats and scarves. Behind them a car, not a van. There was very little on the small table in front of him.

'I've been here fourteen years, moved from Scotland. I work outside, I do car boot sales and stuff like that, trying to make a few pound.' I asked him how much he makes.

'All depends. Some days I've done car boot sales and made £10. I've done car boot sales where I've made nothing at all, and I've done car boot sales where I've made like £100, so it really depends on the day, and where you are. You have to pay to get in. So each car boot sale is different. I think this one today is £25 to come in. It's quite expensive so it's a bit of a gamble if you're going to make your money back or not. I don't have a lot of stuff, you know, so I can only do it like once a week, or sometimes once a month. So I struggle a bit.

'I do have a proper job as well. I'm a driver, that's all I have the qualifications to do,' he says with a laugh, 'so I deliver meat. To different restaurants, for a company. They pay minimum wage, it's per week you get paid, it's not very good, so it's really really hard to survive on that. you know, so this is to top it up.'

Long hours

In Mayhew's day, working days of twelve to fifteen hours were normal. For many people today not much has changed. Most of the security guards I spoke to work twelve-hour shifts. One said: 'I'm still waking up. Started at seven. Give me till twelve, and I'll be awake. Night shifts better. Twelve-hour shift, seven to seven. Used to be eight hours, but everything changed.'

The beadle at Burlington Arcade told me: 'I start at 7.45 till 7.45, so it's a long twelve-hour shift, but in that twelve-hour shift we've got two hours' break, so that's absolutely fine. I live in Thamesmead, which is about one hour twenty minutes from here. Normally I have to get the 6.18 bus and so I get here for, probably 7.35, and then I have to get myself changed and ready. When I go home, I get in the shower, then sometimes after the shower I have supper, and from there go to bed. Because if I stay awake, I won't be able to wake up the next morning, get ready for work the next day.'

Those who are 'self-employed', or with flexible working hours like taxi drivers and couriers, often have to work similarly long hours to make enough money. Safiya, the Tottenham Court Road florist, told me: 'I work eight till eight. I'm working seven days a week at the moment, because I'm saving to take my mum for her sixtieth to Jamaica. Most florists do ten to twelve hours a day.'

Bank holidays

The British calendar is full of festive days, many, though not all, based on religious feast days: Shrove Tuesday (pancakes), Valentine's Day, Mother's Day, Easter. But the most significant of them all is Christmas: traditionally a time of festivity, a time for families to come together, a time for giving. For traders, it can be bonanza time: a chance to make some extra money. For some, it's a time to work; for others a time of particular pressure.

Christmas comes early to London. The famous Oxford Street lights with all the accompanying razzmatazz are switched on in November, and advertising for the festive season appears in the shops as early as October. It all contributes to financial pressure on those who have least – who worry about debt, and the cost and expectation of presents. Most public holidays, religious or otherwise, have been swept up and reclassified as consumer opportunities. Christmas sales traditionally started on Boxing Day, but now often begin long before and spread well into the New Year. So for some it's an opportunity.

Rhoda, for instance, selling her African-themed clothes at Lower Marsh Market: 'Yes, towards Christmas we do a late night. We did one last, two weeks ago. So there are different promotions that go on. Toward Christmas now, you're going to see more traders come because of Christmas.'

Ten days before Christmas, while shoppers scurry for those last presents, the side streets of central London are surprisingly quiet. Office workers often take extra days off, adding what's left of their annual leave to the festive holiday. While shopping streets thrive, market stalls operating in business districts fall quiet, even deciding to close down as their customers stay at home. Between Christmas and the New Year, Oxford Street and other major shopping thoroughfares are full of people: queuing outside shops or pushing past each other on the street, eager for the best bargains. Outside the theatres there are people sitting on the ground from early morning, excited, chatting, queuing for that day's tickets. Other streets fall silent as the roadworks and construction pause, and fewer deliveries of building materials are made.

One market trader was looking forward to closing for the Christmas period: 'Christmas? Yeah, we get two weeks off. I can't wait. Just not to have to get up at two in the morning. I just want to get drunk every night.' Laughing, stroking my arm.

For Delia, who distributes a variety of magazines, it is a different story. There is no work, so there is no money. 'Holiday at Christmas, bank holiday, there is nothing.'

Many employed workers are given the bare minimum of time off: the bank holidays of Christmas Day and Boxing Day. A FedEx driver and a postman I spoke to were back at work on 27 December. No two-week break for them. And many people – doctors, nurses, hotel and security staff – have to work over Christmas. Even those who can choose when they work often opt to do so over the holiday period, needing to make money where they can. Cleaner Viorica told me, 'Yes, I am working Christmas Day. Someone has Airbnb and needs me for someone coming on Christmas Day. I may take Boxing Day off.'

Dubbed the greenest Christmas lights in London, the lights of Villiers Street near Charing Cross are powered using old cooking oil, collected from nearby businesses such as Gordon's Wine Bar and Champagne Charlies. Some years ago in Seven Dials, I came across a lorry and lifting device putting up complex lights, reindeer and sparkly things. A young woman was sorting out the various shapes as they lay on the lorry.

'Must be fun sorting them out!'

'You'd be surprised how often we get them wrong.'

'Is it a full-time job?'

'More or less. We design them all the year. We're doing Carnaby Street, Seven Dials. And,' she said with pride, 'this year, Regent Street.'

Christmas fairs pop up all over the place: in Trafalgar Square, Leicester Square, along the Thames. At London Bridge, 'Christmas by the river' boasts smart German-style chalets offering cuisines and artefacts from various parts of the world; I bought a little Peruvian doll as a stocking-filler. On New Year's Day, another bank holiday, I wandered out at 9 a.m. and noticed some of those who are working: the bus drivers, the paramedics in an ambulance that screamed up Euston Road, a solitary CEO who wished me a happy New Year, and, his apron still on, a cook from a nearby hotel, standing round the corner to have a quiet fag. Having worked at Christmas, Viorica, too, will be working again to welcome people to a customer's Airbnb.

Seasonal work

The evils consequent upon the uncertainty of labour I have already been at considerable pains to point out. There is still one other mischief attendant upon it that remains to be exposed ... Many classes of labour are necessarily uncertain or fitful in their character. Some work can be pursued only at certain seasons ...

Now, the labourer who is deprived of his usual employment . . . must, unless he has laid by a portion of his earnings while engaged, become a burden to his parish, or the state, or else he must seek work either of another kind or in another place.

We have already seen how weather affects the life and livelihoods of people on the street, but trade fluctuates not only according to the weather but the time of year. The problem for many people working on the streets is that their work is seasonal. Chestnuts or Christmas trees in the winter, deckchairs in the parks in summer – but some seasonal variability is less obvious. There can be really tough times when very little is coming in. If businesses have a low season, sales at other times have to compensate.

Chris, a dog walker, is realistic. 'You're never gonna be busy fifty-two weeks of the year. You have your periods where it's quiet. You earn a couple of quid, but then you have another week where you earn a little bit more. And then the next week after that you might earn a bit more. Then the following week it might be quiet again. You might have one day where you only have two dogs to walk and the next day you might have five or six. It's just how it is and I've realised that doing the dog game, just up and down. Same thing for anybody who's self-employed. You never have work all year round.'

Alan, who is now working at the flower stall in Tottenham Court Road, is putting together a lovely bouquet of flowers. 'Yes, of course it's seasonal. They're moaning about the takings as we speak. What can they expect? Of course you're going to have big days on Valentine's Day, Mother's Day and the International Women's Day, then it's half that.'

The book fair under Waterloo Bridge on the South Bank is an institution that has been operating for at least thirty years. A number of booksellers sell a wide variety of second-hand books, from paperback fiction and plays to rare books and prints, arranged in rows of long tables, and scanned by large numbers of passers-by. It is open all year, but in February and March, when I passed, there was just one row of books and one bookseller, huddled in a chair between lockers, keeping out of the wind.

He has been selling from here for about ten years and this is his only venue. 'No, nowhere else. Just here.' I asked him how he coped with work that is so seasonal. 'You have to put up with it, roll with the punters. It's more day by day, week by week, not whole months when you don't make any money. Just more good days in the summer.'

In March there were also few exhibitors at the Sunday art fair in Bayswater. One artist who has been there for many years admitted that he rarely comes in the winter now. This was just his second visit this year. 'I like coming in the summer,' he said. 'Sometimes I even go in the park and do a bit of painting.'

School holidays, especially in the summer, have a different flavour in central London. Tourists flood in – maybe particularly at a time when people wish to avoid future Brexit restrictions – but, although tourist spots like Buckingham Palace, Westminster Abbey, the Houses of Parliament and the museums are full of visitors from other countries and other parts of the UK, the side streets are again quiet. Many commuters are on holiday; office workers no longer arrive at the stations or walk down the streets to their offices. Although noisy, dirty development continues, and sometimes the heat can be oppressive and pollution levels high, residents breathe a sigh of relief.

13

'Can't stop'

The conveyance of goods from one part of the metropolis to another ... is chiefly effected by vans, waggons, carts, drays, &c. The London carriers, carters, and waggoners, may safely be said to be now nearer 8000 than 4000 in number.

I now approach the only remaining part of this subject, viz. the conveyance of goods and communications by means of the porters, messengers, and errand-boys of the metropolis ... The number of individuals engaged in the same occupation in the metropolis was, in 1841, no less than 13,103. Of this number 2,726, or more than a fifth of the class, may be considered to represent the errand-boys, these being lads under 20 years of age.

At present, however, I purpose dealing solely with the public porters of the metropolis. Those belonging to private individuals appear to partake ... more of the character of servants paid out of the profits of the trade than labourers whose wages form an integral portion of the prime cost of a commodity. The privileged porters of the city of London were at one period, and until within these twenty years, a numerous, important, and tolerably prosperous class. Prescriptive right, and the laws and by-laws of

the corporation of the city of London, have given
to them the sole privilege of porterage of every
description, provided it be carried on in the
precincts of the city.

No such privilege or prosperity is accorded to modern couriers. If
anything exemplifies the gig economy, it is the delivery business that
fills the capital with vans, motorbikes, bicycles and trolleys pushed
on foot at a run, all crisscrossing the streets, delivering anything
from food and drink to building materials. By the very nature of
the work, members of the gig economy can't afford the time to stop,
for an interview or anything else. Time is money.

Conditions for delivery drivers have got worse in recent years.
One man, now an Uber driver, explained why he left.

'I used to have my own delivery business. I was self-employed,
collected all the parcels from the company depot, picked them up
with the delivery sheets, put them in the van in the order of delivery.
I was really good at it, used to take me about an hour and a half
at the start of the day then I was out on the road. I could tell you
exactly where any parcel was, if I needed to go back somewhere.
Could take breaks when I needed, made a decent crust. Then they
introduced computerised delivery sheets and it added an extra
hour to my time each morning. And then they started giving the
customer an expected delivery slot, great for the customer, but if
you miss their slot you don't get paid. Look around now, you won't
see any British drivers working for any of these companies now. It's
slavery. I've seen people crying 'cause of the stress of trying to get
round to all their drops. It's no joke. I couldn't take it any more,
got out while I could.'

Another driver agreed. 'Delivery drivers, they can't take breaks.
On the road, under pressure all day long, in the traffic. Too much
competition, and the pay is no good now.'

Unusually, DPD delivery gives customers a time-frame of just
one hour. While it's welcome for customers, I wondered whether it

made life tough for drivers. I asked a man delivering a parcel to me if he found it stressful. 'No,' he said, 'because it's up to the driver to time his deliveries.'

'But there's so little time in between.'

'Not really. I put two mins between deliveries; others thirty seconds. Up to the driver. We're paid by the number of deliveries. How many hours depends on how many deliveries we do. No security like holiday pay – we're self-employed.' As so vividly portrayed in Ken Loach's film *Sorry We Missed You*, a delivery driver, in the words of the *Big Issue* review, is a 'slave to his handheld scanner. He has to make his delivery or be sanctioned.'

The Uber driver had a point when he said, 'You're better off working for one of the bike delivery companies, at least you're getting a bit of exercise.' For, on the whole, those delivering by bike enjoy the exercise and the freedom of their way of life.

Getting the vibe

Giles sat on the trailer of his bike as we spoke. He's a slim, fit man with cropped hair and a smart shiny blue top, rather like those worn by racing cyclists.

'My name's Giles Wiley-Southcot. I'm er' – in a dramatic whisper – 'fifty years old. And I work for Rush couriers; I do a ten-hour day. As far as I'm concerned, I'm quite happy with what I'm doing. The money's not great, but I'm happy to whizz around town, come rain or shine. I log in about quarter to eight and then I'm home, say quarter to six, six o'clock. So that's ten hours, about a hundred kilometres a day, maybe more. Yes, cycling. And I've been doing this now for nine months, ten months. I've lost five kilos and have become very fit, so I really enjoy it. I am very tired by Friday, though. I can't move, my legs are aching. I can't think of anything else.

'It's certainly different from twenty years ago, because I used to do the odd winter in the late nineties, and by Friday you really wanted to strangle someone. It was all much more aggressive.

I find London a hell of a lot more polite now. You go into an office, it's almost as if everyone values their job. And I find that a lot of the drivers are a lot more considerate on the streets as well. Obviously the black cabs, they've got a bit of an attitude, the Uber taxis are dangerous – they indicate to go right, then go left – but apart from that, I dunno, there's a different feel in London.

'Apparently statistically cyclists here are the most aggressive cyclists in Europe. I've seen some really Arctic moves by cyclist commuters, and there is that feeling of competition, pushiness, particularly during commuter hours, between eight and nine and then between four and five and six. I don't mind that though,' he says, laughing, 'because once you're on the street, once you've done your tenth hour, or when you're on your fifth hour, you're wearing your armour, so you're a different individual as opposed to a commuter. You know, this is my job on the street, I'm working it, I'm moving and shaking.

'Cars? No. In nine months I haven't been hit, I haven't been whacked off. There's always going to be an idiotic driver, but come on, keep your head rotating, watch where you're going. There are a lot of cyclists out there who don't look over their shoulder when they make a manoeuvre, *especially when they're going over a red light.*' He whispers the words, and we both laugh. 'But if you're going over a pedestrian crossing when there are people on it, look around, and it's fine. You know, it's high fives with the riders, most of the riders are good lads, there's one or two a little bit funny, but oh well.

'I was in the building industry for quite a long time. It was good and, I must admit actually that two weeks ago I was working with my twin brother for nine days and it's good to have a break from this. Because it can get a little bit monotonous, the sheer hard work of it. On a Friday, I'll sit in my chair, have a stiff gin and tonic, and I won't be able to get out of the chair!' Another laugh. 'Because I'm so tired. Yes, in a way it can ruin a good weekend but this weekend we went out and I survived.

'I was born in Cardiff, lived all over the UK. Lived abroad for many years: Spain, New York, South America, Prague, everywhere. No, I don't miss construction. Nice to dip in and out if my brother has something good to do but I was in fashion as well for a long time. My friend and I were both sides of the camera. Because we were modelling, yeah, I was modelling, that's why I got to all those countries. And then I went the other side of the camera, so I had a studio in Prague where I was the only newsman out there. Back then.' Quietly intense: 'And it's nice to go to these fashion houses and talk the talk with the people in there, and you go into the photographic studio, and I know what you're loading. They're sometimes surprised.

'I live quite central, Brompton area, so that's why I can log in really early, at least it's not a hard commute for me. Yes, I'm married. Twin brother, older brother, sister, parents. I know what people are saying, come on Giles, are you really going to be doing this when – it's something to do whilst you're sorting things out. I'm a qualified personal trainer as well, so I pursued that for a little while. In five years' time,' he laughs again, 'I might still be doing this! Is that a good idea? Not really. But there're guys out there much older than me and they're cycling around. I've seen one chap on a cargo bike similar to mine a helluva a lot older than me, and he,' he says with wonder, 'has trouble walking. I've seen him fall off his bike once and I thought, God you're brave.

'Pay? I can't say. It's terrible. It's an embarrassment. It really is. Minimum wage? Less. Less. And not much per drop – no, it's bad. You get paid per hour and per drop but it's very very minimal. But they're a good crowd and, you know, as soon as I went to see them they told me what it was and I said, I know how the game works. Never mind. It keeps me busy. My wife works, yeah. Accommodation for two. But, you know, no holiday money. Pension – hmm, it's difficult on the money I'm making. No, not from them. We're self-employed. And the only decent asset is what my wife has on her finger!' We both laugh.

*

A well-educated Italian courier alternates cycling with work in an investment bank. He was a punk in his youth – always, he says, something of a rebel. He was adamant that his name should not be used.

'But then gave it all up and studied part time, did GCSE, A level English. Fell in love with finance. Started working for a bank. Did it for a few years, then went back to cycling. On and off. Left the bank in February, so I'm working part time on the bike and sending out CVs, waiting for a job. I got married, so it's no longer just about me.

'It's dangerous. Sometimes you can end up in a conflict, you could win or lose the battle, you could end up crashing. That's very unlike me, but that could happen. You're very vulnerable on a bike. A couple of times I thought I'm going to die right now. I lost a couple of friends.'

'Do you enjoy the riding?'

'I love it. I love the freedom. I love cycling. To be honest with you, I am a bit of a sports freak. I've crossed Europe on my bike three or four times. I've done lots of marathons.'

Duncan is forty-eight, works as a motorcycle courier and is passionate about bikes. He came over from Australia twenty-one years ago, and has more recently become a union rep.

'Initially the work was good, learning the streets of London. I know London better than my home town. It's a hard job in all weathers; it's a dangerous job, but I enjoy motorcycles, so I got better and better at it, knew my way round the country and yeah, so earning more and more money. Then after 9/11 in 2001 it sort of started to decline a bit. I managed to get a contract, so was earning quite good money. I was working at Hammersmith hospital, picking up blood samples from various surgeries, I was doing an *Evening Standard* delivery job in the morning, and then going to the hospital in the afternoon. I did that from 2003 to 2005 and then the company lost the contract to another bigger, so I was on

the circuit, which was ad hoc work, all round the country, basically. So I decided to leave that company and worked for the current company I work for, the Doctors' Laboratories. In 2005 I started working there.

'I didn't hear about the IWGB till early 2017. I heard rumours about a union, but I didn't know the name of that union. But when I finally heard about it, there was a meeting amongst the doctors and the laboratory couriers, so I went along and signed up straight away, and, er, I think later, middle of the year, I became a rep and we started signing up as many people as we could get. Started organising, basically, and we done quite well.

'It's made a huge difference in the company that I work for, because we've got union recognition. So on the first of January 2018 we got our holiday pay for the first time, and we got pension in April that year, backdated to the first of January as well, so we won a lot with the IWGB union.

'I work from nine a.m. to seven p.m., five days a week, Monday to Friday. Up till July this year we were on docket rate, and then we changed, through the union we negotiated an hourly rate with the mileage rate on top of that. The per-job rate was up and down, depending on how much demand there was for work, and the hourly rate means it's sort of flattened out, so there's no bad days any more.'

'And presumably the pressure to do as many jobs as possible has lessened?'

'Yeah, definitely, it has.'

'How do you feel about it all?'

'A sort of mixed bag, because I'm struggling – we've lost out to inflation overall, since 2005. I've never had a pay increase; in 2017, no, 2015, I had a fifteen per cent pay decrease. The company keeps stalling us. We're trying hard to fight but we seem to have hit a brick wall at the moment. But it is a little better than what it used to be.'

'Have you had any accidents?'

'Yeah, many. I've broken my arm; I've got a plate and six screws in my right arm. It's the only bone I've broken in over twenty years. But, yeah, I've had lots of accidents. It's par for the course, pretty much.

'It is quite a solitary job. In previous companies, you'd go a day without talking to another courier, nor will you talk to receptionists picking up packages and stuff like that. But the company I work for has a central hub, so we all come in, so we see quite a lot of couriers during the day. But it's still quite a lonely job. Back in Australia, I was working in a petrol station, see the public all the time, and you get quite skilled at relating to people, but in this job I've closed up a bit. And my people skills have got worse over a long period of time. I struggle a bit with relating to people.

'The best thing? The freedom. It's, when I was, before, when I was a self-employed contractor, if you are good at your job, you can go on holiday for months, come back, and there'll always be a job for you. There used to be quite a lot of courier companies in the late nineties and early 2000s, so if you weren't happy with the courier company, you'd just go to another one and just keep working, so there was a lot of freedom. Now it's changed a lot. A lot of courier companies bought up every other company, so there's very few big companies now. There are just three or four massive ones. Where I work, the Doctors' Laboratories, it's like the last bastion. We were always the best-paid couriers in London, and I feel sorry for the other courier companies – they suffer big time. Their pay has eroded over time and inflation has . . . You just wouldn't want to be working in any other company.'

People carriers

People carriers range from black cabs to minicabs to Uber to the newest kid on the block: the pedicab or rickshaw. Previously the preserve of Asian countries, rickshaws were first introduced to the UK in the late twentieth century. There are now an estimated 1500 rickshaws in London. It's become a popular mode of transport, particularly for tourists. It is of course more eco-friendly than most other forms of transport but, with little regulation, it is also open to abuse. In April 2020, the MP for Cities of London and Westminster said she was planning to put forward a ten-minute rule bill which would bring pedicabs in line with taxis and private hire services. 'Like them,' she said, 'drivers would need a licence from Transport for London to operate, TfL would be given the power to regulate the prices they charge and the vehicles they use would have be of a safe standard.'

Some display fares and would welcome a more regulated system, but they seem to be in a minority. Few rickshaw drivers will agree to be interviewed. Through the lens of this rickshaw driver, however, we get a picture of his competitors.

Jack is waiting for a fare on the edge of Leicester Square. Our interview is accompanied by the sound of a Hare Krishna man drumming and chanting behind us. Halfway through, when the man leaves, Jack gives him the finger. He speaks loudly over the background noise, decisively and fast, with a Canadian accent.

'Well, I'm originally from Canada, and came over here about twelve years ago. I was a foot rickshaw driver in Toronto and I thought I'd come over here for a change – my grandma was here, and they give me a visa based on that. I came over here to do bicycle rickshaw instead of doing it on foot. I got into this back in 1992, when we were just getting over the recession in Canada, and I started making racksful of money to be able to travel round the world and go on adventures and stuff, so I stuck with it. I had no idea I'd be doing it twenty-seven years later over here.'

'Do you like it?'

'It could be better. There's no licensing involved with this, unfortunately. And as such we have a lot of what British people would call cowboy operators. What I would call a bunch of shit cunts. And so there's a lot of riff-raff on the street; we've got a lot of rickshaw drivers who have been homeless for years, using jaggy kind of drugs, criminals, illegals from Third World shitholes. It needs to be cleaned up.'

'So how does your operation differ from theirs?'

'Well, I don't brazenly rip off the tourists for one thing, I don't sleep with my rickshaw for another, I shave on a regular basis, I can speak English, and I'm here legally. We don't have set charges, but we have like industry standards. For example, like er, from here, Hippodrome down to say Charing Cross station' – a distance of less than half a mile – 'would be for two people anywhere from ten to fifteen quid, depending who you asked. And the time of year, and the time of the evening and what day of the week it is. My time is more valuable on a Saturday in August than it is on a Monday in January.'

Back in the 1980s, Jack used to work in restaurants, in kitchens. He prefers what he does now, but isn't that keen on being outside in bad weather.

'Not when the weather's crap, no, but I prefer making my own money, choosing my own hours, not having a boss or anything like that.

'See, I'd work a lot more if I didn't have to come out and work with such a bunch of idiots. You know. I stand in front of *The Lion King*, trying to get people to come on my rickshaw, and I've got a bunch of junkies stood next to me over here, and some guy who can't speak English because he's from Bangladesh over there – I can't work with these people.

'Yeah, it's my rickshaw. I bought it seven or eight years ago. I bought it second-hand for three thousand quid – well, I wanted a good rickshaw. You could pick up a rickshaw for five hundred quid, but you want to sit two fat guys in it and pedal up the hill.

'Of course you get tired. We recently had engines on all the rickshaws, but they were illegal, so the police after several years got to finally get off their asses and do something about it. As such I think probably half of us have taken the engines off the rickshaws and the other half are chancing it. So we'll wait and see what happens over the next two weeks, if this is a one-time thing where the police come down on us for like a week and tell everybody they've done their job and go on to something else. If the police persist, then the engines will come back on and more rickshaws will be confiscated and crushed.

'We get people who are excessively drunk. I tend to ignore them, or I'll point them to the junky or the Bangladeshi who can't speak English, say I'm waiting for somebody or something like that. Then it's somebody else's problem.

'I'm usually away January, February, part of March, travelling around Asia, Africa or wherever. I used to do six on, six off when I was back in Canada, so I'd show up in Toronto for opening day, which is the beginning of April, and I'd go until the end of September, beginning of October, and then take off again.'

'Do you prefer to do it on your feet, or cycling?'

'D'you know what? If they got rid of the bicycle rickshaws and made everybody run, there'd only be ten rickshaw drivers in London because the rest of them couldn't hack it. That would be great.'

He isn't bothered by the traffic. 'People drive in London a little more insanely than in Toronto. In Toronto they drive like wimps. Because they're constantly digging the streets up here. Roadworks pop up with no real notice, and they stay there for longer than need be, so now they've introduced this ridiculous 20-20 thing [new speed restrictions], and it's coming more and more now, on more roads. So traffic's not really an issue. I just go in and out of it.'

'But other rickshaw drivers get in the way?'

'Well, a lot of them do, but if you're a junky and you're trying to operate one of these things, or you haven't slept in a couple of days, because you're homeless' – he makes a doddering sort of hum – 'then you're going to be more accident-prone than someone who has it together a bit more.'

He covers the whole of London. 'Show me enough money, and I'll take you to Heathrow. I live up north London right now. I'm a property caretaker. So they'll have a portfolio of maybe like ten different properties, and I'll have two or three people in each one, and we're there basically to keep the squatters out. They'll do up the property, make sure there's a shower, a kitchen, rooms and stuff, and then they'll put us in there.'

At this point the interview is interrupted by an American customer.

'Hi. I'm from LA. How much to take me to Finchley?'

'That'll be very expensive. Several thousand pounds.'

'Seven?'

'Several.'

'Will you take £100?'

'No. Finchley's a no-goer, I used to live up there. Heathrow's all right, it's flat.'

'Well, will you take me to a club, then?'

'Yes, I can take you to Soho.'

Customer turns to me. 'You can come too. I've got money.'

The metropolitan carriages engaged in the conveyance of passengers are of two classes – ticketed and unticketed; that is to say, those who ply for passengers in the public streets, carry a plate inscribed with a certain number, by which the drivers and owners of them may be readily known. Whereas those who do not ply in public, but are let out at certain yards or stables, have no badge affixed to them, and are, in many cases, scarcely distinguishable from private vehicles.

This might almost be a modern description of the difference between London's traditional black cabs and their competitors, the minicabs. Both kinds are struggling. When asked if they can make a living, they all say, Yes, but it's hard. One said, 'It's all changed today. Compared to then [the 1980s] it's very hard, too much competition, higher fees and costs like insurance, more regulation too. I can earn a living but I have to work every day ten to twelve hours for it to be worth it.'

Part of the problem is the competition from Uber, founded in the States in 2011, which now has branches all over the world. Their employment practices and drivers have had a very bad press and the company is currently appealing against a revocation of their licence to practise in London.

'All the local companies, they are going out of business now. They can't compete with Uber. Even the big London chauffeur and delivery companies like Addison Lee are struggling, they'll probably go out of business, they can't compete on price. And the black cabs, they are struggling with the competition from Uber. They charge a fortune, don't know how they still have any customers. It's all changed 'cause of the technology. Anyone can use a satnav, what do you need three years of the knowledge for now?'

But Uber drivers also complain. 'One of the worst thing is the extra charges we have to pay, since April last year. I blame that Sadiq Khan. He's against Uber, no doubt about it. We have to pay £11.50 daily congestion charge if we drive into central London; black cabs are exempt. How can that be fair? It's all money, isn't it? If I drive into central London I get an extra £1 per job from Uber, so I have to do at least twelve jobs in the congestion zone to make it worth my while. But some days I don't get any other jobs into the centre – what am I supposed to do!'

Nevertheless, the traditional freedom of this way of life is still attractive. 'The best thing is you can work when you want, log off when you want to. I work for Uber and for this other company, a local firm. You can do that now. I'm never short of work. It's hard work, but it's a living.

'I've got this nice big Mercedes nine-seater. It's comfortable, easy to drive. I can take the big premium jobs like families going to the airport with their luggage, or train stations. I've been in this game a long time, why shouldn't I have a bit of comfort?'

Some complaints are universal: 'Sometimes I can't stand listening to people complaining about everything. I ask them if they mind if I turn on the radio, I ask them what station they like, LBC or Smooth Radio!

'I drive nights, I like it but I always have to look out if someone is a bit drunk. I've had someone being sick in my car. He was with his mates, they were all apologetic, said they would pay for the cleaning, but that's no good, is it? The car stinks for three days!'

14

Entertainers

For centuries, buskers have provided a rich source of entertainment for London's residents and visitors. The term 'busker' was used by Mayhew, and it's applicable not only to musicians but other kinds of entertainers. In our interview, magician Jeremy used it of himself. The streets are alive with a whole range of entertainers, from dancers to singers, living statues and musicians of all types. Mayhew said that in his day, street musicians – singers and people playing a variety of instruments, including the organ and the hurdy-gurdy – were thought to number a thousand.

On the whole there is a very liberal approach to busking – such a long-standing feature of London life is appreciated not only by visitors, but by many of the buskers who come from all over the world to perform here. And at popular venues, buskers are generally self-regulatory, taking turns. The Metropolitan Police Act 1839 section 54, which also prohibits kite-flying and sleigh-riding in the capital, was used to arrest some buskers in Leicester Square as recently as 2014, because they were supposedly 'obtaining money or alms' illegally. They were the band King's Parade, winners of the mayor's competition for young buskers, and were released without charge. Public Space Protection Orders (PSPOs), intended to tackle anti-social behaviour in particular areas, have not so far been generally applied to restrict buskers in London, although in 2016 Hammersmith & Fulham Council imposed one on an area outside Shepherd's Bush station.

One man told me that 'in general busking is regarded as a protected activity. Forget the name of the Act – maybe it's the Highways Act? 1980? – which says that reasonable use of public space is essentially a right. So the rule of busking, really, is that you don't block the free flow of traffic. Whatever space you use, you have to make sure there's enough space so that people can comfortably go round you. And there are requirements about noise in some places – a lot of the musicians will crank their amps up really loud, so that you can hear them three or four blocks away, and that's leading to some councils wanting to clamp down on the use of amplification, because it disturbs people.'

Sebastian, an Argentinian busking in Trafalgar Square, said, 'In some places you need a licence, but not here. Not in this place or any part of Westminster. For South Bank, yes, Camden Market as well, the Underground, but not here. Westminster is kind of free. It is good, yeah. It's not so usual in the world to have this kind of freedom.'

But Westminster Council is planning to make changes. There is a petition to resist their plans, but for the moment, in May 2020 they plan to introduce a pilot scheme to reduce busking. Busking on Oxford Street will only be allowed in three places – the north side of the street outside Debenham's, at the bottom of Old Quebec Street, and on the Marble Arch roundabout. The busking regulation applies not only to amplified music but to quieter performers. The one place where amplified music will be allowed is Marble Arch. Buskers will need to obtain a licence and will be allowed to perform for forty-five minutes maximum, followed by a break of at least fifteen minutes.

David, who has been making a living as a busker for many years, was upset at the proposed change. 'It's sad. There have been one or two buskers in town, maybe they've been a bit loud during office hours and some people play after nine p.m. . . . you're meant to stop at nine. It's sad because those people are making it harder. Obviously they get a lot of complaints and it's a real shame.'

*

The most picturesque of the buskers are the living statues: ornately dressed figures in masks, mostly hovering above, and seemingly unattached to, the ground. They have become a common form of entertainment in London and are popular with tourists, who queue up to take photos and pop something in the hat. A figure in a lime-green gown and reptilian hard mask, carrying a Grim Reaper scythe, is often to be seen in Trafalgar Square. I tried to speak to him, but couldn't hear or understand what he said. I then spoke to one across the square who was setting up, spraying his costume with gold, and discovered he was Romanian, with little English. Later in the day, I saw the two of them and some others taking a break, so I gathered that they are all from Romania.

Then one day I saw a startlingly elaborate statue outside M&S at Marble Arch, towering above the passers-by, many of whom stopped and stared with astonishment. It was triple-tiered, with a man at the bottom, another halfway up, and a woman doll at the top. They were swaying in the wind, joined – balanced – by small beach balls. I found that they too were Romanian, and that the one in the middle, Caval, spoke some English. He lifted the golden hood to reveal a blue-painted young face, and I interviewed him *in situ*, holding the recorder up to his face.

'Hello, I'm coming here, and I'm from Romania and my name is Caval, and I like this place. I come here because this performance is everything for me, because my hand is very tired, and my legs, after ten hours. Ten hours, yes. I come here eleven o'clock, and I finish at ten o'clock in the night. Yeah, I know it is a long time. But I like this, this is myself and I say to everybody, Good luck.

'Why here? I am in London for a purpose, because this place Oxford Street it is very popular, so much people are coming here from every country. Money? Not much but not so bad. *Comme ci, comme ça*. It's not much, but it's all right. You know, one day I take £50, it is good for the two of us. I live Dorking, Surrey. I have in England so much time. Four years. But not here – other place,

Scotland, and Leeds, Birmingham, and I'm travelling. I come to England because it's very nice, I've never been here before but I see it in pictures, and I think, wow, look, it's so nice. Everybody says it's good, I go London. I love London. Problems, no, not really.

'No everybody from Romania, but not coming for this work, come for Western Union, for Vodafone, coming for like M[&]S, coming here for our good jobs. For in Romania, you have a job for one month, as a painter for one month, very small. It is £500, you are working every day, every day £500. And here it is £1000, £1500, this is enough, is good.'

I mentioned the other Romanians in Trafalgar Square, but he was dismissive of any who didn't make the effort to learn English.

'I like it so much. It is very beautiful to stay here. Everybody is nice, very nice. They say good luck, see you next time. Not much people tell me you are not good. It is – the school, you know the guys from the school, sixteen, seventeen, kids, they tell me, I push you. It doesn't bother me, because I am here on the street all the time.

'How long will I do it? I'm not sure. Two years, three years, then finish and go my home, for another job, for relax. No, I didn't leave school, I am here for the "Eye for the ears".' This seemed to be some kind of gap year. 'Romania it is possible you don't have the money for the school, it is possible to work one year and then you come back, you pay for the Eye year. Yes, I go back to the school and study to be architect. I think it is good money for everything, for other studio, because I pay for everything, you know. It is good for architect. I am here for my uncle, for my sister, and me!'

A few weeks later, passing through Trafalgar Square, I was touched to see the reptilian statue, standing tall on his stand and in his green gown and mask, bend down to high-five a group of small schoolboys.

Magicians' corner

Mayhew describes a number of magicians, whom he called street conjurers. They often performed in parlours, but sometimes in the street, and they made good money.

'The first pitch we made was near Bond-street. He began with his part of the performance whilst I was dressing up the table. It was covered with black velvet with fringe, and the apparatus ranged on it. After him I began my performance, and he went round for the nobbings. I did card tricks ... All card tricks are feats of great dexterity and quickness of hand. I never used a false pack of cards. There are some made for amateurs, but professionals never use trick cards. The greatest art is what is termed forcing, that is, making a party take the card you wish him to; and let him try ever so well, he will have it, though he's not conscious of it ...

'We did well with pitching in the streets. We'd take ten shillings of a morning, and then go out in the afternoon again and take perhaps fifteen shillings of nobbings. The footmen were our best customers in the morning, for they had leisure then. We usually went to the squares and such parts at the West-end. This was twenty years ago, and it isn't anything like so good now ... Then you must remember, we could have made more if we had liked; for some mornings, if we had had a good day before, we wouldn't go out if it was raining, or we had been up late.'

I met Jeremy, a stocky middle-aged man with a black money apron, waistcoat and hat, at a spot in Covent Garden Market known as 'Magicians' Corner'. He was in full flow, in the middle of a trick with a lemon and a £10 note, surrounded by about fifteen entranced members of the public. At the end, he invited donations.

We waited till he'd lit a roll-up, then began our interview, when he talked in a mellow, faintly American accent, with an upwards lilt at the end of sentences.

'I'm a full-time busker. Er, worked in America primarily. I'm back here for a while visiting family, so I'm bringing my busking to the streets of London, and it's been a very interesting way of earning a living. I started in 2011. Before that I did various things. I've been a teacher, I've been in sales ... What really made the busking happen was I had some health problems, and I'd been out of work for a while so I wasn't quite sure what to do, and I was sending out CVs without much success. I'd known magic when I was a kid, and had been quite serious about it. I'd given it up for, you know, a number of years, but when I was out of work, I remembered coming here as a child, to Covent Garden. I would come here with my magic teacher, and I would watch the magicians busk. And at the time it sort of stuck in my brain and I thought that would be really fun to do, but I didn't have the balls to do it. My teacher was a member of the Inner Magic Circle, a very well-respected magic teacher. So we would come here and watch the magicians, and it stuck in my mind.

'So when I was out of work, you know, what can I do to get back on my feet? And I remembered Covent Garden, I remembered the street magicians. What would happen if I got together a rig, put an act together and just went out on the streets? I was forty-three. Fifty-one now.

'So I went out, the first day, I was in Chicago, and I walked around for about three hours, convincing myself that I was looking for a good spot to work, but it was just because I didn't have the courage to do it. Eventually I said well, I've spent this money getting this gear together. I'm going to feel like a complete failure if I don't at least try, so I just set up my table and I'd been there a few minutes and a coupla older guys came up and said, "OK, what you got?" So I did a trick or two for them. I don't even remember now what I did. They gave me a couple of dollars and I thought, that's not so bad. Then I found a better spot, and that first day I made about fifty-eight dollars for about four hours' work, and I thought, well, this is better than nothing. I'll come back tomorrow. And I just kept coming back.

'I love it. It's a lot of fun. You meet total strangers, and yet, you know, if people are walking through, you have the challenge of seeing total strangers walk past you and you have to find a way to engage with them and have them stop, and have them stay, and have them pay, and you're really giving them an experience that they never anticipated having. No one sets out thinking that today I'm going to find me a street magician, so it's an unexpected moment, it's a kind of discovery. You can really give people this very positive experience, this really great memory.'

Music

Most buskers are musicians. Music on the streets has come a long way since Mayhew's day.

There's a variety of different instruments and a lot of amplified music: in the evenings at Oxford Circus and Piccadilly, and all day in Trafalgar Square. I've come across steel drums at Hyde Park and on the South Bank, and one day walked past a very professional drummer with a full drum kit, sitting in solitary splendour on Westminster Bridge. The music ranges from rock to reggae, from folk to jazz and classical music. A number of music students busk to make a bit of extra cash. People play on the streets and, if they have a licence, in the Underground. At a more commercial level, the individual bagpipers on Westminster Bridge, near the Houses of Parliament, are quite an institution. Handsome in their kilts and regalia, they have been for many years quite a draw for foreign visitors.

David Mwaniki, known as 'The Covent Garden Busker', makes his living busking and can be found most days and in all weathers in Covent Garden or Leicester Square. He's fifty-seven and grew up in London. His parents came from Kenya and settled here in the 1950s. He lives with his second wife in Canning Town.

'So, for the guitar, when I was twelve, my brother was ten, he taught me some chords. He was very good. He was doing all the

Simon and Garfunkel stuff and the Beatles. Simplified chords. He taught me how to do the D and the C, so I learnt the basics.

'When I was with my family, we had a party and I remember just singing along. I was doing . . . a Stevie Wonder song, I think. And they said to me, Why don't you take it up? You can sing. There was a lady who lives near me, and she was an opera singer, she was a vocal trainer. So I paid to go to get lessons, just the basic breathing and scales. She was brilliant. Since, she's died, bless her heart. Lovely lady as well. Really saw the talent, was really good with her students. She knew when you weren't practising and when you did. That was . . . I'd say late eighties, yeah.

'I got lessons from another guy named Chris. Classic guitar, so I had to learn some pieces. A while after the party, I started to sing more, learn some songs, and I went on the Underground. You had to watch for the cops coming. They'd pull you aside or the staff would move you on. Sometimes they'd turn a blind eye, but the police would never and one time I got pulled in by the cops. But he gave me a long lecture and I was being such a good lad, I wasn't being cheeky. He was itching to get me but then he thought, Well, I won't arrest you this time or fine you. But if you do it again, if I catch you again . . . I tried to avoid that station, try another station.' He laughs. 'But one guy, when I started, I was singing and he goes to me, "Listen, you need to sing out. You're a busker. People can't hear you." So that's when I started to get lessons and learnt to do it from the diaphragm.

'I started in Leicester Square first. That was, say, '95, '96. Then '96, '97 in Covent Garden. All my income comes from busking. It is up and down because I spend a lot of money on equipment. It's fun, it's not straightforward because obviously weather depending . . . I have a YouTube channel, "The Covent Garden Busker". Sometimes when I post on there, I get thousands of hits. Not as much as I used to, but it's fine. I used to have better equipment then.

'It's hard sometimes. Like last night was so quiet, so dead. You take the rough with the smooth. But it's a great time for practising, you can learn new songs . . . I do write my own songs but I don't busk them unless people ask me. I've sold CDs, now not so much because people don't buy CDs. Now and again I make 'em up. It's always good to have a batch there.

'Yesterday I made about nineteen quid. Not a good day. On a good day you could make eighty, a hundred quid. In the summer you could probably do two hundred. Those days are gone because obviously there's more buskers now ... you have to queue up, there was more space back then. I just play in the evenings mainly, get to Covent by four, do two or three sets. And then Saturdays I get there by eleven, maybe do two or three sets – or four sets – that day, depends how many people are there. There's a lovely couple that come and see me. They see others as well but they always say hi. It's really good fun. I really enjoy it. Terry, he's been doing it about thirty-five years, I've been doing it about thirty. Well, not thirty. Twenty-three, twenty-four years.'

For most buskers the rewards are more modest. An elderly man with a white beard sits cross-legged on the pavement opposite the British Museum, playing the accordion. He is Romanian and speaks very little English. He lived in Italy for many years so we were able to converse a little in Italian. He has been playing the accordion for twenty years but only for a year in England. He finds English people kind, he says, putting his hand on his heart. He sleeps on the street near Marble Arch, and says he makes enough – between £20 and £50 a week – for food. He kept repeating, '*Buono, buono.*' Good, good.

There are other Romanians playing the accordion, in the tunnel on the South Bank and especially behind John Lewis, at the edge of Cavendish Square. I first noticed an elderly man, but since then I have seen a young man – his son? – in the same place, and a man from Moldova with partial sight. All of them play without a break, often the same tunes, such as 'Under the Bridges of Paris'. A scattering of coins are left on their coat, but few passers-by take any notice.

On a Saturday morning, at Highbury & Islington station, a lone clarinet player with a black woolly hat was leaning up against the

wall. He played for a little while, rather diffidently. There was no one to hear him, so he stopped. In answer to my comment, he replied, 'What d'you mean, quiet?'

'Not much business for you. You seem relaxed about it.'

'Yeah.' He leant back against the wall.

Some people play for their own pleasure, and because playing at home, perhaps in a small flat, is not an option. There may be complaints from the neighbours, or a feeling of inhibition. For many years there was a bagpiper that played on Hampstead Heath – I heard him often, but never caught sight of him. On a Sunday morning in spring, there was a solitary trumpeter on an island in the middle of traffic near Hammersmith station. Sax player Tashomi started like that: 'When I play, I play for hours a day, I play for a good six hours straight and, after a while, it became a bit too much for the neighbours, even for myself. I became irritated because I wasn't at the level I wanted to be at. It was just annoying. So I'd go and play in the park and busk. That was when I first started, it was a way to keep playing and practising outside of the house.'

Paul, who has stopped playing for the time being, has the same problem, 'I can't practise at home. It's a small flat and the tenor saxophone would drive the neighbours mad. Practising as you know, for me it's long notes, it's kind of stuff that I don't know, it's making a lot of mistakes, it's getting very frustrated. I don't want to be performing like that for people to hear so when I go back to playing, the first thing I do, I find somewhere to practise.'

But even outside, there's a tension between busking and the needs of residents, especially with amplified music. Michael said: 'I used to play here [in Hoxton] with the mandolin in Goldsmiths Row. Once people started moving in' – there are new flats near by – 'I kind of knew the end had come but I continued. And after the third week of doing it, a woman come out and said, "Don't do it please, I just want my Sundays quiet", and I couldn't really argue with that.

'I'll chance my arm but if somebody tells me to go, I'll go. I mean it's the beauty of having an amp, you can just go twenty yards up the road. I don't want to be hated, that's not the purpose. If a hundred people could tell you that you sound, you know, beautiful, one person comes along and says the opposite and that's the one that affects you, isn't it?'

Art

What is the cheapest, most public way of expressing art? In Mayhew's day, people chalked on the pavement:

> A spare, sad-looking man, very poorly dressed, gave me the following statement. He is well-known by his coloured drawings upon the flag-stones:
>
> 'I was usher in a school for three years, and had a paralytic stroke, which lost me my employment, and was soon the cause of great poverty. I was fond of drawing, and colouring drawings, when a child, using sixpenny boxes of colours, or the best my parents could procure me, but I never had lessons. I am a self-taught man. It's 14 or 15 years since I started in the New Kent-road, and I've followed up "screeving," as it's sometimes called, or drawing in coloured chalks on the flag-stones, until now. I improved with practice. It paid me well; but in wet weather I have made nothing, and have had to run into debt . . . The Waterloo-bridge-road was a favourite spot of mine for a pitch. Euston-square is another. These two were my best. I never chalked "starving" on the flags, or anything of that kind. I don't do as well as I did 10 years ago, but I'm making 15s. a-week all the year through.'

And the practice continues. In Trafalgar Square, for instance, a number of people sit on the ground and draw pictures on the pavement; some draw flags, and invite members of the public to place money on a flag of their choice – a particular attraction for visitors from other countries. If permanence is not an issue, the pavement provides an extensive and easily accessible surface to display people's artistic endeavours. It is remarkable that, in the days of such sophisticated electronic communication, people should still resort to such an ancient practice to make some money and display their art.

Others use more durable media for their pictures, often directed specifically at tourists as souvenirs of their London experience. There are long-established collective opportunities for artists to display their work: for instance, the art fair by Whitestone Pond at Hampstead Heath in the summer and, all year round on Sunday mornings, on the railings on Bayswater Road between Queensway and Lancaster Gate. The show, licensed by Westminster City Council, has been established for nearly sixty years and bills itself as the largest regular open-air show in the world.

When I visited, on a bright early March afternoon, there were only about eight exhibitors, and most of the works were unframed oils of a chocolate-boxy kind. I chatted to a couple of older long-term exhibitors. Echoing the experience of market traders, they were agreed that the fair wasn't what it had been. It used to stretch all the way to Hyde Park and, said one sixty-five-year-old artist, 'you couldn't cross the pavement for people'. He, like a lot of other artists, now sells through the internet.

He has been coming to Bayswater Road for forty years and had sold nothing for the previous two months. And, yes, he comes throughout the year, every week. 'If you need to make a living, you have to. You have to pay for the licence, which is about £140, then you have to pay the council every month, whether you come or not. I think it works out at about £7.50 a week. Sundays and bank holidays only.' His paintings were spread over a wide area. 'If the ones on either side don't come, you can spread out.'

The other artist, who was sitting in his car, taking an order from a regular customer, asked me not to give his name. 'You've seen the level of paintings here. I wouldn't want to be associated.' I could see what he meant. His own were mainly watercolours of local scenes, selling unframed for £20, though there were some framed oils selling for £50 to £100. When I commented on the cheapness of the unframed pictures, he admitted to doing them from photos; at that price, he couldn't afford to take too long. 'But that's the expected sort of price, here.' I asked if he made a living. He said in the twenty years he's been coming he has never made a loss, but he now sells mostly from galleries, and in the past he did commercial art, which gave him a cushion. 'Unless you're one of the lucky few who make a living from the beginning, you have to teach, or do something else.'

*

Some draw or paint to order: portraits or, indeed, caricatures. I chatted to a man in Trafalgar Square, who insisted on drawing me as we talked. Anthony is Jamaican. In a bright yellow sweater, hair with a few grey hairs tucked up in a black Rasta hat, he was sitting on a little chair with examples of his art displayed bedside him.

'I've been doing this since I retired, I would say about a year. I'm sixty-six. I was a commercial artist. I was born in Jamaica, came here at the age of seven and was brought up in Kensal Rise, north-west London, went to school there, did everything there. No, I didn't go to art school. That was my mistake. I should have gone to art school and obtained a degree. It would have put me in a better place in life, but I didn't. It didn't cause me any problems, but I could have had a better position in terms of work. You know, if I had a degree, I could teach art because I'm quite gifted in art. I've always been an artist from when I was little, but having, you know, those papers would have made life much more easy for me.

'I wasn't freelance; I always worked for a company. The first company I worked for was in Kensington, doing graphic design. No, tell a lie, it was designing garment labels' – pointing inside his back collar – 'yeah, labels that go in your garment. That was before Letraset, computers. In those days everything was done by hand – lettering, everything. And then came computers that changed all that.

'I love doing it, man. I love it. And people seem to like it, which makes it a bonus. I chose to do this because I was good at it. Caricatures, yeah, I was good at it, and I enjoy doing it. What do I enjoy? Art. People too. I'm a people person, I love people. I enjoy interacting with people.'

Anthony's sisters and brothers still live in Jamaica, and he tries to go there every year, 'because I hate the cold, so wintertime I want to run somewhere, right? And I run to Jamaica because it's hot over there.' The interview ends as we are interrupted by someone asking for a photo of us.

Anthony finishes his drawing of me and hands it over.
'I've left out some of the lines.'
'What do you mean, lines?'
'Laughter lines.' Right.

Unexpectedly, walking along the South Bank, I came across some-one else who produces things to order – a poet. In Mayhew's day poets wrote ballads copied sometimes a thousand times, but did not produce unique poems written for individuals. Luke was sitting on his own at a little card table between the Globe Theatre and Tate Modern, with an old manual typewriter and a piece of cardboard saying 'POET. Give what you like'. It was a showery day, and he had to keep an eye on his typewriter. He was a bit nervous to begin with and needed prompting. A halting, thoughtful delivery.

'I've been doing this for two and a half years, in this spot. Never done it before but have been writing for a very long time. My friend made me do it, that was the immediate thing, but I'd been kinda envious of him. I saw that he was making a bit of money doing it, enjoying himself, improving as a writer, getting big rewards outa it, so I wanted to be involved before he pushed me into it.

'You know, there are not a lot of avenues for poets either to be read or to ... make any money whatsoever, particularly if you are not willing to spend a lot of time ingratiating yourself with other people and kind of moulding what you do to pre-existing formats. In some ways it's an ideal solution. Every poem probably doesn't have much more than one reader, but it does have one quite attentive and critical reader. And you end up with two oeuvres. You have one of your own, written in your own time, and under your own name, and then you have this anonymous one, distributed all across the world. Kinda treasured possession by various different people. That's quite ... I like it.

'They ask me to write a poem about a particular subject, very often love poetry, it can be anything. And ... I will write that generally in about three, four minutes, because you have to, or

people will get impatient, and if you have a queue, then you will lose custom if they're waiting too long. You work to that kind of time frame by necessity.'

I asked if it was hard to write to order.

'It's about as hard as I would like it to be. And I suppose also it's about as hard as you make it . . . because it depends somewhat on the kind of standard that you're holding yourself to. What degree of repetition you allow yourself, what length you want to write to, how trite, how platitudinous you're going to be. Er, it, it all determines how difficult it's going to be, you know. I try, I do try and push myself to write at the peak of my abilities, such as they are.

'Yes, they are pleased with what they get. I'd be horrified' – he laughed – 'if they came back and wanted their money back! They're quite good most of the time. The reality is you can't write a masterpiece every single time, when you're writing fifty, sixty poems a day potentially, all in a very very brief space of time, and also very often about the same subject, again and again. I've written more love poems than any man alive. It's good practice. I'm doing the same stuff again and again, and you know I'm not always absolutely thrilled with the results. I try to keep fairly consistent.'

I expressed my amazement at the volume that he produced.

'In summer, you can do . . . it depends, it's like anything, sometimes it's working quite well, and sometimes, like today, it's not. You take it as it comes. All the year round? Yeah, I do. There's a limit to what you can do in winter because once you get to about the three- or four-hour mark, your toes are about to drop off. There's nothing you can do about that. You just have to leave.

'This is the spot that my friend had found worked; he established himself here, felt comfortable here, so we just carried on here, you know. It is a great spot. It's a kind of bottleneck. You can't play music here because it's residential, so I don't have to fight with the musicians or whatever, because I'm quiet. I have a good relationship with the people living in the houses. It's ideal, really.

'You'd be surprised how few spaces there are where you can make this kind of thing work, in London at any rate. It's quiet enough, yeah, but also just where you won't get moved on, so if you go downriver a little bit, then I think Qatar owns it, or something? The whole stretch of riverbank around Tower Bridge and so on, and they've got their own private security and they'll move you on. This is increasingly the case throughout the city, you're getting private ownership of land, they make their own rules. No, you don't need a licence, or pay anything for being here.

'Before this? That's another reason I started doing this, because I was doing a whole series of things that you find ... you've got too old to do. Like kinda working in coffee shops, working in bars, builder's labourer, these kind of things where you reach a point where it doesn't feel possible to carry on. I won't make a fortune but so far it's been all right. You don't want to tempt fate but, yeah, just about. So far. And when people ask you to do it in other contexts, when you're out and about to do a wedding or some kind of thing, you have that as well.

'I love it, yeah, I mean it's made me. It's probably the first time I've felt more or less happy, really, in my skin, sort of life-changing. It's just the very simple thing of being able to spend your time and make your money by doing this ... thing that you think you're supposed to do, that you think you're good at. And er not just doing that but getting this constant drip of approval every day, and people being amused or touched, or some kind of connection being made in that very brief period of time. All that stuff is good. Even making coffee was nice in that sense because you're doing something for someone who wants that thing and they like it when you do it.' We both laugh. 'It's a good kind of feedback loop, you know. It makes you feel better about yourself.'

'Anything bad about it?'

'Erm ... well ... I mean you get ... I was talking to one of the other buskers, who does something different, and he was saying that some days you kind of go home in *tears*. Which I don't go home in tears but, you know, I guess ... I kinda, I *do* know where he's coming from. You know, I think maybe for him it was more ... he plays his music and everyone ignores him, right? He doesn't have an amp like a lot of these young kids, you know where they're just playing stadium concert level of volume, er and I think it comes out when he plays er and no one kind of looks at him let alone gives him any money, it really hurts, and I think for me it's a *little* bit different, I mean I do have quiet days, which are not so nice, but it's more, I guess, if you feel you've kind of poured all this stuff out er and nothing really comes back. You give this thing away, you never see it again, you never see them again, er so, if you're kind of feeling delicate' – another little laugh – 'then, then sometimes maybe that could feel er a little bit sad, I don't know. Most of the time . . . I'm kind of too robust to be bothered, but it can be challenging, potentially. As I say it really depends on what state you're in on any given day, as to how much that will affect you.'

He said there was no abuse or rudeness from passers-by. 'Almost never. It's exceedingly rare, maybe two or three times, but even these are very very mild. In a different part of London that might be different, but it's mostly wholly positive. Yeah, amazing, extraordinary. I don't know what the explanation is.' He laughs again.

Sebastian is forty-one and has been living here for about fourteen years. 'I started life in Argentina, but I grew up in Spain, and I moved here when I was twenty-seven, initially to just spend the summer. I was driving, a bit of adventure, I was in Potters Bar for five years. I was bored. I moved to London, and I ended up staying. I live in London. I like it.'

He told me how he got started.

'Well, I just picked up a guitar and had a normal life until later. I was sixteen, and started learning – like, some friends showed me some chords – then took some lessons, then got more interested in flamenco music and jazz music. I started in different places, like privately. I studied music, harmony, theory, jazz guitar, flamenco guitar, and then I mixed all those things into my own thing, which is why I like it. I used to have a band here in London for nine or ten years. We released a couple of CDs. But that finished and I realised. Been solo for the last few years. No, I'd rather not sing.'

While he waits for his turn to busk in Trafalgar Square, he plays chess with passers-by.

'Yes, I play chess as well. There was a couple of guys I used to play, because we wait here, you know, we queue, sometimes it's for hours. You have to do something. We used to have some boards sometimes and then people came to play with me. I make a *little* bit of money. But it's nice ... the kids, people have a good time, sometimes. Old gentlemen that haven't played for years, they get all excited, they tell you some stories, it's a connection with people. You just have that feeling, you know, it's like anybody can be involved. You can be a child, everybody plays chess. It doesn't matter. It's just because you're there. A lot of different people come together and you play different people. It's quite a unique way of meeting people that are so different to you. I do enjoy it a lot. And also, I like playing.'

People perform on the streets for different reasons: to make money or to express themselves, and for many it is the only way to combine the two. Hard as it is, according to Sebastian, it is possible to make a living.

'You can make a living out of music. I do. You can, if you work hard enough. You have good times and worse times, but on average it works out; it's just like having a job, a normal job. In my case, not that much, but it's not bad, so it's OK.'

15

Getting the message out

Not everyone is on the street to make money. Some use the wide arena as an opportunity to get the message out.

Campaigning

London has a proud history of protest and campaigning. Some choose to extend their protest beyond a one-off march or vigil.

Tony is in his seventies and is often to be found at a little stall opposite the Chinese Embassy, what is called a 24/7 protest site. There's a petition to sign and leaflets to take away. There is usually music playing with someone there praying, sitting or kneeling, facing the embassy across the road.

'I practise a spiritual discipline called Falun Gong, which is being very very persecuted in China. It's had millions of people, there's lots of evidence about people who have been victims of the Chinese Communist Party. As you may well know, the Chinese Communist Party is very brutal – they don't like anyone who believes in anything. Muslims, Christians, LGBT. They admit they've been taking organs from so-called criminals, which shocked the world, but the world didn't say too much about it, because a lot of money is being made at the moment from taking them from religious people. Prisoners of conscience, Christians and Muslims and Tibetans, some of the practitioners of Falun Gong.

'They say at least a million and a half people have been killed for their organs, so we're trying to tell the world very urgently, because the FG believes in the humanity virtues: truth and compassion and tolerance, which are sometimes difficult to practise, but they make a huge difference to people's lives and would obviously make a huge difference to the world. We actually feel that what is under attack in China is human nature's basic decency, so it's not just China, and also because everybody takes its orders from China, no one's got the courage to publicly criticise China. The government seems to do nothing at all, and so we feel very concerned that humanity is in very grave danger, which it is anyway.

'This has been going on since 2002 and it's going on in many countries and many capitals all over the world – Australia, Germany, France, Canada, USA, lots of places. We want to get people thinking what is this thing, Falun Gong, why is it so important, and why do we feel so strongly about it? And I can say straight away that any human being can benefit from this. Whether they would take it up and keep doing it, I don't know, but erm, I was so deeply moved by it ... I've done T'ai Chi and meditation – I was doing meditation in India in the 1970s, but I'd never come across anything like this, and the fact that it is being persecuted massively by a present-day government and kept quiet by the rest of the world's governments really struck me that this is something really serious. I've been waiting for this all my life.

'I've been here since it started. We were discussing a 24/7 protest seventeen years ago, 2002. We were asking ourselves do we need to be 24/7, and I said yes, absolutely, but I had to be honest and say I'm not doing nights.' He laughs. 'It's not just me, there are loads of us, probably, em, with a turnover of, em, quite a few, maybe twenty people. There are people who do it on a regular basis, and if there's not someone to finish a shift, which is usually about four hours long, then somebody gets phoned up. There's maybe two hundred, a hundred and fifty of us in London.

'How long will I continue? I don't know. This is the driving force in my life, it's not just a hobby or something like that, I'm totally grabbed by it. I felt almost finished about eighteen years ago when I started doing this. I was absolutely amazed, a lot of things were happening at the time, but everything seemed to converge and happen at the right time, like a jigsaw puzzle. I'll always want to be part of this, because, give you an example, a few times when I didn't do the exercises, when I just stopped, and you're supposed to do a little on a regular basis, just stare into space, and this is such a rare thing, that anything like this can happen to anyone. so whatever else I do, I will still have this as my base. It's like having your breakfast in the morning and having your dinner at night, and much more than that, for someone or something to show you that there's a meaning in there. That's absolutely priceless, isn't it? You can't buy that with millions of pounds.

'None of the authorities have objected. In fact, Westminster Council, they've actually spoken with me a few times and with other people who have similar appeals going on all over the place, in town centres, in Chinatown and Trafalgar Square. We've always enjoyed good relations with the council. They know what's happening. They understand that what we do is not something bad. And the police.'

Some sleep on the streets in solidarity with their cause.

Noah is a gentle elderly man with a long, straggly whitening beard and hair. Though he has an address, he is currently living in a tent and sits with his very friendly dog in a prominent position on Great Portland Street, behind a couple of tables with an assortment of DVDs, books, bags and other knick-knacks, which people have given for exchange. Not for sale, though sometimes people give donations. It's just to remind people to recycle, not throw things away. Behind him are giant posters and banners saying 'Humanity Faces Extinction, The Truth About Global Warming'. We sit on a couple of newspaper-covered canvas chairs.

Noah refuses to answer any personal questions or talk about how it feels to be on the streets, answering everything in the 'we' mode.

'Tell me about yourself.'

'This is a protest site. This is the Noah's Ark campaign and is about raising awareness about the extinction of life on earth, including the human race, as a result of global warming.'

'And what about you as an individual? How long have you been doing this?'

'This is my life. This is what I do. We open protest sites to protest against consumerism which is destroying the planet.'

I try again. 'Where were you born?'

'Well . . . I was born on the earth because this is my planet. I don't really go into personal information, because that isn't the point of what we do. It's not about individuals, it's about the issues.'

'How long have you been living in a tent?'

'Tents, caravans and treehouses are part of our culture. It's an alternative way of life.'

'Do you feel safe?'

'What do you mean, safe?'

'Sleeping here on the street.'

'It's not really about safe or not. This is England. We're supposed to be safe in England, aren't we? As environmental activists, we're perfectly capable of dealing with any kind of trouble. The main trouble comes from government and police and other agents of the state. If necessary, we can fight. We can defend ourselves.'

'So are you reliant on what people give you or do you buy stuff?'

'We're self-sufficient, we have an alternative lifestyle; we try not to support the capitalist system. It's a form of post-apocalyptic survivalism, that's what we call it. We feel as though the financial system has already collapsed. We are aware that global warming is destroying the planet, causing the greatest mass extinction in history. We know that our industrial civilisation is collapsing around us and it's obvious from the news day after day after day – heatwaves, hurricanes and melting Antarctic, hundreds of millions of climate refugees – that things are getting worse and worse, and we don't support the capitalist system. We get food from supermarket skips, we do everything we can to avoid giving any support whatever to the system that is destroying the planet.'

*

Dan is standing in Trafalgar Square next to a large white chalked stylised image of several women, headed with the giant word 'MegaWomen'.

'Are you a woman of God? Then I trust you.

'My name is Dan. I'm sixty-five years of age, last June 1st. I've stopped work after fifty years, working in twenty-eight countries of the world, with three hundred and seventy staff. The company still operates now. I've had fifty glorious years. We're a facilities management company, and we build railways, airports, councils, buildings, and we wanted to make a difference. The last job I did was Dubai metro for ten years, and this year we formed this.

'MegaWomen are the women who have the least amount of things in life, but lack the opportunities. So we provided the opportunities, the jobs, the future, the careers, and gave it to people who – the people on the streets are homeless, they have nothing. It's easy for people to say get off the streets and go and live in a hostel, but you need money for this, you need deposits, you need careers, you need jobs, you need security. But most of all you must have the trust of the people around you, so this is where I choose, for twelve months, on the 1st June last year, after fifty years' work, I decided to retire and give back to the people who have nothing. We do twelve months, a fixed period, and I live on the street, sleep in sleeping bag, we have tents, by the kind permission of the Saudi Arabian owners there, No. 1 the Strand.

'I have fourteen women there on average each night and it's designed to be for people, women who have come into trouble, who have been raped, harassed, chased, all the badness, the robbery – they come to us at two o'clock in the morning, standing in the clothes that they have, scared to the living daylights. And they want help. They hear by word of mouth on the street. Everybody knows that if you come into any trouble whatsoever – because the police cannot help you, right? – there's no shelter, there's no address you can go to to get admission. So I do this from experience.

'I say, everybody come to No. 1 the Strand, the arches over there, in front of Waterstones, and we are there every night. We have clean tents, clean sleeping bags and mattresses and pillows. They have food and drink. They have first aid. And we have a doctor and a nurse who sleep there as well. Along with two security guards, we have microphones and loudspeakers, cameras, video recorded all night, and we finance this from the donations we are given publicly.

'This is the first place where you can come and see how we live. And when you're on the streets, you don't have hairdressers, you don't have dentists, you don't have doctors, but we provide these services, so when they come and need help, they come with just the clothes they stand in. We have other women there who have the competence and the trust and we say you don't have to worry any more now. This is the start of your new life. They can stay as long as they like, and what we do is we put them through a twenty-eight-day programme, and get them rebuilt, we take them to the nurse and the doctor in the morning, we liaise with National Health doctors who will treat homeless women immediately on the day. So you go to the surgery, and you know you're going to see a doctor that morning.

'My slogan is "What small thing can I give you today that will make the biggest difference in your life, every day?" And you give that thing to the person in the morning. It's not the big things, we've learnt. We've learnt the small things are the things that help you progress – have you heard of Maslow? We use Maslow's triangle. OK? We say, you stand at the very bottom and this is your new life.

'We have helped 8342 women in the same predicament from all different nationalities. We give them work, and we give them a future, we give them the apartment to buy or rent or sublease. Because of the financial crunch, we bought from Keel, the construction company, two hundred apartments from them, for cash. We sold all our houses, and we paid the cash for the apartments, and they gave us sixty-eight per cent discount, from the crash. And we got new apartments, and we put the women in there, so they had the advantage.

'I said I'd do it for twelve months till 1 July. Till I find out if there's a position where we can hand it over, so that the good that we've learnt we can then, because some of the women, they too, the success is a real success, they go to the normal work, they do their improvement and they have their life back, their new life. But they've never forgot where they came from, and they can come back there. And we'll give you a sleeping bag and a tent and you can stay the night, and they come there voluntarily to help the other people and also to prove that it is possible. Because it's very very very hard to ask a woman to believe, to change her life, and put her trust in somebody she's known for a very short time.'

Preaching

For some, the message is a religious one. David 'The Covent Garden Busker' combines his musical life with evangelism.

'We run a course called Streetwise, which is in Stratford, in St John's Church, the big Anglican church on the Broadway. We run it from ten till three and people will hear about us online. They come, they learn how to do a sketchboard [an interactive whiteboard]. We do things like tricks as well, illusions, we use that in the gospel message, rope tricks. I don't do most of the tricks but some of my colleagues do, they're very good, very professional. We do it in an entertaining way.

'We might do a sketchboard, we might do a chart and ask, "What is the answer?" Some people might say, "Learn." Education is good but you might be forever learning and never come to the knowledge of the truth. We talk about points and then we bring the cross in and say, "Look, Jesus did come and he died for our sins. You can have freedom." There's an eight-minute to ten-minute message and then we give an appeal and we've got a team in the crowd who are there to talk to people. Different churches get together. There's probably about ten of us, or sometimes less but we meet, we pray, we go out, do an hour, then we go and we do a debrief. They're a wonderful bunch of people.'

Mayhew was familiar with preachers and tracts. In his day,

More than one half of the tract sellers are foreigners, such as Malays, Hindoos, and Negros. Of them, some cannot speak English, and some – who earn a spare subsistence by selling Christian tracts – are Mahometans, or worshippers of Bramah!

It's strange that with more sophisticated ways of spreading the word available, people still resort to handing out leaflets. Nowadays they are given away, not sold, and it's mainly by Jehovah's Witnesses, who are very used to proselytising. They are best known for going door to door, but they are also to be found at various spots on the streets. I came across pairs of them a number of times, next to a little stand (a bit like a clothes horse) displaying a variety of leaflets with titles such as: 'Where can we get the answers to life's big questions?' They were invariably friendly and open to discussion.

One pair were standing at the corner of Oxford Street and Great Portland Street: a woman and a tall, very young Afro-Caribbean man.

'Do you do this full time?'

'We do shifts.'

'So you have another life?'

'This is our life. The most important part of it. But, yes, we do have jobs and things.'

Another day, a trio near Portland Place. Two youngish men and a woman. Cheerful and friendly. 'We're at this venue for three hours. We have eighteen venues in central London. Yes, quite a lot of take-up. Conversations and people taking leaflets and so on.' For an interview, they said, I would need to go via their website.

There was another pair at Marble Arch, a serene presence round the corner from the mayhem of Speakers' Corner. They have a version in Arabic too: 'The Bible is universal.' Both came to their faith around the age of sixteen, and they evangelise door to door too. The young man tries to do seventeen hours a month, as well as holding down a nearly full-time job in security. The woman is a carer.

Many of those handing out leaflets seem to belong to no particular religious denomination. Walking down Tottenham Court Road at 9.30 a.m. on a Monday morning, Stephanie, a small Afro-Caribbean woman, offers leaflets bearing the message 'Tell me the Truth' to passers-by. No one takes up her offer. Having initially refused as I normally do, I ran back to get one and asked her about what she was doing. She works as a cleaner from 7 to 9 a.m., apparently, then comes out to do this. 'It's my gift. Everyone has a gift, and this is mine.' When I asked which was her religion, she replied, 'The message is just Jesus Christ. If you confess your sins, you don't need a religion.' It was all rather individual and attractive – until in the leaflet, produced somewhere in Northern Ireland, I saw the usual references to sin, repentance, heaven and hell.

'I'm going to work out now,' she said, 'to look after my body, my temple. If the Spirit wills it, we will meet again.'

There's no shortage of invitations to some kind of spiritual or religious life. In Bond Street one Saturday evening, I came across two women standing with a magazine in English and Spanish and a placard saying: 'Is this life all there is?' Outside Goodge Street station, a Japanese man was handing out *Happiness* magazine; in Oxford Street, a man came up to me as I sat outside a café and said: 'My English not good, but,' patting his large Bible, 'Jesus loves you.'

Most days, a group of volunteers look after a table in Leicester Square giving out leaflets and copies of the Qu'ran in many languages. The first time I visited, I made the mistake of offering my hand. The young man explained that through 'respect for women, particularly my mother' he was unable to shake it, and that I would have to wait for his boss for an interview. I did not make the same mistake the second time, a cold February lunchtime, when their table was the only offering in the square. This time the table was covered by a tent, with 'Ask us about Islam' and 'Who is Allah?' written on the roof.

The two young men there, Dawood and Iftikher, were friendly and helpful. They had been volunteering for two months and two years respectively, one earning his living in security, the other in a mental health charity. They said they gave away fifteen to twenty copies of the Qu'ran a day, mostly in English, and that since they were not selling anything, Westminster Council did not charge for the space. Our chat was interrupted by the arrival of a more author-itative man, who told me that the stall had been there since about 1990, then insisted on engaging me in a theological discussion. I mentioned that I had heard that only the Arabic version of the Qu'ran was authentic. He said that translations were acceptable but that, in a beautiful phrase, only the Arabic 'has the flavour and the sweetness'. We talked about my concept of Jesus, and the Muslim one, about the Trinity and one God, and many different aspects of faith. Despite many commonalities, where we differed he was insistently dogmatic, and I left.

Charity

For some, charity is both a way of earning money and of making money for a good cause. 'Chuggers' working for various agencies or charities accost people on the streets and ask them to sign up. Among these is Bella, studying forensic science. We meet at the end of her shift, at 6 p.m., and sit outside Pret a Manger near Oxford Circus. She is concerned about me getting cold and offers to buy me a drink.

'Yeah, I've had a few jobs in my time: retail . . . I coach football at the weekends as well, so do a lot for people when I can. I work for a charity right now. I used to work for a fundraising agency, and they would like, work like for different charities, but now I'm working directly for Barnardo's charity, so yeah.

'I've only been at this agency since Monday because they liter-ally, I mean Barnardo's used to have an indoor team, fundraising from door to door, but now they've opened a street team. We meet at seven forty-five in the morning at the station or at a coffee shop near the site. We just talk about what we'll get in the day, what we're going to do in the day. Usually the target is to get three sign-ups, and it's only over eighteen years old and a fiver a month, so it's not really a lot. The last charity I worked for was £10 a month and over twenty-five. We'll work from ten o'clock till twelve thirty, have a half an hour break, then start again one till three, then another half-hour break, then work usually from about three forty-five till six.

'In the old job I was paid hourly, and also paid commission, so every eight sign-ups I would get in a week, I'd get £80, and then every one sign-up after that, it was £20 extra, so that was an incentive. But this job is fixed, it's only hourly, no commission, no nothing. £10.50. £10 in the other place.'

I ask if she likes it. 'Yeah, I mean I love interacting with people, I find it so, like, warming. I mean I get rejected all the time, but even if I get no sign-ups in a day, meeting people and having nice conversations with people just brings me up and makes me feel good about myself.

'People are rude to me, yes. Can I swear? I was in Holborn once, and I stopped some lady, and she shouted at me, and goes, "Don't even try it, you bunch of cunts", then moved away. People tell me, go get a real job, what are you doing on the street? You're irritating people, why are you wasting the time? Or stop bothering me, or this stuff.'

She laughs. 'I'm like OK, I'm bothering you, but I'm doing it for a good cause. At first it was like, it makes you feel so low and so small, but you just have to take it on the chin, like, there's one horrible person. Let's say I meet ten horrible people, I meet one nice person, that will completely switch my mood. It makes me feel shit about myself, but when I speak to that nice person after, I say OK, you know, there are nice people out here. Not everyone's an idiot like you!' Another laugh.

I ask her what she would say to someone like me who likes giving to small on-the-ground charities, and won't give to someone like her because I don't want to pay for her or for big ads.

'OK, I'd say the charity I work for now, every pound that gets donated, 91p goes directly to the charity, which is very high. And the rest of the money goes directly to making another pound. I mean paying for people like me. At the end of the day, people do have to get paid. Like you said, there are small charities, but without anyone on the streets, or adverts, they won't benefit from it, because not many people will know about them. But if people aren't comfortable with it, I wouldn't stand there and force you. I'd say, I understand that, it's OK.'

Most chuggers are, like Bella, young and filling in time between studies, or saving up money during a gap year. But Eric has been working in the sector for eleven and a half years.

'We get paid a basic wage on an hourly rate. There are fundraisers out there who do it by commission, but if you want my honest opinion, it can be valuable, but I think it's unnecessary pressure. If you're having to sign people up to get paid, then you've got to put more pressure on. If you get an hourly rate or a daily rate, whatever it is, then that takes away that pressure. You know you're going to get paid anyway. A lot of it is the charities. They don't want people to be pressured into it, we want to inspire people to pay for as long as they possibly can.

'All the agencies I've worked for give an hourly rate as well or a daily rate. I get the London Living Wage. It's not a lot, but then it is a very valuable agenda. I love this job, you know. I often say to my fundraisers, how many people can you name that actually save lives every day? Apart from the charities, fundraisers do. We do the fundraising for organisations to go out and help people. And save lives. Save animals' lives. Help the environment, whatever they do.'

Even though he is now thinking of moving on, he says, 'There'll always be a spot for fundraising in my heart. When I first started, it was a job, but I've developed this love for it, a passion. I'm forty-six. I've been doing it since I was thirty-five. A long time. Over eleven and a half years I've been fundraising, I've generated between five and six million pounds, and that is from me, myself. Obviously there's many, many fundraisers out there. It just puts it in context how valuable a job it is.'

Free newspapers

Times have changed for the newspaper trade. Although there are still kiosks selling magazines and newspapers, not only have many papers gone online, but some of the printed papers are now free. The *Evening Standard* is the best known. Published since 1827, it became free in 2009, in the expectation that its circulation would more than double to over 600,000 each day. At that time there were more than three hundred vendors of the *Evening Standard* and a number have remained to staff the distribution points. A spokesman said the 'vast majority of vendors are paid hourly, while the rest are paid a margin on sales'. Other papers followed suit. The London edition of *Time Out* became a free magazine in September 2012, with distribution the following month of a record 305,000 copies per week.

London is peppered with people giving out these free newspapers, especially around tube stations. The *Standard* is daily but others, like *Time Out*, have their special day. And Delia distributes them all.

Knowing that Tuesday is the day that *Time Out* is given out, I had earlier met two young women at Oxford Circus station, each of whom said that their shift finished at 12.30 and agreed to be interviewed. But, given previous experience, I wasn't surprised that neither was there at the given time. I did, however, see the back of a short black woman in the familiar red tabard as she faced an onrush of passengers coming up the stairs from the tube, energetically calling out, '*Time Out*, FREEE, last copy.' I agreed to take that last copy and she agreed to be interviewed. She dropped off her gear, and we went to a local café and sat down. I offered to buy her a coffee, but she declined; since she is known there, they were happy for us just to use the chairs. Delia spoke fast and sometimes the speed of her delivery, together with her Nigerian accent, made it hard to catch what she was saying.

'My name is Delia, the short form of Cordelia, and er I do a lot of distribution of magazines and cards and anything that is readable. I do that almost every day of the week on the streets of London. I enjoy it because it's something that people can pick up and read it, and the next time they say, Oh, do you have this, do you have that, and I am happy to give it out again. Different magazines, different booklets, some religious, some secular.

'I do it because I think, number one, this is a very literate society – people actually read them, that's why they pick them up. Secondly, the public, the general public, they do not go to the internet that day, this is a Monday to Friday, and they are going to work, and they pick it up and they have it. Also we have a lot of free literature, like free *Evening Standard*. People advertise there and that's the only way, really, they make money. People are taking it and reading the adverts, in't it? If people are not reading it, the people wouldn't have these papers any more.' She laughs. 'So the fact that people are taking it and reading the adverts, that's what keeps the paper free.'

The number of hours she works varies. 'Anything from sixteen hours to twenty-eight hours. Monday to Friday. Obviously we don't do weekends. Most of the people are not concerned about the weekends. So the free papers are not at the weekend. But Monday to Friday is very busy. Most of the time I would say, on average, it's only Monday . . . Tuesday I do five hours of *Time Out*, the others are usually two or three hours. So five hours on Tuesday, seven hours most days. Only one day I do five hours of this, plus four, that is nine hours, like today.

'Yes, we get paid per hour, which, obviously,' she laughs, 'is not always the best . . . Like today I've done fourteen bundles. You have to give them out if you can, but you have to stand for the five hours for the pay, rather than stand and do nothing. For *Time Out*, pay for the five hours. It seems to me you should be able to do two per hour. They are fifty in each bundle of the *Time Out* magazine. So it's entirely up to your speed, what happens. I already finish – in three hours I finish my ten, so I go back for more.

'I've been doing this for the past three or four years. I also do literature for the church. And that's my church, next to the BBC. Yes, All Souls. I am going there for leaflets and do it now once a week. We do it at night, seven to nine, Thursdays. I live in Camden, so not far.

'If there was a negative, it would be that they could pay more. I think they want to keep it down, maybe it is their first job, or to keep the papers free. *Standard* is free, *Metro* is free, *Time Out* is free – all of them are free. I think they can pay more – that's the only downside. Most people are nice, if you are nice. Because it depends on your reaction: if you are smiling, and the way I talk to them: "Morning, *Time Out* is free, FREEE! It's true, what I say to you. It's free. You have nothing to lose."'

Pat is a small elderly man standing outside Goodge Street station, behind a container with piles of copies of the *Evening Standard*.

'My name is Patrick Simpson. I've lived in London all my life, except for seven years I lived at Eastbourne, and I was also in the army at the same time, 1947 to '52. I was born and brought up in Holborn. I've been doing the *Evening Standard* since 2007. We sold it then, then they decided to let the papers go free and I've been doing it voluntarily ever since. I love what I'm doing. The bloke who was in charge at the time, when they broke up, and sorting the papers out, and paid for them, he decided to keep the money, so I never got any money from them. So I'm happy to do what I do. I'm not a spring chicken no more.

'I'm eighty-eight. I worked at the National Hospital, Queen's Square, for twenty-five years as a porter, then I went from there to the University of London on security, and I was there for thirty-three years till 2007. The bloke who was in charge of the papers at the time, he asked me would I like a job, because I got to know him quite well. And I said, yes, I don't mind, so that was that. We worked up the top of Tottenham Court Road by the tube station there, and I loved what I was doing. Then they moved me back down here, selling the papers down here, and they decided after that when we finished, you know, selling the papers, and when it went public like this, he decided to keep the money. So that was it.' I tried to clarify how he was cheated of his pay, but all he would say was: 'I did mind at the time, but I'm OK about it now.

'It keeps me going, it keeps me not sitting on my bottom all the time. Because I had an accident round the corner in Goodge Street, had a lorry go over my feet, and I had a broken toe, and they had to cut the toe off because it went all black. Yes, I'm standing, but not all day. I walk a bit – I like walking – I just like getting on with things. I do it three till five every day.'

He says 'Thank you' to a customer. 'I love doing it. Because it gets me going all the time, keeps me moving, which is a good thing, because when you get to my age – Thank you. Have a nice evening – when you get to my age, what do people do? Come on. They sit on their bottoms all the time. That's not for me. I live alone now. My wife's gone, God bless her. I've got two girls and one boy. My eldest daughter talks to me quite a lot because she's got multiple sclerosis, she lives over Stamford Hill. My other daughter, Ruth, she lives in St Ives in Cornwall, and she's got two kids of her own. Grandchildren? I've got great-grandchildren. You want them, you can have 'em! I've got eight granddaughters and eight great-granddaughters and one grandson. I'd like to spend time with them, but I can't get down there. Getting on the train and all that. I can't do it, because of the platforms.

'The best thing about doing this job is that I'm talking to you. I talk to other people and that, and it keeps my mind going all the time. The worst thing is sitting on your bottom all the time. The weather is difficult at times, but I'm quite used to the weather.'

A number of people get paid for delivering or giving out leaflets for different companies. Zack, outside Westminster Abbey, handing out leaflets for a bus tour company, says, 'I've been doing this job for one week now. We'll see how it goes. If I sell well, then I could stay for quite a long time; if I don't, then I'll be out before two months. The deal is basically I need to sell a certain amount, probably in each week, in order for me to stay on, for the company to be satisfied with my performance. So I can obviously get the money to pay rent at home, etc. I'm paid by the hour, minimum wage, but if I want to get more, I get the commission for the extra sales I make. There is no security, no.

'I do enjoy it, even if people reject you at every opportunity. You eventually learn to live with it. It's just ignoring, it's nothing bad, malicious, it's just like you don't exist.'

He thought Brexit might be problematic for companies like his. 'Because London is an international city, we rely on international workers, especially workers from our nearest neighbours, in Europe. Without them there will be a huge effect not only on my work, my industry, but I think on industries across the board.'

Like many in his situation, Zack is used to insecurity.

IV

Survival

16

No Fixed Abode

'Everyone has the right to a standard of living
adequate for the health and well-being of
himself and of his family, including food,
clothing, housing.'

Universal Declaration of Human Rights,
Article 25, 10 December 1948

'At the end of the day, though, homeless
people aren't any different – they're just people
without a house.'

Former managing director, now homeless

'There's more and more people on the streets.
There's a lot, a lot of them. Even wee girls.
They'll never cure it. On the one hand they're
getting the people off the streets, on the other
there's more and more coming on the streets.
West End, East End, north London, it's mad.
Pure madness.'

Mo, an Irishman begging

Rock bottom

Some people, the most desperate, are almost invisible, even to themselves. Yes, they have a past (though one that they very often would wish to forget) but the present and future are a blank.

*

While I was sitting in a square in the sun, a thin young man approached me for money: tentative, with a sidelong look, expecting, and inviting, rejection. I invited him to sit down and be interviewed. Excited, he went to fetch his bike. Saying he was smelly, he refused to sit on the seat next to me, but sat on the ground. I had to move across to be close enough to record. A couple of young men sitting across the square laughed derisively as they saw us talking. Throughout the interview David picked at scabs, scratching, grunting with effort, and lighting up as we spoke. He was a hesitant speaker, needing frequent prompting, and was visibly moved during our conversation.

'Will you lend me the tenner, and do the interview later?'

'No, sorry.'

He laughs. 'Just trying it on. What do you want me to say?'

'Your name, who you are. Anything, really.'

'Hello, my name's David. I'm from Wolverhampton, When I was fifteen I went to live with my cousin. Do you want me to tell you ...?'

'Anything.'

'When I was a little kid ... my little brother killed himself, he couldn't handle all the shit, but I didn't have the bollocks, I didn't have the balls, sorry, I didn't have the guts to kill myself. He was fourteen. I was fifteen. And then I got into drugs and that was it. Once I got into drugs, I didn't look back.'

'How old are you?'

'I'm thirty-four.'

'What drugs?'

'Crack and heroin, and spice, but I'm trying to stop the spice now. I sleep in parks, on the floor, usually in St James's Park or Embankment. I can put my head down anywhere, really. I think that's what got into my head when I was a kid, my mum did that, I think that's what it is, so I've just realised, thanks, just realised. Everyone just abuses me, all my life. My mum and dad, they pretended to people that they're good and stuff, you know? They presented as good, Daddy loves you and all that.'

'Were they nice to you?'

'Nah. In front of other people, yeah, but I don't give a fuck – sorry, I should care, shouldn't I?'

'When did you come to London?'

'Seven, eight, nine years ago, something like that. I've been here years, people don't realise because I change my appearance all the time. I was rude to the wrong people.'

'Do you get any help?'

'Nah, nah. I let the people who want to help give a little help, don't waste it on me. If someone gives help, I just mess it up, you know? I don't know, miss, I don't know. I don't know any more.'

'Do you get enough to eat?'

'Yeah. In the long run.' He laughs. 'In the long run.' There's a long pause. 'My head's all messed up now, you know what I mean?'

'That's the drugs.'

'I've been off them before, you know? Yeah. Not long. I think I can help other people do it. I like to see other people do well,' he says with more determination. 'Just because I can't do it by myself, people don't get that about me. They say, "Why do you want other people to do well?" Because I do, so what?' He shouts: 'IT'S THE ONLY WAY YOU CAN CHANGE ME BY FORCE. I CAN'T BE FIXED. I'M UNFIXABLE, HA-HA. All my so-called *friends*, or whatever they are, they've all been fixed, the rats.'

'Do you ever get a bed for the night?'

'No, no. How long have you been doing this?'

'A few months.'

'D'you like it?'

'I love talking to people.'

'Yeah?' He laughs again. 'I do as well.' Another laugh. 'They just don't like talking to me.'

'Well, I do.'

'You're great, you are. Thank you. I don't like to talk. I don't complain. I don't like complaining. Some countries, the children don't have shoes on their feet. The worst thing about being on the street? The two-faced bastards that call you friends. Any good things? Drugs. They're not good, though, are they? I don't think there is. Talking to you. I like the rain. Dunno why.'

'What would you like to happen?'

Long pause. 'Just get a little bit of money in me pocket. I dunno. It doesn't seem to make ... You're right, yeah, money doesn't seem to make people happy, does it? Everyone be nicer to me.'

'Are they horrid?'

'Yeah.'

'Strangers?'

'They listen to rumours and that. People spread horrible rumours about me and people listen to them. Me, I used to listen to rumours as well, I wish I never. That might be my crime, listening to rumours, people listening to my rumours, that's what I did.' He groans with effort. 'That's all ... I've got a bottle. It's a normal thing for me, though.'

'Ever have a job?'

'Yeah. Not for very long. I'll tell you the truth, only for a couple of days.'

'Did you like it?'

'No, terrible.'

'Did you get paid?'

'Yeah. I want someone to say, here's a couple of hundred quid, go and sort yourself out. I could get a couple of hundred quid, I could, but I dunno.' He mumbles something about a nun and how she has helped him. 'Yeah, she just writes a letter, you might have heard of her from the Cardinal Hume Centre. Dr Hickey, she's been there years. In a surgery, in Victoria, you must have heard of her.'

'Well, I wish you well. I wish you a happier life.'

'You're nice. Well, you look nice and you seem nice, but they say you shouldn't be fooled by a smile. I think it was you that said that to me? You know your book, yeah? I really want to read it next time. Can I read it?'

When he filled in his consent form, David scrawled a large N/A (not applicable) across his contact details. No address, no phone, no email. Almost invisible.

When I was growing up and reading the court reports in my parents' newspapers, the term 'No Fixed Abode' carried the expectation of wrongdoing. It was a term of abuse, and to some extent it still is. Mayhew called rough sleepers 'vagrants'.

In Mayhew's time the sight of homeless people and beggars on London streets was a common occurrence, and so it is now. Bundles in sleeping bags lie in doorways. Some people hide away out of sight; others congregate in groups along the Strand and Euston Road, or on the Embankment. Some have dogs; a few wheel their possessions through the streets in supermarket trolleys.

For most of the twentieth century it was a different story. From the 1920s on, there were a few tramps, 'gentlemen of the road', many of whom were survivors of the First World War trenches, suffering from what now would be recognised as PTSD. But rough sleeping was rare and begging something only seen in India and other developing countries. It was a shock when beggars appeared in London almost overnight in the 1980s after a change in social security reduced benefits for those under the age of twenty-five, and disqualified altogether those younger than eighteen. Neither voluntary agencies nor local authorities had the resources to cope with the increase in the number of rough sleepers in London.

Since that time, and in spite of the efforts of successive governments and the voluntary sector, the number of people sleeping rough on London's streets has been rising rapidly. According to statistics released by the Greater London Authority, from January to March 2019 outreach teams recorded 3217 people sleeping rough in Greater London, a 31 per cent increase on the same period in 2018. In Westminster alone, 986 people were seen sleeping rough, 268 more than the previous year. Of these 48 per cent were British or Irish, 38 per cent were from central and eastern Europe; 15 per cent were female and 8 per cent were over sixty. There are also a lot of immigrants and refugees on the street, who aren't counted in the official figures.

For those sleeping rough, some conditions have improved since Mayhew's time. There's the National Health Service and the benefit system, and the sight of children sleeping rough is not something you will see on today's London streets. However, many homeless people report a problem in finding medical help, and many don't claim benefits – out of pride, an inability to cope with the complex procedures, or because they don't qualify. Westminster Homeless Action Together (WHAT) reported that of those surveyed, 61 per cent said they had no income of any kind.

Increasingly, an address is used to define our identity. Consider how often you are asked for an address, indeed all your addresses for the past three years, how access to many services – credit, a bank account, any number of public services, such as public libraries and bus passes – depends on having one. Without an address, car insurance becomes invalid, you cannot vote and will have difficulty in accessing medical care or any kind of insurance. Even a post office box needs a residential address. Some homeless charities, recognising the need, allow rough sleepers to use the address of a day centre so that they can vote, or register for some services.

Sleeping rough

Imagine spending just one night on the streets. Am I allowed to be here? Will I be arrested? Wondering how to keep warm, how to keep safe, away from prying eyes, where to put my belongings, where to pee, clean my teeth, get a drink of water, wash, change or wash my clothes. It is astonishing how clean many street homeless people are. Yes, there are day centres which provide showers. But you need to know where they are and when they are open, how to find them when perhaps you don't know the city and have no money for travel. And maybe there's a language problem. Not to mention mental health issues or drug or drink dependency, which can be caused by the stress of being homeless if it wasn't there before.

One size does not fit all. No two stories are the same and not all the people on the streets have come from a chaotic background. Many were in good jobs. In 2008, the housing charity Crisis said that a quarter of the people using their services had had a stable home and work life before becoming homeless. It used to be said that we are all two salary cheques away from the gutter; now Shelter says that eight million people are in danger of homelessness after just one month's loss of pay.

Forty-nine-year-old Lee, sitting on the ground near Trafalgar Square, is newly on the streets. He told me: 'I had a nice little business for myself, but when my marriage fell apart I turned to drink, and that's how I lost my home, because I didn't realise I was depressed so I kept hitting the bottle every day. Basically, I had about £80,000 in the bank, and I spent it in a year on drink and cocaine, you know, so I've learnt my lesson the hard way.'

A few years ago, around 2014, Tim ended up in a supported living hostel in Brixton. 'I had, in societal terms, quite a dramatic fall from a salaried job with seventy-five staff, a lot of responsibility and a great love of what I was doing. Eighty thousand a year was my basic salary, but the way it was structured, I got a commission, so I was taking home about £140,000 a year.

'These things creep up on you, but I've always loved parties and I was part of the rave scene. I found myself enjoying what I thought was the benign effect of drugs at the weekend but I also found myself being exposed to slightly harder ways of taking the edge off things, as it was put at the time, which culminated in me smoking quite a bit of heroin.

'Going from owning two flats, from working damn hard, to staying with a friend on the floor of his hostel room. I was staying in his room at the top of a house. There were basic amenities, it was warm, but it was about nine foot by six foot. I had to slightly bend my legs to sleep on the floor. So there was a single bed in there but I was on the floor. I was in a bit of a state of shock and he moved the bed round to give me more room. I could not believe quite what had happened to me. I put my stuff in storage but that place eventually burnt down so I lost everything. I was really shocked. Out of love and friendship, my friend said if you have to work in London come and stay with me.'

Big Issue seller George also has a professional background. 'Worked in the NHS for many years, psychology, worked in psychiatric settings and clinical psychology for years on end and, aah, oh – big life change for me came around the time of the financial crash.'

The difference in backgrounds is reflected in people's appearance. Many homeless people are diffident, lacking confidence, and have what one might class as a characteristic gait, shuffling, trousers sagging, dirty and smelly – not surprising without easy access to washing facilities. But remarkably, some are smart, managing to cope with the practical and emotional difficulties of keeping clean and retaining some vestige of self-respect. Some 9 per cent of people on the streets manage to work, which is a tough ask after a night on the pavement. Indeed, one man reported that his job centre said it was pointless for homeless people to apply for jobs, because nobody would give them a job in their state.

But Robert from Hungary is still trying. 'I'm educated, but here' – at The Connection day centre, attached to St Martin-in-the-Fields – 'no one cares. I didn't mention it on my CV, that would look ridiculous. Highly educated. I finished university. Science, I studied. "What job you looking for?" "Kitchen porter." Doesn't come together. I don't want to mention it because it just looks ridiculous. But my life is here, I've been here now thirteen or fourteen years.'

Public response

I think most passers-by either take the sight of homeless people so much for granted that they don't notice, or they don't know what to do. We all cope as best we can with the sense of guilt, embarrassment, uncertainty and suspicion that the sight of a beggar induces. Professionals working with homeless people advise us not to give to individuals, but to charities who help them. The dilemma for us all is: do we give to someone who, homeless or not, may just be desperate for something like the next fix? The need is there; do we have a right to make a judgement about it? Occasionally I give money, but in general, I offer to buy something to eat. And I always engage, meet people's eyes, ask how they are doing. What most people want is to communicate with another human being.

I heard many accounts of verbal and physical abuse. Darren in St Martin's Lane can't sleep for fear of attack, while Linda in Great Portland Street talks of abuse: 'I've had some people throw food at me, tell me to get a job, being spat at, because they think I'm involved in drugs, things like that. Some people think that all of us are on drugs, or we drink, or are bad people. We're not all like that.' David, defeated by crack and cocaine, says: 'Everyone just abuses me, that's my life.'

These experiences are common. Six in ten rough sleepers in a recent survey said they had been insulted by a member of the public, and one in ten said that they had been urinated on. More than one in three have deliberately been hit, kicked, or experienced some other form of violence while sleeping rough. Three in ten female rough sleepers experience sexual violence at some point while homeless.

Graham Walker wrote in the *Big Issue* that abuse 'nails their fate to the streets. It affirms what you are already thinking about yourself. Trying to stand proud in the street is a huge ask for a homeless person and I've seen people take time out of their little world to go and abuse a homeless person and I'm convinced that abuse just keeps them there longer.'

I was more surprised to hear stories of people's kindness, which, with an increase in public awareness, I think has grown over recent years. Sometimes it is to do with the demeanour of the person concerned. Those with a sunny disposition are often on the receiving end of considerable generosity. Race, sitting with his back against a building just up from Oxford Circus, holds a big piece of cardboard, on which he's written in big thick letters in various coloured pens:

> Don't worry
> Be Happy
> SMILE
> Because you're amazing

Some more writing, then, in very small, barely visible letters:

> Donations welcome

As we talk, he greets passers-by: waves, shakes hands and accepts a banana – 'She always brings me bananas.'

Lee, in the next doorway, tells me that 'the smallest things in life, like, you know, a meal, make you happy. Last night, a guy called Yahim, every week he goes to the Pizza Express, and every week he buys me a pizza. You know what, that just makes my week. And I says to him, thank you so much. And there's another guy, he comes from the BBC, he comes to see me every day, and he's so encouraging and he says he's in awe of me because of my spirits. Well, you've got to keep your chin up, haven't yer?'

Causes of homelessness

The causes of homelessness are complex and individual, but there are some common underlying societal factors, notably housing benefit cuts, the lack of affordable housing and insecure private sector tenancies. The Resolution Foundation, a think tank working to improve the lot of those on low incomes, stressed high housing costs as the cause of poverty in London 'perhaps more so than at any time in the past'. Since the massive sale of council houses under Margaret Thatcher, the supply of 'affordable' housing has dwindled, and too many people are homeless or live in damp, overcrowded, poorly maintained properties, reminiscent of the 1900s.

An architect and long-term resident of a council estate in west London told me that estates struggle to survive. Those that have done so usually have a mixture of tenants, including private tenants, who have no rights at all; housing association tenants, with a variety of rights; and council tenants, whom the council has a duty to rehouse – but only if they are named on the tenancy agreement. I spoke to one man made homeless when his mother died. It turned out that hers was the only name on the tenancy, so he was evicted.

The provision of new social housing often depends on negotiations at the planning stage of large developments. Although local authorities are legally obliged to provide a percentage of social housing, they are often under pressure from specialist lawyers hired by large developers to reduce it. It is hard for councils to resist the temptation of international finance and the argument about the 'reasonable use of ratepayers' money'.

Housing charities have warned that renting privately across most of England has become unaffordable for people on benefits, and analysis by the BBC has shown that the gap between rent and local housing allowance (LHA) has more than doubled across most of the country since 2016.

Housing is not only unaffordable, but insecure. No-fault evictions, where private landlords evict tenants at short notice without a good reason, are commonplace. One woman said: 'I keep getting evicted through no fault of my own, and each time that costs me over a thousand pounds. So every time I save money, which I could put towards a deposit, it's gone.'

Rents and living costs are increasing and services are being cut. Without government support, a sudden increase in pressure like losing a job or becoming ill can quickly force people into homelessness. Serious benefit caps have also been introduced in the last few years, meaning that many people have to top up their rent from the living component of their Universal Credit. Eventually people can't afford to continue, and become homeless.

The criminalisation of domestic squatting has also had a deleterious impact. The bouncer Pixie talks about how Brixton used to be: 'For example, Rushcroft Road used to be a street full of squats and now it's just million-pound flats . . . d'you know what I mean? And squats were a vital social safety net for a lot of people, especially young people who may be having real difficulty with abuse at home. They couldn't get housing benefit if they were under eighteen, and if they were being abused at home a squat could be a real haven. Apart from that, it was a way of life that left creative people free to write, paint and make music without the burden of having to find the rent every week.'

When external factors combine with difficulties in personal circumstances, homelessness is often the result. Maureen Crane's survey on older homeless people found that for the 'lifetime' homeless, their situation was triggered by disturbed family homes, and by discharge from orphanages or from the armed services. For the 'mid-life' homeless, triggers included the death of a parent, marital breakdown, and for transient workers, a drift to less secure work and housing. For the 'late-life' homeless, it followed widowhood, marital breakdown, retirement and the loss of tied accommodation, and the increasing severity of mental illness.

The WHAT survey in 2016 found that almost 39 per cent of women and nearly 22 per cent of men said homelessness had been caused by a traumatic experience. Such experiences can take many forms. For several people I talked to, it was the death of a child. Raymond told me: 'I was married, I set up my own kind of business and I lost it, but this is way way back. It was in security. Then I left from there – and I had a nervous breakdown, because my daughter died, at about five weeks, and my life became upside down. Because, yeah, I was put into a situation where it was bad.'

Domestic abuse

According to the 2013–14 Crime Survey of England and Wales, domestic abuse will affect one in four women and one in six men in their lifetime. Many young people from abusive homes have to leave and are deemed to have made themselves intentionally homeless, so they get no benefits. Among women, this is the single most quoted reason for becoming homeless.

Linda in Great Portland Street said: 'I was in a violent relationship, and I lost my children. I became very depressed, started self-harming, couldn't leave my house because I had anxiety, couldn't pay my rent so I lost my home. So now I'm living on the streets.'

An anti-slavery co-ordinator talked about the complex problems of one of the women she's been working with: 'This lady – this girl – she was coming out of an orphanage and she was talked to and taken by an Asian gang in the west of London. She was thirteen years old so they took her to their place, there was sexual violence, sexual exploitation and she was forced to take drugs. Eventually she was forced to sell drugs. Finally she escaped them at the age of seventeen. She became homeless. Since then she has high trauma. She's still addicted to drugs and she got a boyfriend – this happens very often with women rough sleepers. As soon as you have a boyfriend, even if you have an abusive boyfriend, it's better than having no one in the streets. She was indeed a victim of modern slavery for sexual exploitation and forced criminality; she was a victim of domestic violence and she was still an addict.'

Breakdown of relationship

Over twenty years of talking to rough sleepers, the cause of homelessness that I've most often heard cited is the breakdown of a relationship.

Lee says, 'I'm not scared of anything. I was more scared of being married.' He laughs a lot. 'I was only married for four months, but I was with my partner for twenty-four years and then she had an affair with my best mate in my own home. That's how it all fell apart. My best friend got thrown out by his missus, and I invited him into my home, and he started having it away with my missus, and that's how it all fell apart. If that hadn't happened, I'd still be at home and happy with my wife, but he basically brainwashed my wife against me. In the end she wouldn't – I used to cook every day and she wouldn't want my food and he was in her ear'ole all the time. But you know what? If she can do that to me, she wasn't the person for me. And I can walk around with my head held high. I've done nothing wrong but I'm the one who's paying for it. But you know what? I'm going to take that on the chin. It's only going to make me stronger, if only to prove they're wrong.'

Some people survive the breakdown of a relationship, but if there is an underlying vulnerability, that might lead to drink, drugs and/ or mental breakdown. Typically, over the years, the story I hear is of a middle-aged man who after divorce leaves the house to his wife and children, thinking he can cope, becomes depressed, takes to drink, loses his job and ends up on the streets. Generally a number of factors combine to render someone homeless; it's when several traumatic events happen that maintaining a home becomes impossible. George's story is an example:

'I had not long before that bought quite a big house, a big detached house – this is going back to 2006 or something. My mother was unwell at the time, she had Alzheimer's, and the idea in part of getting the house was to have a granny flat for her, keep her out of the care sector. Then it all went pear-shaped after the financial crash; I was on a temporary contract. I split up with the woman I was with, and everything that could go wrong went wrong. My mother died, I had to sell the house, the house ran into what's called negative equity where the house value was less than the mortgage and basically I was financially wiped out.'

Addiction

Sometimes drug use starts off as a social game, part of the scene, then becomes indispensable, ruling the rest of a person's life and often leading to loss of job and home. For the rave generation in the

1990s, Ecstasy fuelled a movement. Drug use was fun and communal. Many connections were made and the spontaneous creativity had an impact on the fabric of social culture in London and the rest of the UK. Many of those people went on to live pretty 'normal' lives; others came down into heroin use and lost everything.

Addiction, whether to drink or drugs, is both a cause and an effect. It's usually a result of deep-rooted unhappiness – a coping mechanism, whether to deal with difficulties in a past life or on the streets. McGinlay, who came out of the care system and spent years in hostels and squats, eventually recognised the roots of her behaviour.

'I binge drinked for a really long time, and now I've had therapy I realise that a lot of that was to do with my PTSD symptoms. As soon as I realised why I had those symptoms and that it was perfectly OK for me to have those symptoms, the desire to knock myself out, so to speak, which is what I was doing, became less desirable.'

Although I found no mention of drugs in *London Labour and the London Poor*, opium and other narcotics were readily available in Victorian London. People could walk into a chemist and purchase laudanum or cocaine, which was welcomed for its uses in anaesthesia and as a treatment for such ailments as toothache and hay fever. Addiction is well documented in Thomas De Quincey's 1821 work, *Confessions of an English Opium Eater*, and later in the century in some of the Sherlock Holmes stories.

In today's London, heroin and crack cocaine are the drugs of choice on the street, with dealers offering one-on-ones (a £10 bag of each that people usually inject together). Some people use one or the other, and some people still smoke heroin. The move to injecting can be situational – you're just around it – or economical, because it's cheaper to get high if you're using intravenously. While the statistics from the 2018/19 Home Office Crime Survey for England and Wales suggest that drug use is at its lowest since measurements began in 1996, the problems caused by addiction and the crime it fuels are evident on our streets and in our prisons.

Drew is American. His newly acquired drug habit led to the break-up of his relationship. 'What happened ... the first time I became homeless, was I basically started using, snorting heroin and stuff like that, essentially because I couldn't get any anxiety medication from my doctor. But she [his girlfriend] eventually found out because she's urrgh : ... neither of us ... our lifestyles ... I came from a like pretty strait-laced middle-class family and she's from a you know academic type family, and so to find a syringe of brown liquid in your coat pocket is definitely not the way she thought that would go ... and it went downhill from there.'

Ishwari is an attractive, small, well-dressed woman of Asian origin. It was only at the second meeting that the pallor of her skin and her dirty fingernails become apparent. She was upfront about her problem: 'I guess right now, as a snapshot answer, I'm somebody who's homeless. I'm thirty-nine, just had my thirty-ninth birthday. Very emotional person. Kind of have a bit of a raging drug habit at the moment. Struggling with A-class drugs, which I've been hooked on for about four years now.'

She grew up in Surrey. 'I'm the eldest and from a high-class Hindu Punjabi Brahmin family. I'm just a black sheep basically. Then I got married, I had a love marriage so I ran away from home. That was another bad thing. Married a Mauritian guy. Had four kids. And ... he wanted to explore his sexuality and gave me an ultimatum. He said that if I don't explore this with him, we would have a divorce. And I felt quite passionately about being married to him, I felt like I sacrificed my family and everything to marry him. And I couldn't do it so I left. Since then, that was my journey on my own.'

While sleeping on a friend's floor in a hostel, Tim was actually managing to work. 'I was still taking drugs ad hoc and at one point, and I'm not proud of this, I went from smoking heroin on the foil to actually injecting it. And it blew my head off. When you do that, you feel fucked for days afterwards, at least I did. And my work must have noticed. I have very blue eyes and I'm told it's very easy to tell when I'm stoned. And there were times I would lie to my friend about it, telling him I was fine as I tried to put my trousers on my head – that actually happened.'

There are many different attitudes to drugs. Some, including those working in the homelessness field, feel that some drugs are not bad in themselves – it is only when they take a hold and blot out all other considerations that the damage is done. Given the social fall-out from the war on drugs, some people are starting to question the wisdom of prohibition, and wondering whether we should follow the example of Portugal, where the decriminalisation of drugs has brought about a dramatic fall in overdoses and in the prison terms served by addicts.

One thing that everyone we spoke to agreed on is the danger of the drug 'spice', which appears to induce a catatonic state. Dan, who runs a private women's shelter, calls it 'the most complicated evil thing – it's rat poison, really. There's eighty-five components in that spice. I've been on two training courses with the police and social services, and the information I had on the street about what it actually did to people day to day – it totally destroys certain parts of your brain. And then it degenerates the rest of your body and it changes your personality, your looks. You can tell, you can spot people who are on spice, every day.'

A formerly homeless case worker reported an occasion where someone had spiked a roll-up.

'I bumped into a friend of mine – who I thought was a friend of mine – who I was homeless with, haven't seen her for a while, and she offered me a roll-up. Didn't think nothing of it. Took the roll-up. And it had spice in it. I lost two days. I still don't know [what I did for two days]. I just felt … not good. I ended up taking tablets. Something like Naproxen. It's scary, 'cause I wasn't aware at all. I don't even know where I'd been. When I realised what had happened I went to A&E. I was expecting [stomach pumping] but they didn't do that. I'm still angry about it.

'There are a lot of homeless people that say, "Ugh, I had spice last night." Because I think they've been picking up butts. And if they're on script [a prescription drug] or anything like that and they go and have a pee test it comes up on that. I've got about twenty clients that are on it. I don't know how many clients I've got. It's maybe about a quarter of them. They say, "At least I'm not taking heroin or drinking." It's quite scary really. This one guy, he takes it ... it's just like *The Walking Dead*. You gotta stay clear of picking up butts and even taking drugs off people.' Spice, he says, has 'a smell to it'.

Freddie, who sleeps under Waterloo Bridge, told me, 'My mate died the other day, on spice. You probably know about that. Really bad drug, spice. I don't take spice ...' Even the severely addicted David is trying to give it up.

A less visible addiction is to gambling, but it has a similar effect on the addict's life. Lyobimir is a homeless man from Bulgaria.

'When I came here ... I already have an education as a chef, I started working as a chef but in one short period I lost everything. First I cut my tendon and I went to hospital, but after the first surgery there was an infection on my finger and they did six more surgeries. I was almost killed in the hospital with the sickness. This was in 2015. September, something like that. I was sick for a long time. Through this period my girlfriend left me, and when I went back to work, maybe a month after, I crashed my car.' He laughs. 'I went back to hospital for a few months. Maybe during this period something happened with my head, because I started gambling. I thought this is because of my depression, I tried to escape from my reality, that's why I started gambling, and I lost everything. My flat, my savings, everything.

'When I started gambling, I started lying to people, I started taking money from them, because this was an addiction. I started thinking about bills – "I cannot pay my bills today so I will take some money from someone." I go in this circle and I went down, I lost everything, I lost my relations, my friends, my social status.

'When I came back in London, I rented a few different rooms for short periods but I kept gambling during this period, so all my income that was coming in I put back into gambling. I was in this circle. Find job, start working, lost money, go back on the streets for one or two weeks, I meet some friends ... and last year actually,

I realised this is my issue, my mental issue. I stopped work, I was on the streets and I really starved actually, then one friend told me about this place.'

'This place' is The Connection at St Martin-in-the-Fields, where they are helping Lyobimir sort out his issues, and he has found a talent for art. 'I think that I cannot go back because the past is the past, you know? But I will try to repair my life, maybe some different way, maybe I will try to repair some of my relations from my past. I can't go back to the same, maybe similar but not the same.'

Coming off an addiction is hard and needs skilled support. Some people simply aren't ready. When asked if she had tried to kick her drug habit over the past four years, Ishwari confessed, 'Yeah, no, I haven't. I haven't really, to be honest. I've experienced being without a few occasions, and the sickness is so scary that I just try and keep myself above that. Because it is like ... people have described it to me as your bones ache and your muscles ache. Even the beginning symptoms of like, sneezing and sweating and yawning, I hate that so much that I just try and keep myself above that, so I never have to face that kind of pain. It's really horrible. Psychologically I don't think I'm ready. I think drugs provide me with that really nice cloud, like a hug from my mum.' She laughs. 'It sounds really crazy.'

Mental illness

Disease among rough sleepers is rife. A quarter of those interviewed in the 2016 WHAT survey said they had chronic health issues and almost half (47 per cent) said they avoided seeking help when not feeling well. There's no cholera now, but TB and gangrene are still present – and so, too, are problems with mental health.

If someone didn't have mental health issues before arriving on the street, they are likely to develop them. As Lyobimir recognised, 'I'm looking now at my personal feelings, this is most important. When I talk to someone, I explain this all the time: people on the street, living on the street, including me, most of us have mental issues. We have an addiction, we have a problem, we have mental issues. Most of us had some life before, some flat, some job, but why they are now here?'

After his breakdown following the loss of his young daughter, Raymond managed to make a positive out of his position. 'Because I've been on what they call sickness benefit, they're not allowed to employ me, I've been told. So they won't employ me, so I have to do voluntary. And that's what I do.'

Magician Jeremy even jokes about his medication in his act. 'I'm bipolar, so it's mental health issues that have caused the problem. But after a year it was like OK, we got the medication right, things were getting better, and everyone that I spoke to in the mental health team was asking me: "Well, what did you do?" I told them that I'd been a busker, and they were all like, why don't you do that again? For a while I'd been so unwell, I couldn't foresee even working again, but I felt better, and I thought, yeah, I'll do it again.'

Samaritans recognise that spring is a particularly difficult time, and a bad time for suicides. After the winter, others perk up, but those with depression don't. A number of homeless people reported their suicidal tendencies, like Carrie, who I met living in a tent in Fitzroy Place. Another woman, who has been diagnosed with complex PTSD, said: 'By the time I'd reached eighteen I'd already been physically attacked at school, I'd been physically attacked by my mum, I'd been raped three times and constantly sexually abused in that area of Paddington and I was on the brink of suicide. I didn't want to live any more.

'And I tried to attempt suicide on several occasions because I did not trust any adult, I did not trust the care system, I did not feel safe in any so-called home situation. So, I actually felt safer walking around in parks or being out in nature rather than being in concrete or in a so-called home. There was an element of danger being in a building that has a roof that is classified as a home. Whether that be a foster home or whether that be a hostel in my later years, there's always been this element of violence that I've been exposed to.'

And the resources to help simply aren't there. A case worker said:

'I think it's important to bear in mind that hostel workers are not mental health professionals, indeed they are often not even health-care professionals. Therefore when someone is in acute crisis there is not much that hostel staff can do other than advocate for their clients and link them with appropriate services. Due to cuts, there is a shocking lack of specialist resources available for people in this kind of crisis, and I think the complex nature of most of our clients' needs – addiction, challenging behaviour, lack of engagement with services, etc. – makes it even harder for them to successfully access this type of support.

'In terms of whether hostels do enough to prevent people from reaching the point where they might feel suicidal – in a word, no. Again, this largely comes down to huge cuts in services which have caused workers' caseloads to double and clients' support needs to soar over the past six years or so. Yet no further resources are given to services to effectively support these higher-need clients. As a worker it can sometimes feel like we are so focused on firefighting that there isn't the time to do the slightly softer stuff' (which might include supporting people to fill their days with something they feel passionate about, helping them focus on building positive relation-ships and improving self-esteem).

Many people on sickness benefit are not allowed to work, which does nothing for their chances of improvement. A homeless woman told me: 'I'm not allowed to work because of my mental health. I've had mental health since I was a child, really. There's been some people trying to help, but the council and that, it's no good for a child. Six years old, that's no good for me.'

And a homeless man: 'They say I can't work because of my mental illness, psychosis and all that, and [my girlfriend] can't work because of her mental – she's more knackered than me, she's got more mental issues than me, know what I mean? Half the stories she still ain't telling me, I don't really know her background. She chopped her hair off the other week, chopped all her hair off, that's how crazy she can become.'

The problem is magnified for those with no recourse to public funds (a status identified as NRPF). One woman from Mauritius was deserted by her husband when he left her for a woman she had befriended, and she ended up on the streets. She cried as she told me her story: 'I say, please God find me somewhere. Because I want to kill myself. But now I am on tablet, I am on treatment. Two times I try to kill myself. One time I try to cut my hand' – she shows me her wrist – 'when I was with my husband, and one I took those tablets and I was in hospital. When I die, everything finish: no pain, no problem. This is not me, a person like my mum, family love me . . . I had to give my cat away, I had to give my fish away.' She cries again. 'My cat, he was very close, you know. My house was so beautiful, everyone who comes say . . . We have flowers in the toilet, beautiful flowers.'

Leaving institutions

The numbers of homeless people who have come from some of our major institutions make it clear that such places do not prepare people for life on the outside. Figures released by the multi-agency Combined Homelessness and Information Network (CHAIN) show that those with a prison or care background are more likely to remain on or return to the streets. In a welcome development, the Homelessness Reduction Act 2017 ruled that certain public authorities, including prisons and social services, must notify a local housing authority in England where one of its service users may be homeless or at risk of homelessness and agrees to the referral. Service users should be asked if they have a history of being in care, in the armed forces or prison, and, if they are approaching discharge from hospital, armed forces or custody, whether they have accommodation available.

Prison

One of Mayhew's most famous interviews is with a returning convict, and the 'Statements of Vagrants' are peppered with mentions of prison. We don't transport people any more, but prison continues to be a part of the lives of many sleeping on our streets. The CHAIN report showed that a third of people found sleeping rough in 2015–16 had served time in prison. Even if people have homes before they go into prison, they often lose their tenancies while inside; landlords often dispose of their possessions, sometimes even their ID, which makes it hard to establish themselves on release. Family relationships are scarred and often dislocated. The vast majority of prisoners who are serving short-term sentences get little help with housing, education or jobs. The Howard League for Penal Reform reported that around a third of people about to leave prison said that they had nowhere to stay. UK-wide, up to fifty thousand people a year leave prison with nowhere to go.

Many rough sleepers come from prison, and many go back in, leading to what is called the 'revolving door' of prison and the streets. In 2017 the charity Crisis reported that 73 per cent of rough sleepers experienced some kind of criminalisation and 15 per cent of those imprisoned in 2018 were homeless at the time. The laws they break may relate to illegal drugs, or to thieving to support a habit, but what is not generally known is that sleeping rough without visible means of support is in itself still illegal. The Vagrancy Act 1824, which refers to 'vagabonds and rogues' and was very much in operation in Mayhew's era, is still in force today.

The Act makes it a crime to sleep 'in any deserted or unoccupied building, or in the open air, or under a tent, or in any cart or waggon, not having any visible means of subsistence'. People can face up to £1000 in fines and a two-year criminal record. Since, by the very nature of their lives, most rough sleepers are unable to pay any imposed fine, they can still be sent to prison. The law is most commonly used informally, the threat of arrest being used to move on those sleeping rough or begging. Despite moves to repeal the Vagrancy Act, in London between 2011 and 2015, 2442 people were arrested for begging in a public place, an average of about 500 a year. On top of that, many councils opt to use civil powers provided under the 2014 Antisocial Behaviour Act, such as public space protection orders that ban begging, rough sleeping and related activities. Breaching a PSPO can lead to a £100 fixed-penalty notice, but offenders face a summary conviction, sometimes a criminal behaviour order (CBO) banning an individual from future begging and imposing a fine of up to £1000 if they fail to pay. Violating a CBO can result in five years in prison.

Freddie, currently sleeping rough, has spent much of his life in prison.

'I'm originally from south-east London, an area called Penge – you might know it? My mum and dad are still alive. I've got two brothers, one's doing a life sentence. I've got an older sister and then there's me. I've been in prison twenty-seven times, I've been in and out of jail all my life since fifteen. Last time I got out of jail was 15 August last year, and I've knocked it all on the head. No more criminal activities from me. But I come out of jail homeless – I was in jail for forty-five months, see? And the problem was, when I was inside, I was inside that long that when I come out it was on licence, but I was only out for four days when I got a recall for missing just one appointment.

'Just missing one appointment without doing a criminal activity, they made me do the whole licence, the whole sixteen months, no sorry, the whole nineteen and a half months, just for missing one appointment. And that was bang out of order. The reason was, I reckon, because they didn't want me back out because I was NFA. I had nowhere to go, no address, that was the problem. But I consider that I've been out since 15 August last year, I've been working with St Martin-in-the-Fields homeless unit. I really can't remember my key worker's name, but she's Irish, I know that.

'I know a bit of good news. I've got a partner, I've been with her since last year, November, and the good news is she got offered a studio flat this morning, and I'm very happy for her, but because she's got mental issues, she's a bit worried because she had to go on her own with a key worker, she wanted me to go wiv 'er. She was a bit worried and panicky, I said go, just go, it's good news. So, really and truly I'm just waiting for her to come back. It's in Streatham. Hopefully it's gone good today for her but, erm, I don't know what to say, up 'ere, it's not really good.

'I don't understand about the government. No one will help. That's how mad it's got me; I've just lost it all. Because I don't think no one's going to help us. I said to my pals, give it fifty years' time this country will be a ghost town, it'll be all tents, desert, it'll be bad, it'll get worse. Everyone's trying to get in; give it thirty years, everyone'll be trying to get out, that's how bad it's going to get.'

The armed forces

Mayhew interviewed a number of beggars who had returned from service in the army and navy, or pretended to. In the decades after the Napoleonic Wars, the future of returning servicemen was a serious problem. In our day, too, members of the armed forces find it hard to return to civilian life; many suffer from mental health problems, and some end up in prison. In 2018 the British Legion estimated that there were about six thousand homeless veterans in the UK. In London, CHAIN reported that 6 per cent of people seen sleeping rough in 2018–19 had served in the armed forces at some point in their lives.

I talked to Stephen on the steps of All Souls Church, Langham Place.

'I'm an ex-soldier, Coldstream Guards, and I ended up on the streets. I didn't have any money, I didn't, I didn't know what it was all about. And it was the guys that were here, and if you come back later, at ten o'clock, you'll never see so many tents, so many boxes. So the next thing is, is one minute I'm a hero because I worked for the country, I lived for the country, and I said I can take a bullet for the Queen, I can die for the country, but I couldn't save my son, because that was another story.

'Everybody that's on the streets has a story. They don't want to be on the streets at the beginning, but they end up on the streets, and it can happen within . . . a night. The guys, there's more men on the streets. And there is ladies on the streets as well – I don't know that story, I don't get women, I don't understand women, I don't, er, you know I . . . I was married, and I said to my wife, I don't understand this, I don't get this. I've worked and worked and worked and put money in the bank and everything else because we got a son coming on the way, and then I gets another son and he passed away seven months later through negligence, and I couldn't handle that.

'I will always thank the army. When we went to Ireland – we went to Hong Kong, we went to New Zealand, some of the guys went to Brunei on a guard and everything else. And we did cere-, ceremoni-, ceremonial duties, we did Buckingham Palace, we did Tower of London, we did St James's, we did Windsor Castle. You know. So there we are, doing our job and we're as proud as can be, and when we went to Ireland we came back with every man. Some of them came with wounds and some of 'em came with injuries and everythink else, and that was sorted out, but there was other guys that have been doing what have you, and I got out, because the shit hit the fan one day and I got the blame for it, and I went woah, I didn't join up for this.

'A year later I emigrated to New Zealand. I came back, and they told me, your mate's getting married at the weekend, and I went, Really? So I ended up at his wedding, and what a day, what a wedding. That was 1989 – and then, six months later, I'm at his funeral because, boom!

'So, *then*, I comes out and I work, I work, I work, I work, and I lost my son. I couldn't understand it. I couldn't handle it. And I end up on the streets. Yeah, there's no answer, there isn't any answer. I can't say to you because this living on the streets is not you'll get a gentleman or a lady coming out of the BBC and they'll go "I fancy that life" because nobody does, nobody does, because it's not natural, but things happen in your life and things take place. There's other guys, I know where they are now, that was in the same battalion as me and they're on the streets in other parts of London, in other parts of the country. They'll be there now, I could take you there.'

When asked whether the army hadn't looked after him, Stephen replied, 'Not in those days. No, no no no no no. Because the army thought they'd done well, they thought they'd trained us well to look after ourselves. Right? But what the army does …

think of this, there was seventy-two of us when I joined up, and only eighteen of us made it. They was breaking them. They were breaking the guys.

'The first time I was on the streets was 1991, and I was on the streets for five years. I was selling the *Big Issue*. The *Big Issue* was the greatest thing for me because I sold the magazines and the place is there now. If you go to High Street Kensington you've got a bench there opposite M&S, and then at the back of it you've got St Mary's Church, and there was an Irish fellow who slept on one bench and I slept on the other bench, and I just worked and worked and worked. And the media, the BBC got hold of my story, and I went down to the Passage one day in Victoria and they said we want to do a story on an ex-forces guy . . .

'So there's the BBC and they're doing this story and the next thing it was John Major, he's got back in. On the Friday he's doing this great story of how he's going to clean up the streets and everythink else, and on the Sunday they tell my story. Within three weeks I got a studio flat. And I bought it. And I met a beautiful woman, a glorious woman, and she gave me two children and it was the second child that we lost through negligence . . .

'Everything that the government do they think that the answer is money. It's not, it's not. How is it that you can have people come from all different countries and within a few weeks they've got a flat, they've got a job, they've got stability, they've got whatever.

'I ended up in prison. I was fighting, and the next thing is I was fighting against the judge. The judge says if you go back to your house, and I went, It's my house, I bought the house, I built the house, I changed the house. My business was there. My wife was there and everythink else, but what I was fighting against – a lot of the guys, some of them ex-forces, will probably say he's right, and some will say not . . . But what kept me going was my enthusiasm. What kept me going was, What's next? Life is wonderful. Life is amazing. It's like today, because of all that's happened, I've stayed away from here for three months, thinking. I've got accommodation. When we've finished this conversation, I'll go back. It's because the government said get this man off the streets. I've just come here for the reminiscence and the joy that I've had on these steps.

'Being on the streets, it's the people that come by,' he says, a bit tearfully, 'there's beautiful people that come by every day, and they just go, You've made my day. And inside of me they don't realise that they're making my day.' He breaks off to greet a passer-by. 'You see what I mean? It happens. It works.

'And the worst thing is, when you get rejected. By the Church. When you get rejected by the government. When you get rejected by your family . . . You as a guardsman, as a soldier, you could fight anything, anything, anything in this world. But you know the one thing you can't fight? Is rejection.

'Do I miss the army?' A long pause. 'Not now, because it's changed. It's changed in a big way. Because, the country's changed, and I've said it to many young guys: Would you die for this country? And they go, no.'

Now Stephen spends his time going to the parks and feeding the squirrels and the birds. 'I just keep going here and there and everywhere. I've got my benefits. I'm nearly sixty. When I'm sixty I get my army pension. Now, what a lot the army guys don't realise is that they're entitled to that. You've got the British Legion, SSAFA [the Soldiers, Sailors and Airmen Families Association] and all these other organisations and this is what is going on. You've got great organisations, but they don't want you to claim, because if you don't claim, they get it. I know for a fact that they said to me oh, we had to have a whip-round for this guy that passed away, and I went, what are you talking about? There's twenty grand, there's £20,000 available for him. And they go, I never knew that. I said no, because they're not telling you that. Right? . . .

'Who came by the other day? I thought he was going to be the greatest prime minister, even better than Churchill, right?, was Tony Blair. I wrote a letter to him and I said to him, please do not go with Bush, right? It's not our war. It's not our war. Anyway, I gets this letter back and the folks said to me, how have you got a letter from the house of 10 Downing Street? And I said because I wrote to them. Anyway, I opened it, and they went wow. And it was from the secretary and he says, we've logged it.'

'Thank you, Stephen.'

'My pleasure, my pleasure, and I just hope people realise that the greatest thing – do you know what you have done tonight? It's something very special. You've come along and spoke to me. And that's what it's all about. The best is yet to come. A new chapter is opening – I'm looking forward to learning what it is.'

*

I remember two earlier encounters with ex-servicemen. In the late 1990s, when a few of us went out with tea and sandwiches, a well-known resident of the notorious Cardboard City in Waterloo took us on a conducted tour. 'No one comes down here, not the police, not the social. They're too scared.' He had served in the army for many years and proudly pointed out his immaculate patch. He had been trained to be orderly, so his shoes were lined up outside his cardboard shelter, polished and ready for use. Then, in 2007, at the annual service for people who had died homeless on the street (see Chapter 20), I recognised his description as a man who had run his life – and helped to run St Martin's soup kitchen – with military precision. He was seventy-nine when he died, and had been homeless for over twenty years.

A few years later I met a man sitting on the ground, his crutches beside him.

'What's wrong? What are they for?'

'I lost my toes. I was in the army.'

'Why isn't the army helping you?'

'They do what they can.'

Then, seeing my obvious distress, he said, 'It's all right, sweetheart.' But it wasn't. It isn't.

Residential care
One of the major differences between today and Mayhew's time is that we no longer have children begging or sleeping rough on the streets of London. There are protection measures in place. If home

conditions are inadequate, children can be taken into care by the social services. Though some people are homeless for twenty or thirty years, there's no story to compete with Mayhew's '70 years a beggar' – 'I have been a beggar since I was that high – ever since I could walk'. Nowadays, children are not brought up to be beggars, but many face a lifetime of homelessness (and usually begging) from the time they leave an orphanage or care home at the age of sixteen or even earlier. Some are even criminalised while in care. Many stories show that the care system is failing its vulnerable residents. In London, some 11 per cent of rough sleepers have a background in residential care.

The former soldier, Stephen, is one, as is Race, who has been homeless for five years. I saw him wearily walking down the road. 'Need a rest. Not feeling so good. Smile? There's my teeth. Had 'em all out, top and bottom. No one told me to clean my teeth.'

Like Carrie, in her tent near Fitzroy Square, Darren became homeless when he left care and has known nothing else. From his pitch in St Martin's Lane, he says, 'Stood here selling the *Big Issue* here for fourteen years, homeless for nineteen years, on and off. Born Kingston, ended up in care, scattered everywhere, went on the street when I was fourteen. Work? Only *Big Issue*. Did bits when I was in kids' homes, when I was younger, years ago.

'In five years' time? Not standing here. Oh, dunno, hope to be out of the country by then, go travelling. Work? Yeah, hopefully. Anything outdoors. Like it. Used to it.' We laugh. 'No, don't see children or ex-partner. Like being alone. No, I don't know how things could be better for homeless people, I never see homeless people. I haven't been in a day centre since 2007. Day centres, hostels, none of it. Homeless people, can't stand 'em, can't be in same building as 'em. Washing? Travelodge once a week, only place, Sundays they're cheap. No, none of the agencies give me nothing, Only the *Big Issue*, that's it.'

Temporary housing

Rough sleeping is the tip of the iceberg. Thousands of families are in temporary or inadequate housing, and the extent of homelessness is hidden by people sofa-surfing or in insecure accommodation. According to the Ministry of Housing, Communities and Local Government, more than 86,000 households were in temporary accommodation at the end of June 2019. Insecurity is the norm in the privately rented sector, where many daren't complain about inadequate conditions in case the landlord decides to turn them out. Shelter also found that 55 per cent of families in temporary accommodation are in work, and that this rise in 'working home-lessness' is being driven by a combination of expensive private rents, the ongoing freeze on housing benefit and a chronic lack of social housing.

McGinlay, who has been diagnosed with PTSD, said, 'Even when I got housed into a private studio, where I am now, it was still under construction so I ended up squatting anyway even though I had a flat.' She laughs. 'So my flat was like a storage space but there was like concrete and mud everywhere and cables running through my flat and there was a group of ten workmen coming through my flat. Even them acting like that triggered old memories of people being intrusive in my home.

'It's not that I can't maintain a flat. I've had three flats to myself as well as flat sharing, squatting, as well as camping out in parks, but when you've had my kind of history as a woman and you've got ten strangers walking in and out of your flat, it's a little bit hard to make it all nice and rosy and like put out the dinner table mats, and put the flowers out and make it all homely. And then this is another thing about private landlords. They piss me off. We didn't get any notice of this construction work, we were just told by the workmen, just another few weeks, just another few weeks, but this went on for over a year.' The landlord obviously told the hostel that the room was fit for habitation so they could start to get rent before the work was completed. The process of moving on from hostels to the private sector is rife with the kind of behaviour that can leave vulnerable people in challenging living situations.

At a party to commemorate twenty years of the Quaker Homeless Action (QHA) mobile library, I met a woman of eighty-six who told me that currently she's living on just over fifty pounds a week. She has a small pension, because she hasn't always worked in this country, but they have taken away her sickness benefit, and are threatening to do the same with her housing benefit. She says it is all because she has a foreign name and, having lived in Switzerland for many years, she sounds foreign. She is having to prove that she was born in London. She feels that as the country builds up for Brexit, the Home Office is putting pressure on 'foreign' people to go.

She lives in temporary accommodation: a small flat in one of fifteen large houses bought by a company from Tower Hamlets Council, who couldn't afford to bring them up to proper standards. She is allowed to live there while they do it up around her. She talked of water leaking into her flat as they first did up the bathroom above her, then the kitchen. Her possessions have been moved, and she climbs over other people's to her bed. 'But,' she says, 'I'm not complaining. I have a key to my door and a roof over my head.' Her friend, the same age, has a flat where he only has to pay £10, no council tax, and, she says, 'still he complains'.

Whatever the societal contributions to the extent of homelessness, for each individual it is still a personal issue. Sara, formerly homeless herself and now a project worker with other homeless people, commented: 'This is what society makes us feel, regardless of if you've lost your job or if you've got a really bad physical or mental health problem. It's still your fault. No one's gonna say well that's unfortunate, or that's rare so I'm going to give you extra time. People are like see you later, your choices have led to your bad life and that's on you. And that's bad.'

17

Hanging on

The first instinct of the well-to-do visitor is to breathe a thanksgiving (like the Pharisee in the parable) that 'he is not as one of these'. But the vain conceit has scarcely risen to the tongue before the better nature whispers in the mind's ear, 'By what special virtue of your own are you different from them? How comes it that you are well clothed and well fed, whilst so many go naked and hungry?' And if you in your arrogance, ignoring all the accidents that have helped to build up your worldly prosperity, assert that you have been the 'architect of your own fortune', who, let us ask, gave you the genius or energy for the work?

Then get down from your moral stilts, and confess it honestly to yourself that you are what you are by that inscrutable grace which decreed your birthplace to be a mansion or a cottage rather than a 'padding-ken', or which granted you brains and strength ... It is hard for smug-faced respectability to acknowledge these dirt-caked, erring wretches as brothers, and yet, if from those to whom little is given little is expected, surely, after the atonement of their long suffering, they will make as good angels as the best of us.

Sleeping rough has serious consequences. Almost six hundred people died while homeless in England and Wales in 2017, and the figure in 2018 was 726: a rise of 22 per cent in one year. The average age of death was just forty-four for men and forty-two for women, about the same as for people in the general population born in Mayhew's time (i.e. in the 1840s) compared with today's figures of seventy-six for men and eighty-one for women among the rest of the UK population. A homeless rough sleeper is nine times more likely to commit suicide than the average person.

So, for an individual who finds him- or herself on the streets, what are the options?

The *Big Issue*

The *Big Issue* was launched in September 1991 and is now published in many countries of the world. With the motto 'a hand up not a hand out', it is one of the positives for contemporary homeless people, who currently buy the magazine at £1.50 and sell it at £3. Selling the magazine doesn't generally enable people to live a self-sustaining life – many are still homeless – but offering the magazine to customers leads to greater self-respect, which in turn may lead to getting a job. It's an opportunity to be proactive, for people to stand, literally, on their own two feet, rather than sitting or lying on the street begging and appealing to the pity of passers-by.

I spoke to a number of people selling the *Big Issue* – there are a lot in central London. Some are still homeless; others are not.

A cheerful young *Big Issue* seller with a northern accent told me: 'No, I'm not homeless any more. I was, but now I sell the magazine to help towards paying my bills.'

George, who has been selling the *Big Issue* for some years, is a lively outgoing Scot who used to be a familiar face outside the BBC, but now has moved on. He has his own little business editing academic papers for people whose first language is not English.

'Well, ha, ha, ha, ha! Have you a year and a day? My name is George. I just came to London and the first thing I had in mind was no longer viable, and I erm, I found myself on the streets, and totally unprepared for it.

'I walked about, I was round about Covent Garden in central London at the time. I saw people sleeping in the Strand. I had a kinda indoor sleeping bag, with a waterproof, in case his couch' – he had been staying with a friend – 'hadn't been that comfortable. And I ended up, just for a couple of nights, just walking up and down what I thought was a fairly safe place, the Houses of Parliament. I was in my fifties. And then I saw the Charing Cross police and I told them the situation, what had happened. And they suggested, actually, that I sell the *Big Issue*. Very kindly, you know, the lady took a bit of time checking out the hostels that were available, and she told me of a hostel out towards Wembley like you get for about £7 a night. Yes, this was the police, Charing Cross police station. I think just being based in Charing Cross, there's a lot of rough sleepers round about the Strand, and they have a kind of specialised homeless unit. I'm not too sure if that still exists, but it certainly existed then.

'So that's pretty much what I did, I went and registered with the *Big Issue*. They've moved since then, and that was the only place that I must say it was an open door, it was easy to go in, it was helpful and within ten minutes I was out selling magazines. You know, and a few other things and people and organisations, I contacted them, but everything seemed to be a number of major hurdles that had to be jumped before anything could happen, so I've been eternally grateful to the *Big Issue* for that. I was in Covent Garden at the time, and I sold a few on Covent Garden and got enough money together to go to the hostel I'd been told of and paid for a couple of nights in the hostel, and um so that was my experience, limited as it was, of sleeping rough and walking about and not having a place to stay in central London.

'When I started selling the magazine, it took me about twenty minutes before I could mumble out, "*Big Issue*."' He laughs. 'I used to buy the *Big Issue*, and it was a little bit uncomfortable and now I'm used to it. And I know so many people through it; you almost become like a regular feature of the place, and I know so many people who tell me personal things, things that are important in people's lives. It almost feels like a social network that I'd be reluctant to lose. I'd like to maintain it to some degree, maybe in a different way. Maybe I could have a different role in *Big Issue* land, something like that. I do, em, I try to keep positive in whatever I'm doing, you know.

'I've had ups and downs in life. Times in the past when I've had a big house, holidays abroad, and aspects of life that were relatively comfortable, and I've also been hungry and not known what to do about it. You need to keep yourself jollied along. The situation I'm in just now with the *Big Issue*, I enjoy it, but I'm sure I could find myself in other situations and keep myself jollied along in these situations as well. So I wouldn't say I'm reluctant to leave *Big Issue* land, but I'll make the most of it while I'm there.

'You're welcome.' He takes a donation, but insists on giving me a magazine.

Darren, Ian, Livia and Iva also sell the *Big Issue*.

Darren: 'I've only slept two hours since Friday.' This was Monday. 'My things got wet. No, the *Big Issue* don't help. I haven't asked them because then you get into outreach workers and benefits.' I saw him again in November, when he said: 'I'm cold. I wake up cold. This is my last year. Twelve years I've been here; it's too much. You used to earn money doing this but not any more.'

Oxford Street, Sunday afternoon in January. An older man on his knees, calling out in a hoarse voice: 'Won't someone help me sell the *Big Issue*?' I buy one. Ian has small tattoos on his face and hands. He has only sold five and is worn out. He started late because the supplier didn't turn up and he had to go to a pub to get the copies himself. Ian has been homeless for twenty-seven years, and used to sleep in the Bullring in Waterloo, where I used to take soup and sandwiches in the 1990s. 'My address,' he says proudly, 'was No. 1 the Bullring. But it was dangerous in them days. I still sleep in Waterloo, at the back of the church. Yes, I sometimes sleep inside. At Christmas I treated myself.'

Livia is Romanian and has small children. I asked her how she found out about the *Big Issue*. 'One lady, she speaking English, she help me. Before, in 2010, 2011, the big office. She drove me here, I make it. That lady she help me. Now, I make about £15. Before in 2013, 2012, I made more. £30, £40, £25, £35, now too much people with the *Big Issue*. Now all day, maximum twenty-five one day. Maximum, but not every day. Sometimes.'

'And do they help you, the *Big Issue*?'

'No, me no need help. I am young. Twenty-nine. That's why no charge help. Some friends help here, I know a long time.'

'Romanian?'

'No, English. Here I have no friends Romanian.'

'And the future? In five years?'

'Me no memory for that. No think future. Only the present.'

Iva is in her late twenties, and too nervous to be interviewed. She has been standing outside the same shop selling the *Big Issue* for ten years. She came over from Bulgaria because friends were here and she had no job. One friend told her about selling the magazine, and she's been doing it ever since. She lives with friends. She has no address or National Insurance number, so cannot get a job. People in the shop and her customers are her friends – they give her food, clothes, even cooking equipment. She has no children. She does not want to go back to Bulgaria – there are no jobs, and her family are here.

As with any good idea, there are those that try to take advantage. Sometimes people manage to get hold of old copies and try to pass them off as if they were real *Big Issue* sellers. I saw one man clutching a different magazine as if it were the *Big Issue*, and asking for money. There are also bona fide *Big Issue* sellers who 'don't have' the right change, or who beg – something that is forbidden under the vendor agreement they all sign.

Benefits

In order to access benefits, people have to jump through a number of hoops. Even British citizens have to prove their eligibility under the Habitual Residents Test. Local councils can deem you intentionally homeless and 'discharge their duty to house' you if you lose your home through 'anti-social behaviour' or failure to pay the rent, or if you have nowhere to live after leaving or being sacked from a job that came with accommodation. Those leaving an abusive home may not be believed and may also be deemed 'intentionally homeless'. People seeking a new life in another area cannot easily prove a local connection in the new area; indeed, some people coming out of prison are not allowed to return to their old haunts. And many of the increasing number of rough sleepers from outside the UK are ineligible. Those without permanent leave to remain in the UK, including those from the EU, are not allowed to work or claim benefits, a regulation that leaves many in destitution.

Benefits currently include disability allowance, the personal independence payment and employment support allowance. These are sickness benefits, but will soon become part of Universal Credit, the 'simplified' benefits system first introduced in 2013. Universal Credit is a benefit for working-age people, replacing six benefits, including what used to be called jobseekers' allowance for living and housing benefit for rent. Merging them into one payment was designed to make claiming benefits simpler.

But the new benefit has been beset by problems. The fact that all claims and updates have to be done online is problematic, and a waiting time of at least five weeks before the first payment is made means some claimants fall into debt and have to resort to food banks. Advance payments, which are meant to help, actually increase the number of people in rent arrears, as people usually use it to pay for food and fuel not rent, and then have to pay it back.

As Professor Pat Thane, FBA, wrote in January 2019, poverty in modern Britain reminds us of the past:

The substitution of Universal Credit for many benefits, and the slowness and complexity of its roll-out causing long delays in payment, is increasing poverty and likely to do so further in the future. The government argues that Universal Credit increases incentives to work, just as administrators of the nineteenth-century Poor Law justified low, punitive benefits as essential correctives to the innate idleness of the poor. Awareness that the Poor Law perpetuated poverty by driving people into low-paid work, damaging society and the economy, was among the early pressures for state welfare. Thereafter, state action brought sustained improvement. Since the 1980s, 'rolling back' the state and welfare has returned us to a situation sadly like the 1900s.

The system was meant to be fully live by April 2017, but as a result of the problems, the roll-out has been delayed to September 2024.

Vic's story is just one of many. He is not homeless, but is largely unable to work as a painter and electrician because of severe arthritis. I asked him how he could work.

'I can't.'

'What are you doing for money?'

'I'm struggling. I live on £100 a month. I'm on the sick, but I get £800 a month, and I've got to pay £678 rent. They only give me £578 towards it, and I've got to find the other £140 out of my money, and that's why I've got £100 a month to live on.

'Yeah, since I've been on Universal Credit, it's completely ruined me. It's taken away all me money – the system doesn't work. Loads of other people in the same situation – people losing houses. Can't afford to pay the rent, because they pay *you* the rent for you to pay the council, so people when they're short of money, they're not going to pay all the rent, they're gonna pay some bills. And then they're gonna find out they're in trouble with the council and they're going to get evicted – it's just a complete cycle. I was warned a year ago that UC would ruin me. I've only been on it for three months, and it's completely ruined me.

'I've gone to see the Citizens Advice, they say there's nothing more they can do. That's what everybody gets. That's it. Having to pay £140 out of my own money towards my rent each month, it's what takes everything out of me. It leaves me completely with no money, then I've got to find £75 a month for council tax. Let alone my electricity, and food.' A hollow laugh. 'Gets depressing, but there's light at the end of the tunnel, I suppose. That's the way I look at it. You have to. I'm just glad my daughter's around to cheer me up, or I go and see them to cheer me up. Oh, well, summer'll be here soon!' It's October. We laugh.

Not surprisingly, many homeless people don't apply for benefits. Former soldier Stephen does, but he understands why others don't. 'There's guys on the streets and they won't go and claim, because they're ashamed and they don't realise what they're entitled to. I keep saying to these guys: Are you claiming for this? Are you claiming for that? And I understand it.'

George told me: 'I've never since I've been here claimed any benefits. I did to begin with, the first hostel that I got into to cover me for a couple of weeks, but I started selling the *Big Issue* and I paid that back. I don't mind that, because I like supporting myself, and I'd rather not be on benefits if I'm able to. I'd rather get out there and do that.'

Darren: 'Don't want benefits.' With a dredged-up remnant of pride, 'Never had them in ten years.'

Jason: 'I never get benefits. I never bothered to try.' He laughs. 'It would be nice if I was entitled to it, would come in handy to me right now. I'm signing on with the Home Office, you know. I don't even know if I have residency status or if I don't. I came here in year 2000. Them run everything, you know, if they say you have to do it, you have to do it! I don't have no one to help me, you know I am not that good with education.'

If homeless people don't sell the *Big Issue* and can't or won't get benefits, there are few survival options available.

Begging

I think a beggar's life is the worst kind of life that a man can lead.
A beggar is no more thought upon than a dog in the street, and
there are too many at the trade.

STATEMENT OF A VAGRANT

After I left my master, I tried hard to get a place; I'm sure
I did, but I really couldn't; so to live, I got watercresses to
sell up and down Oxford-street. I stayed at lodging-houses.
I tried that two or three months, but couldn't live. My
mother had been 'through the country,' and I knew other
people that had, through meeting them at the lodging-
houses. I first went to Croydon, begging my way. I slept
in the workhouse. After that I went to Brighton, begging
my way, but couldn't get much, not enough to pay my
lodgings. I was constantly insulted, both in the lodging-
houses and in the streets. I sung in the streets at Brighton,
and got enough to pay my lodgings, and a little for food.
I was there a week, and then I went to the Mendicity, and
they gave me a piece of bread (morning and night) and a
night's lodging. I then went to Lewes and other places,
begging, and got into prison at Tunbridge Wells for fourteen days, for begging. I only used to say I was a poor girl
out of place, could they relieve me? I told no lies. I didn't
pick my oakum one day, it was such hard stuff; three and
a half pounds of it to do from nine to half-past three: so I
was put into solitary for three days and three nights, having
half a pound of bread and a pint of cold water morning
and night; nothing else, and no bed to sleep on. I'm sure
I tell you the truth ... That's about two months ago. I'm
sorry to say that during this time I couldn't be virtuous.
I know very well what it means, for I can read and write,
but no girl can be so circumstanced as I was. I seldom got

money for being wicked; I hated being wicked, but I was tricked and cheated. I am truly sorry for it, but what could a poor girl do?

'HOMELESS PEOPLE ARE MORAL PEOPLE. THEY DON'T WANT TO STEAL, THEY WANT TO LIVE OFF PEOPLE'S DONATIONS. THEY DON'T WANT TO GO TO PRISON.'

A man shouting in Percy Street in the West End, about 8.30 a.m. on a weekday morning. His only audience is a few people walking to work. No one takes any notice.

Although only in recent times has it again become a phenomenon on London streets, begging is the first and most obvious way of trying to cope without money. Mayhew says that 'the majority of the Irish street-sellers of both sexes beg, and often very eloquently, as they carry on their trade; and I was further assured, that, but for this begging, some of them might starve outright'. Asking for money is done in a variety of different ways, depending on the temperament, mental state and background of the person begging. Some walk up and down the street, accosting people and asking for money for a hostel. Some hold cardboard cups and sit outside tube stations and supermarkets; a few prostrate themselves, with signs saying 'I am hungry' beside them. Some walk up and down inside train or tube carriages and ask passengers for 'a little change'.

The woman on the train was tiny, well spoken, English and obviously educated, over forty, with a ballet-dancer physique. She was neat and tidy, wearing a bobble hat and skirt with a rucksack. She was standing and a young man offered her a seat.

'No,' she said, 'I'm one of those troublesome people. I'm homeless, I don't suppose anyone can give me any money?' The atmosphere in the carriage froze (as it usually does when people beg on the tube). Then the young man offered her some money, and the whole atmosphere changed.

Mo, who has been on the streets for some years, only begs for what he needs.

'I'm from Bangor, Northern Ireland. I was born 16 April 1959. I've been in London thirty years, on and off. Came over here to work. At first the work was brilliant, good wages, everything. Then everything just went down the pan. The jobs started to get less and less. More they brought the people in from Eastern Europe the wages dropped. That was in the eighties, nineties, know what I mean? That was when it started, but it wasn't as bad then, it's worse now. You could get three of them' – he's referring to the Poles who came to England in the first wave of immigration from the EU – 'for one of us, so we lost our wages. Minimum wage.

'A typical day, sleep most half the day, then we get up, go out begging, get our money, go do what I have to do, buy drugs. But I don't buy drugs, I buy beer.' He laughs. 'You know I'm an alcoholic. So I get drunk the night before, get up, go out and beg, 24/7, that's the way it works.

'I sleep at my mate's house. Sometimes he lets me stay, if the girlfriend goes away. She works for TV. I think she does documentaries or something like that, she goes away for weeks and weeks. When she is around, I can't stay, I sleep in the block of flats up there. There's no caretaker, so I have a wee kip up the top. If it's a good night, the park. Or maybe in a doorway. Or it's up by Old Street. Just crash out.

'I don't go to any of the homeless day centres. I get enough money for my food and that. That's the way I live. As long as I get enough money to get myself some fish and chips or a kebab or something. I'm getting pills from the doctor, for these bad acids. I've been sick with food poisoning this last couple of weeks, been sick and diarrhoea. Bad, man. It lasted for three days then it went away, then I got it again.

'I'm not greedy, I beg for what I need then I go. Some boys sit there all day. I don't beg anywhere else, that's my spot. We all got our own spots. There might be another guy begging there, and I don't mind, but when I turn up they get up. I just give them five or ten minutes.

'It [this life] suits me, I just love it. Every day is different. Every day you meet different people. Sometimes I just sit there and chat to someone all night. You know, you get to know the people, and they are nice to you. I've been at this spot a long time, since that was Costcutters. Must be twelve years ago, when I first started begging here, I had to fight for that spot. You know these other guys coming down, I had some fights.' He laughs again.

'It all depends how long it takes. Sometimes I have to sit there an hour, two hours, three hours. Last night, it was three hours. Usually people are good to me. Sometimes people buy me food, you know, which is handy. But I could use a bit of money.' Another laugh. 'I usually start after the kids have come out from school.' He feels bad about begging while the schoolchildren are around: 'They come, you know, I get up, I walk away. They are all right, they don't bother you . . . But now I just drink beer, about five cans, I drink that 9 per cent stuff.' He laughs. '£5 or £10 is enough to get tipsy. Sometimes I can get it in half an hour, twenty minutes, all depends who's walking past!'

Jason, in his mid-fifties, hates begging and tries to get work when he can.

'I'm just a guy going through struggle like any other guy on the street. It's not easy without a job in London. I'm originally from Jamaica, been here nineteen years. Sometimes I find it rough, sometimes get a little work. I don't like stealing, I don't like to beg people. Usually it's cash in hand, these people pay me to move boxes, do removals, that kind of thing. I find it hard to beg, I feel so shamed to beg. I do a little begging already, but it's not funny. I'm used to work for my money.

'I used to go to the Dellow Centre [a day centre for homeless people] in Brick Lane in 2003, and sometimes I used to go to the Whitechapel Centre' – he's talking about the Whitechapel Mission in the East End – 'but I don't even go there any more. You have to pay for your meal there, even when you don't have no money.

'I'm not a drinker, but I really smoke. I ain't gonna tell you no lie. I'm a smoker but I cannot take drink, man, not for me. I smoke on my own, but sometime me and a friend have a little smoke, but it's not a regular thing with me.

'I move around and stay sometimes with different people. If I have money, you know, I can stay somewhere, but if I have no money they kick me out. These people are so funny in England, I can't even sit on the sofa without money, no matter how cold it is. That's why I'm really out here now to try and find a little change. Give somebody a little fiver, have a fiver for myself, you know. Nothing special.

'So I have a guy that calls me sometimes, for removals, that's the main thing I do, but I do other things too, I do a little painting job sometimes. But I don't have the right papers, so that's one of the difficulties. I would get a job. I'm still strong and fit. Have a guess how old I am. I'm fifty-six, born 1962, fifty-seven in March coming up.

'So a good day for me is I've got money, and it's not cold like this,' he says with a laugh. 'I don't like it cold, no one like it cold. I have good friends, I'm telling you. And if I'm with friends and have a little something to eat I just kick back, have some food, nice people, associate myself, have a drink you know, on a sunny day. That would be nice!

'You know, life is getting more difficult in London, everyone can see that. People who are coming to London think that life here is going to be easy, and it's not like that. People still come, every year it's getting harder. Even people coming here in 2000, and now it's 2019 it keep on getting harder. I'm telling you.'

Drew hates begging too. 'Yes, at one point, though I just say if I'm gonna sit here that long and people are going to start recognising me, then I might as well start . . . put a fucking cup out. Whenever I ask for money, I couldn't make that leap but . . . if it comes to you, you having had put the cup down, trust me, I circled around it quite a few times and looked at the spot and wondered am I really doing this?' He'd rather read, do anything and not think about it, 'but at the same time you just want a beer to feel like you're a human being'.

For Lee, 'It's quite degrading for me to be begging but I haven't got a choice at the moment. I don't claim benefits. So if it weren't for the kind people out here, I'd starve to death.'

Christopher was sitting on the ground at the back of the Oxford

Street Debenhams, talking to a pigeon. It's injured, apparently, and he feeds them. He says the English like animals; they just don't like to admit they like pigeons. His crutches, in use because of an accident, lie beside him. He's in temporary accommodation and hopes to be given a place in Brent Cross in a few days' time. He's begging to pay for food. A couple of paperbacks, which he gets from charity shops, are on his coat beside him. I return a couple of days later, but he's gone. Maybe the Brent Cross accommodation worked out.

Sometimes, begging just doesn't bring in enough, especially if there's a habit to feed.

Shoplifting

One man, now a black cabbie, told me: 'I used to go into supermarkets and buy some little thing, and get a big box. Go out, then go back in and put more stuff in the box, and wave my receipt at the security man. "It's all right, I've got a receipt."'

Mat told me of a more sophisticated, and highly successful, approach. 'When things got really bad, I was on the streets for a while. Until I found a way, a couple of guys cut me into a thing they had going, which was going to Morrisons supermarket on Seven Sisters Road and stealing a bag of meat every day. You could steal it, about £140 worth, and take it to a pub and sell it to pensioners. You know pensioners, they love their meat, and you could sell it for half price to them. Other things were very difficult to get rid of, but meat wasn't.

'So you'd wake up every morning, go to the supermarket, and steal a rucksack full of meat. It took one of us to do it, one of us to take the tags off, and one of us to be lookout and load the rucksack on.' Mayhew was familiar with this ploy: referring to 'duffers' visiting small chandlers' shops in the obscure streets in London. One of them goes in, leaving his mate outside to give him a signal if 'the enemy' turns up.

'The security guard must have known,' said Mat, 'but he never said anything. I mean I did eventually get done for it, but that was about a year after doing it most days, in the same shop. And the owner of that pub didn't mind so long as we didn't actually go inside, so we used to stand in the doorway to sell it. You know, one of us would walk through the pub, which would alert everyone that we were there, then they would all shuffle up, get their meat.

'That was enough to get us started on the day, we'd get enough for a fix, then I'd go and shoplift other things. At that point I had nothing, so I couldn't buy things to sell. Some nights I'd spend on the streets and then go round there, and other nights I'd sleep there, and we'd all get up around eight or nine 'cause we weren't very comfortable.' He was staying in someone's flat where they rented out spaces on the floor. It was actually a 'shooting gallery', where people could buy and inject themselves with drugs. 'I remember being knackered all the time, and I was diagnosed later with severe anaemia, and this is so ironic, stealing a bag of meat every day, and having an iron deficiency. An irony deficiency, hah! We did not eat one steak from what we nicked, from £120 to £150 worth of meat every day. Sometimes we went twice a day.

'Sometimes when it was getting a bit on top, they were watching us, we'd you know buy something, like four or five boxes of corn-flakes in a trolley, and hang the meat off the back, then just walk out with it. We couldn't have done it without working together as a team, covering each other, and looking more natural. The person who was lookout would draw the most attention. I got nicked after about a year, I was leaving with about £95 worth of meat and they stopped me. I was lucky it was under £100 worth, and I had no previous, I got off lightly. A copper took me aside and said, "You're hanging around with some really horrible blokes, you don't want to end up like them." You know, they'd grown up doing this all their lives and had been caught before, whereas I wasn't from around there so I'd never been caught before. I'm no better than them as a person, though, that's for sure.'

Two homeless women explained that shoplifting was one of their sources of income, along with begging, dealing drugs or, as a last resort, sex. The need for money was especially urgent if, like Ishwari, they needed to feed a drug habit.

'I'm a prolific shoplifter, so I make around two to three hundred pounds a day to try and support my habit when I'm feeling well.' She gets Universal Credit, 'but mainly it's from shoplifting'. And she gets caught.

'I have, yeah, many times. Well, because I have a clean police record, I just get a slap on the wrist. Touch wood. Even though I do it every day and they would class me as a prolific offender, because it's never more than a hundred pounds at one time, in one shop, it's at their discretion if they want to press charges or take it any further. But mainly 'cause I'm only doing things like Tesco's and Sainsbury's and things like that, it doesn't really go any further.'

'They don't want to be bothered with the paperwork?'

'That's right, that's exactly what it is.' She laughs. ''Cause then the store would have to do it and then if they follow it up with the police services they would have an equivalent amount of paperwork to do.

'Basically, I'll try and keep something for the morning, so whenever I wake up I have some heroin so I don't experience the symptoms. I take some and I'll be OK 'cause obviously doing what I have to do I try to dress a certain way so that I won't draw attention from store detectives or workers in the supermarkets. I try and get ready. I get my clothes really from what other people have thrown away in the TRAID boxes and outside charities like Oxfam in Dalston and stuff, try and go through and get some smart things. Yeah. They have boxes everywhere and people leave clothes outside. So I get my clothes from there. You know, I can't even remember the last time I purchased some clothes.' Another laugh. 'I get dressed and then I'd go hit a shop. That'd maybe take me an hour or so. Then I'll cash up so that'll be like twenty, thirty pounds.'

She sells the stuff at 'local caffs, local newsagents and things like that. Whatever the price is in the shop, I'll sell them on for half price. So they're happy 'cause they're not paying VAT, not paying taxes, and they're paying half price, cheaper than cash and carry. Sometimes they even give you orders, like we need this and this and this. So I'll go out and I'll specifically look. Then, say I got up at nine o'clock that day, the first hit will be done by about ten, half ten. Then I'll do what I've gotta do to feel better. Then it would go again and again. In a day it might be like five, six times before eleven o'clock, twelve o'clock at night before the shops shut and that's it. And by the end of the day I'm so tired. I haven't got time to think about anything.

'That just takes all of your focus, so that's it. A hundred per cent of my focus. I'm thinking, right, from here where can I go? So you gotta plan the logistics – I've done this shop, done this shop, need to go here, duh duh duh duh. You see what I mean? That's my day, every day.'

One man in his late fifties had a more specialised approach. He makes most of his living from selling drugs. When asked if he had ever shoplifted, he replied:

'Not really, it was too on top. But, saying that, we had the book thing – bestselling books. This was when *Football Factory* was out, *Mr Nice*. We used to get so many bestsellers in the week and sell them on the Holloway Road at the weekend. We were hitting Waterstones at Angel Islington. The security in there was bollocks.

We used to go in there and get a holder full of bestsellers. I used to go in every morning, more or less. If I couldn't get rid of them on the Holloway Road, I'd sell them to a shop in Liverpool Street for a pound each. We used to get a fiver on the Holloway Road and we'd have thirty books at a time, so that adds up. We got interest from the police but when we got stopped with them, we'd say they were water damaged. They knew they had a problem with prolific shoplifters at Waterstones but we'd have the barcodes off so they couldn't prove they came from Waterstones. In the end, they got right on top of that. About three times I had to run out of that shop and jump on to the back of a number 19 bus. I was fitter than I thought.'

18

Destitution

At the bottom of the heap in our society are the hidden people: the asylum seekers and forced migrants, the 'ghosts', as they have been described, who have no right to remain, no recourse to public funds, and who are not allowed to work. They have no official status, they are destitute, and are to all intents and purposes invisible. And many of them are women. They sometimes sofa-surf for years until they run out of friends able and willing to put them up. What is left to them then but begging, thieving or prostitution?

Individuals in this situation rarely self-identify – I could not find them just by talking to people on the streets. I had to reach them through specialist organisations which try to help asylum seekers and victims of trafficking – and even then, some organisations, seeking to protect their clients from further hurt, will not allow interviews.

In their report, *Out in the Cold*, the Jesuit Refugee Service (JRS) lays out the stark facts:

> The destitution of those whose asylum claims have been refused is created by government policy. The Home Office aims to create a 'hostile environment' for undocumented migrants. This crim-inalises many everyday activities, such as driving and work, and makes it extremely difficult for undocumented migrants to access vital services, notably healthcare. As criminal convictions and

unpaid medical bills count against an applicant in the immigration system, these policies also serve as a further impediment to regularising immigration status. Especially pertinent to homelessness is the Right to Rent Legislation: the 2014 Immigration Act declared that undocumented migrants did not have the 'right to rent', and introduced civil penalties for landlords who did not check immigration status. In the 2016 Immigration Act, criminal liability was placed with the landlord: landlords can be imprisoned for up to five years if it is found that they had 'reason to believe' that the tenant was in the country irregularly. Also, landlords can now evict undocumented occupiers more easily, without any court order, and the Home Office can order them to do so . . .

62% of refugees have been street homeless in the last year
47% of refugees do not have a regular place to sleep

. . . The 2014 Act prohibited banks and building societies from opening current accounts for individuals who do not have immigration permission or a right to be in the UK. All undocumented migrants and all those claiming asylum in the UK are liable to being detained in an immigration removal centre. In the UK, there is no time limit on detention, and some people are held for years. In this, the UK is very unusual among European countries. Those surveyed in the Day Centre live in perpetual fear of detention.

Asylum seekers arriving in the UK are forced to live in accommodation provided by the National Asylum Support Service (NASS), in what the *Guardian* on 27 October 2017 called 'squalid, unsafe, slum housing conditions'. The public meanwhile is largely unaware of the conditions into which 'traumatised people are routinely dumped'. Testimonies from asylum seekers and frontline workers detail accommodation that is infested with vermin, insecure, damp and dirty.

The houses are often owned by big companies which buy them up, becoming housing providers for people placed there by the government. As housing benefit is not available for those without recourse to public funds, the funding comes direct from central government, and, by cramming people in, companies can make a lot of money. Homelessness as a cash cow.

Agencies like the JRS and the Red Cross can help with food and advice, but they cannot provide accommodation. Social services, faced with a mother and child, can take the child but can do nothing for the mother. One woman from Botswana, faced with that choice, refused to be parted from her baby, saying she would rather sleep under a tree. A compassionate policewoman – 'I'm a mother; I wouldn't give my child up' – took her to one of the few places that can offer accommodation to destitute asylum seeker women: the Catholic Worker Farm.

The CWF is on the outskirts of London and provides a home, a community, for destitute asylum seeker women, helping them get their papers and lives in order. It seeks to establish a life that is as near normal as possible for women who may have been trafficked, tortured or suffered from domestic abuse. In its eleven-year history, it has helped five hundred women, referred to them by agencies like the Red Cross, as well as by health visitors and social workers. I met two women there, both of whom had suffered domestic abuse.

Amira is from a middle-class Pakistani family. She is thirty and has been married for three years. She was living with her husband and his family. She sighed, and explained what went wrong:

'All was not good with me. You know, mentally, torture, everything. Everything. Not good. That is why I leave them. I live with whole family, that's why I live there. When I came here the problems start. The sisters not good, and the mother and the father. Like what you did, what you did, little little things, so I was fed up, so that's why. I am waiting for my immigration. My husband, he took everything from me, my passport, my jewellery, everything my parents give me.'

Simone's husband turned against her as soon as they arrived in

England. We sit on the sofa, and she tells me every detail with a deadpan face, dispassionately, without a break.

'We came from Guinea. I was living with my husband in Lewisham and he hit me. He say he will never do it again. And then after a few weeks, he hit me again, and then one day he hit me and he kicked me out. And then I go out and I was on the corner and I was crying, and then my neighbour come ask me, "What happened?" And I told her, "I don't speak English." At that time I don't speak any English. And she ask me, "What is your first language?" I told her my first language was French, and she say, "OK, I know one woman and she speak French. And I will call her and you explain to her and then she translate to me."

'And I say OK, and then I go out, I sleep out, and then early morning, he open the door and I come in and he say to me: "Everything I tell you to do, you do it. In England I am your god. If you don't do what I want you to do, I will kick you out. And you will sleep out. You see the homeless, they sleep out, and you will sleep out like them." And I say nothing.

'Then, after a few weeks, my neighbour one day she see me, I was coming out and she called me, and called the woman who speaks French, and then I tell her about what happened in French, and the woman translate for her in English. And the woman told me: "Here is England. He don't have the right to hit you. Call the police."

'I say, "I can't call the police. I'm scared." And she say, "No no no no no, you have rights. He can't hit you in this country. In this country that is not acceptable." I say, "No, I can't do it." And then after two weeks, he hit me again. When he hit me, my neighbour heard, and she called the police.

'I was sick, and I went to the GP, and they say, "We don't know you." I have pain everywhere, and they say, "Where is your passport?" I told them my passport is with my husband, and they say, "We can't do anything for you, because we don't know you, we don't know what you did." And I just cry. And from the GP to my house is not far.

'The police came and I explain about everything what happened, and the police take me to the hospital, and after they take him [her husband] to the police station. The police ask me if I have any family in the UK, and I say, "Yes, I have two cousins here in the UK." They call one, and she don't pick up, and they call the other one, and he pick up, and I take the phone and explain everything to my cousin and he come meet me at the hospital.

'When the doctor finished with everything, when I explained about everything, and she report everything on paper, the doctor ask me, "You want to go home with another, like carer to sleep there?" because they see I am too much afraid. My cousin say, "Can she come with me at home?" And I say, "Yes, I will go with my cousin, because I am scared to sleep in the room, and my husband's house." The woman say, "No, your husband is in the police station now," and I say, "OK, but I want to go with my cousin," and then after that I went to my cousin house.

'Then after one week, my cousin tell me, "Look, you can't sleep here," because he had already called the social services, and told them I am a victim of DV, domestic violence, and he said to me, "You know, they don't want to take you any more, the social services, I can't keep you in my house."

'And I say, "Why?" And he say, "I can't keep you in my house, because I have a lot of family, they come sleep here." I say, "OK, what can I do now, because I don't have anywhere to go?" And he say, "Look, let's go to the police station, I will drop you at the police station, and they will find you a place, because here in the UK I am not your family. The police is your family. You can check with your husband." I say, "OK," because I don't have choice, and he drop me to the police station, and they say they don't have nothing for her.

'He just drop me and left me there. I can't speak any English. He was telling me something I can't understand. And I just tell them I don't know where I am going. They say, "OK, it's fine. Tomorrow morning, we will take you somewhere." I say OK, and I go out, and sleep there on a like bench, sofa, in reception. I sleep there. It was too cold, too cold, I was frightened like this' – she shivers – 'and in the early morning, they just take me to my house, and I take my two jackets, because I don't have jackets, and put on jacket and two trousers in a little plastic, and they take me to the Lewisham … Lewisham somewhere where they take homeless people. And when the police drop me there, they ask me my name, my family, about his job, about everything. I tell them. And they say we can't take you any more, because you are not prisoner, you don't have jail. And then I cry and I sit down there, and they want to close the office, and they call the security guy, and then I go out and go down to the bus stop.

'And then I was cry and cry, and one woman come and ask me, "Why do you cry, why do you sit here alone and you cry?" I say, "I don't have anywhere to go," and they say, "Do you have family? Can you call your cousin?" and I say, "I don't have top up, I don't have top up." The woman call my cousin then I take the phone and I cry, "Please, I don't have anywhere to sleep. Take me back, please. Please. Take me back."' By this stage she is beginning to get emotional, and single tears run down her cheeks.

'And he say OK, and then he come and he take me back into the house, but the woman, the wife, she is not happy because she is my husband's family as well, and after one month, the woman sometime don't give me food. I just sleep on the sofa, and she talk loud about me, and sometimes she call my husband, and she say in my language, "She is sleeping on my sofa," something like that. I just keep quiet.

'And then one day, one woman call me to the social services, and I don't forget that and it's Athena, called Athena. They ask me about everything where I am now, and I tell them I am still in my cousin house. I explain everything, and she say, "OK, I will call you tomorrow back," and the next day she didn't call me, and my husband come to my cousin house and he say he will kill me.

'When I hear his voice, I go to the bathroom and I come out of the bathroom and I go to my cousin son, they have like a terrace, and I want to jump but his son scream, and he hold me, and I don't know what to do and I sit down in the corner. And he come and say: "I want to kill you. You make me trouble, you take me in this country, and I'm in trouble now. They can write on my paper, I don't know what they write, you abuse people, something like that. I have no job now. I can't do anything. Because of you. I will kill you. I will kill you."'

Then, she says, her cousin called to the husband, 'Get out of my house, go, go out from here.' 'His wife say, "What your cousin did was not good. She called the police." And I say, "It's not me called the police. I don't call the police." And then after that he go, because my cousin say, "If you don't go, I will call the police again."

'Then in the early morning, the social services call me, and ask me about everything, and I cry. Then they ask me what happened yesterday, and I told her, "I'm scared now, he wants to kill me." And then the next day, early morning, I went out to have a little bit fresh air, and when I come, the woman closed the door, and I knock the door she don't open the door. And then I go out from like eight to seven. I knock the door and I heard her put the chair there, she locked the door and she don't want to open the door.

'And then when I come' – this was in the evening – 'the cousin open the door but I don't say your wife closed the door. I just kept quiet, and then I went to the kitchen, because I want something to eat, and she come tell me, "This food is for my child." I say OK, and I just drink the water and go to the lounge and then everybody go to sleep and I sleep. I explain about everything to this woman and they take me to the Solace Woman's Aid.'

I asked how long it was from when the trouble started till she got the aid place. 'One month. One month and I think, like thirteen days. Then I went to Solace Woman's Aid and they find a solicitor for me. They give me a room, accommodation, everything, but my case is difficult because my husband writes a letter, sent to the Home Office: "I'm here because of paper, blah, blah, blah." After he hit me the first time, he called the family and told my dad, "Your daughter called the police on me." And they called my cousin, but I said to my brother, "I never called the police on him, it was my neighbour called the police," and my cousin explained to my dad that maybe tomorrow the police will call her if she wants to charge him and my father tell me, "Don't charge him." Everyone in Guinea called me and said, "Don't charge him, he's husband."

'And when the police call the next day, I tell them I don't want to charge him. And then when I went to Solace Women's Aid, after I stay there eight month and one week, and they tell me, "Look, your case is difficult, because your husband write a letter to the Home Office, telling them you just married him for paper, blah, blah, blah." And then they say we don't have plans for you any more now, you have to move to the Catholic Worker Farm. And then I move here. Here is five months.

'Sometime I feel a little bit sad, because now the Home Office give me settlement but I feel a little bit sad, because I left everything in my country for this man. I had my job, and I left everything for him.' Her voice breaks. 'I help him. I did everything for him. I gave him love, I give him everything, but when I come here, he treat me like this.'

Dennis and Easton came to one of the six Crisis winter shelters together with volunteers from the London Catholic Worker. At its centre in Haringey, the LCW offers accommodation and hospitality to people with no rights to work, welfare benefits or accommodation of any kind. Like the church winter shelters, they close over Christmas, so it was a boon to have somewhere for their guests to stay.

Dennis is originally from Belarus. He is forty-one, though he looks at most thirty. He first came to Britain in 2008, and made a claim for asylum. He was given accommodation near Heathrow. He didn't give his reasons for claiming asylum, but he did mention the need to get away from the Soviet system. As so often, his claim was refused.

He has therefore been living outside the system, with no recourse to public funds, since 2009. He says there is no shortage of food, and there are places to go and stay warm in the winter. He was quite smartly dressed, finding it easy to get clothes from some of the different groups that do handouts on the streets. He is not allowed to work and doesn't beg so has very little money; he can only get occasional fare money from services like the Red Cross and Jesuit Refugee Service. Basically he lives hand to mouth, day by day. When asked if he had any plans, any hopes, he looked quite thoughtful, then resigned, and said he couldn't really say. He can't see any route out of his situation, and his energy, his attention, is all used up in the daily task of surviving. He seemed to accept that this was how his life was going to be.

Easton had a manuscript book in which he kept his carefully handwritten poems. He also showed us a video on his phone, of him reading one of his poems at the Poetry Café. Crisis has a DJ and an open mic space in the evenings, and one of the volunteers suggested he could perform some of his poetry later in the week.

Easton came to the UK in fear of his life. He had witnessed a violent incident in his neighbourhood in Kingston, Jamaica. A man was murdered and the people responsible, notorious Yardies, wrongly believed that he had testified against them. In a place where everyone knows everyone, he knew he was not safe, so he got the next flight to London and lay low. He was managing, earning enough for accommodation by working in the informal economy, until one day in 2016 he was picked up by the police while chatting to a friend in Stratford town centre. They took him to Harmondsworth detention centre. It seems he was able to make a claim for asylum but this was refused; then he was released, but not given any route to regularising his immigration status. He goes to sign on once a month at the Borders and Immigration Agency centre near London Bridge, but it seems he had not had good advice from anyone. His poems eloquently express his bitterness and frustration with British 'justice' and 'human rights', and he agreed to share one of them:

MI NEVER PLAN

Coming from yard,
Say mi a go abroad,
Never know life would be so hard.

Say mi a go a england,
Thinking england is the mother land.
So, when mi reach the air port in a england,
Me didn't even have an escort to take me about
But some-way mi find mi way out.

Jump in a taxi cab,
Tell the driver to take mi to a hotell
That him think would be heaven and not hell

After settling and making mi-self comfy,
Not knowing that the authorities them a watch mi.
Have mi pon CCTV like mi a movie star.
Them watch mi near,
Them watch mi far,
But one thing mi try not to get a scar.

Anyway, one thing mi do wrong,
Mi never mek a plan.
And the wrong mi do is stay in england too long.

But through mi was running for mi life
When mi leave yard, say mi ago abroad.

Mi never violate, only that mi over stay,
Them say 'mi wrong'
So them a fi put mi in a detention.

But while in a detention mi had was to sort out a plan,
So mi pay attention to the rules and regulations,
Thinking of getting out of detention
Because mi never plan to fi stay a england too long.

Now mi still in a england.
Everything a go wrong
Because mi never mek the right plan.

So man, always think before you plan,
That when you plan,
You plan is the right one.

Robert from Hungary is thirty-eight and homeless, although if you saw him on the street you would never know. He is clean-shaven, smartly dressed in a suit, tie and overcoat, and wears a felt hat at a jaunty angle. He uses The Connection at St Martin's day centre for showers, meals, advice and support. He managed to make light of the problems of arriving in a strange country.

'When I first arrived, it was hard. No help, I didn't have any help. I was on my own, really. I was with Hungarians in a shared house, but no help. I had to realise that they were so selfish. I didn't speak English at all when I came. I even had to ask my friend when I went home, like, What is a CV? I asked someone on the street how to say, I am looking for a job. I asked a Hungarian woman on the street. That was funny.

'I had to learn English. Picked up words, expressions, from the street. I tried to say how they say it. I remember a time when I actually spoke some English but I had no clue what I was saying, like when you sneeze and people say "bless you". I don't know what I'm saying, but that's what you say. Or when someone gives you something like a coffee and you say "thank you". When you have no clue what you're saying but you know that's what you have to say. It was really funny.'

But he was more serious when he spoke on the subject of support:

'We haven't talked about the homeless situation and how stupid the whole system is. As I said, I don't get any help. I worked all my life, and now when I need help I don't get any. Nothing at all. And those people who never worked, get some benefits, accommodation.

'When I used to sleep in the city, there were these people, they found me on the street, sleeping. So they tried to get me in a place called No Second Night Out. And they tried to get me the benefits, because that's their priority. They said it's impossible, because of nationality. It's called an A8 country, those who joined the European Union later. Different rules or laws for these countries. The problem was I didn't have a constant five years, because you have to have only a break of five days between two jobs in five years. It was literally four years I worked for Wetherspoons, that was the pub actually where I went. Four years. And then I went to work elsewhere . . . I can't remember where. And there is a gap. And that's the problem.

'I'm registered here with the Workspace. It's not the Connection, it's the whole system. Even if they try to help you here, they have handcuffs, you know? When I don't get benefits, it's not Connection, it's just the whole system's so stupid. Right now I need help and I don't get it. Nothing at all, no penny.'

'Because you don't have a status,' said one woman, 'people use you, abuse you.'

Clearly Easton, Robert and thousands of others need expert advice and advocacy to negotiate the Home Office systems. But people who work in the field of providing advice and other assistance to forced migrants and asylum seekers talk about the arbitrary nature of decision making. Perfectly sound and well-evidenced claims are often refused, even on appeal. The system seems to be creaking, if not actually falling apart, under-resourced and low on the list of priorities of the government and the public.

Trafficked

One day centre has made the connection between homelessness and modern slavery. Maria, who works there with people who have been trafficked, explained that homeless people make perfect victims.

'What nobody thought before and we are seeing now – we kind of opened a Pandora's box here – is that actually homelessness is completely linked to modern slavery, because when you escape your traffickers you often don't have your documents and you sleep rough until you find a day centre. So you become homeless after escaping your traffickers.

'You may also be recruited because you are homeless, so it's most of the vulnerable people. Recruiters work with dreams as bait, and the most vulnerable people to it are these people who don't have money, who are in poverty, who need a job, who need a roof. And rough sleepers and homeless people are ideal, tick all the boxes. What we are seeing as well now is that unfortunately, due to gaps in government support, when a person leaves the safehouse after receiving government support, they might become homeless as well, and re-enter trafficking again.'

A number of nationalities are involved, primarily British and Romanian. She told us how it works. 'What we are seeing here is that Romanians tend to be recruited in Romania. They are told by a friend of a cousin or a friend of a friend, Go to London, go to Victoria, there will be someone waiting for you and they'll take you to a nice spot for work for two or three months or six months. It happened, for instance, a person left the orphanage at eighteen years old, a family picked them up, put him in their farm. He worked there for six years then the family said, "We have another job in England. We'll take you to England." So they took him in their car and when he arrived here he was enslaved for seven more years. He had to sleep in a caravan without light, without electricity, without water. There was always a dog patrolling outside so he didn't dare go out, even to go for a pee. Working on a farm picking fruit and vegetables. He was beaten up with a broom – there's always an element of physical abuse in all the cases. He was never paid. He had some mild learning disabilities. He was in his twenties. He escaped, he became a rough sleeper.

'The latest one I had, he was told to come here because he was a decorator, for a decorating job. He came here, he met a couple, they took him to their place, closed doors, took the passport and all the certificates and forced him to work in a car wash for four months. That was in north London.'

19

The homelessness industry

'When I went away, homelessness was a problem.
When I came back, it was an industry.'

Fr Padraig Regan, Chaplain to
the Passage Day Centre, on his return
from a sabbatical, early 1990s

1861: Asylum for the homeless poor of London is
opened when the thermometer reaches freezing
point . . . want being the sole qualification
required of its applicants.

2017: London Mayor today announced plans to
open homeless shelters in London every day the
temperature is forecast to drop below zero.

Then and now

DESCRIPTION OF THE ASYLUM FOR THE HOMELESS

The only refuge for the houseless now open which is really a
home for the homeless, is that in Playhouse-yard, Cripplegate.
The doors open into a narrow by-street, and the neighbourhood
needs no other announcement that the establishment is open
for the reception of the houseless, than the assembly of a crowd
of ragged shivering people, certain to be seen on the night
of opening, as if they knew by instinct where they might be

housed under a warm and comfortable roof. The crowd gathers in Playhouse-yard, and many among them look sad and weary enough. Many of the women carry infants at the breast, and have children by their sides holding by their gowns. The cries of these, and the wrangling of the hungry crowds for their places, is indeed disheartening to hear. The only sounds of merriment come from the errand-boys, as they call themselves, whom even starvation cannot make sorrowful for two hours together. The little struggle that there usually is among the applicants is not for a rush when the doors are opened, but for what they call the 'front rank.' They are made to stand clear of the footpath; and when five o'clock – the hour of admission – comes, an officer of the Refuge steps out, and quietly, by a motion of his hand, or a touch on the shoulder, sends in about 150 men and boys, and about 50 women and girls. He knows the great majority of those who have tickets which entitle them to one or two nights' further lodging (the tickets are generally for three nights), and these are commonly in the foremost rank. The number thus admitted show themselves more or less at home. Some are quiet and abashed; but some proceed briskly, and in a business-like way, to the first process, to wash themselves. The Asylum for the Houseless Poor of London is opened only when the thermometer reaches freezing-point, and offers nothing but dry bread and warm shelter to such as avail themselves of its charity.

Like being booked in to prison

Here, Mat describes his experience of LACS, the Lambeth Assessment Centre.

I had been bouncing between the streets and shooting galleries for several years and I was desperate for somewhere warm to lay my head at night. I was picked up off the streets by an outreach team and taken to LACS in Vauxhall.

It's depressing walking into a hostel. It's got an institutional feeling. Stark, white walls and there's a reception that makes you feel like you're being booked in to prison. Sounds echo, you know, they're harsh and nothing about it feels like home. You know you have to do this to get housed – to go through what might be weeks in this place followed by years in some other type of hostel. There's a sinking feeling that you're worthless, unable to sort things out for yourself and you notice the cameras everywhere watching your every move. The atmosphere bristles with anxiety, anger and depression. Over the next few weeks you are assessed mentally, physically and at times what feels like morally. It's a process that can strip you of what's left of your esteem and for many it is difficult to deal with.

Walking into a hostel is an experience that hits all of your senses at once. Sounds are loud and echo, there's a smell of boiling veg that tastes like my gran's cooking, the taps in the toilet are sticky and it looks empty, with plain white walls and basic furniture that wouldn't be out of place in a cheap office.

To every sense it seems to be the opposite of what a home is meant to be.

On returning in March 2020, Mat was able to cast a more objective eye:

The foyer is smart and the two staff that man the reception are polite. The paint is fresh but there is nowhere comfortable to sit and that's true of the whole building. There's a fridge in the reception and every few minutes someone comes in for a handful of the Pret Sandwiches that have just been delivered. Someone tells me that they're fed up with avocado.

On the left is a room in which the doctor sees everyone who comes through the assessment centre as part of an overall assessment that will decide what type of hostel people are placed in. The main recreation room is big and as it's lunchtime it's full. Noises echo and clash with people bellowing their orders to the residents who are helping to dole food out from the large hatch.

At the other end of the room is an extremely loud television that fights to be heard over the fifty or so sets of cutlery that grind, clash and clang against the porcelain plates.

There is a maze of corridors but every inch of the building is covered by CCTV and there are intercoms in each room. Apparently staff can listen in on these even when the button to talk is not held down. Rooms have single beds and are small and basic but always warm. There is a large courtyard outside of the recreation room next to the railway line where people hang out, chat and smoke. Although people are meant to stay in assessment centres for no more than a month, some people are spending a lot longer in them as the system becomes clogged up, with no flats to move people on to in the social housing sector and benefit caps excluding unemployed people from the renting market.

Gone are the workhouses, almshouses and paupers' lunatic asylums of Mayhew's day. Enter shelters, day centres, hostels and food banks. Those who die without the means of paying for a funeral are no longer buried by the parish, but by its modern equivalent, the local council.

The service for people who have died homeless in London was packed. I've never seen St Martin-in-the-Fields so crowded – with homeless people, some formerly homeless, and representatives from the multitude of charities that work with homeless people. It is not only the number of homeless people that is shocking, but the number of people and hours, and the amount of money, involved in trying to support them. It's an industry. Mayhew lists the organisations that worked to support homeless people, and I imagine the numbers now are comparable – even if the less moralistic attitude of today's workers is not.

There are hundreds of organisations working with homeless people – the big ones, such as Crisis, Shelter, Centrepoint, St Mungo's, The Connection at St Martin-in-the-Fields, The Passage – and many smaller ones. Technically, hostel, day centre and outreach workers work for charities; since 2003, however, they no longer receive grants but are generally commissioned by local authorities, which draw up service specifications and invite tenders or bids from 'service providers'. Those whose outreach workers are commissioned to deliver services for local authorities, and who receive public money, have to toe the line in the way their services can be accessed. Access is generally by referral by a select number of organisations; self-referral is rarely acceptable. The tension between immediate help and the need to move people on is not restricted to government services, but extends to the charities who receive funding.

For those who can access them, day centres offer a lifeline – providing not only showers, clothes and food, but access to specialist support for addiction or mental health issues, and classes in a variety of subjects, including English, computer skills and art. Some people discover unexpected talents.

Those of us who worry about the plight of people we see sleeping on the street have been heartened by hearing of Street Link, an umbrella organisation that can be contacted to report individuals sleeping rough. However, the experience of those on the receiving end is not always positive.

Linda: 'The people from Street Link and people like that, people who bring food and things. But that's it. They come and see you at three o'clock in the morning, to come and stay somewhere, but what's the point? We get up at seven. We've just got ourselves dry and then they wake us up and say come and stay over. We get soaking wet again and get up seven o'clock in the morning. What's the point in that? They should come and see us first thing in the morning. Why come and see us in the early hours of the morning and wake everybody up? That's stupid.'

Mo: 'They mess you about as well, you know, outreach, they come and say be there at such and such, and we'll come and see you. You're sitting there waiting then they don't turn up. Then you leave and they say, We came, and you say, No you didn't, then they get ragged with you. Jokers! Then they put all the blame on you, it's not right. So if an outreach worker comes to see me now I just tell 'em to go away. I haven't seen anyone for the last year. It's been so long, they just leave me alone.'

Hostels

Among the general public there is considerable confusion about hostels. When homeless people beg to get money for a hostel, they're talking about the kind of hostel used by backpackers, which often have special rates for homeless people. It was one such hostel that George came across when he found himself on the streets.

'The initial hostel at £7 a night was twenty people in one room, in bunk beds, and there were mice running about the place and people coming and going at all times of day and night. It was uncomfortable and you're not too sure who you're sleeping with, and snoring like you would not believe existed, like wounded *animals* every night. What is that? There's an elephant in here that's severely injured. Oh, heavens above. But it was a roof over your head, you could have a shower, you could get laundry done there, you get a semblance of normal life.'

Selling the *Big Issue* has enabled him to pay for a better hostel. 'You know, I'm still in a hostel but I have my own room in the hostel and it's en suite, quite costly, and I do pay for that.'

Ninety per cent of homeless accommodation projects consist of hostels. Every year in England 200,000 single people experience homelessness, and many of them have support needs apart from their housing. Hostels provide a roof, a bed and a measure of the support needed. If people meet the criteria set by the local council, if they are entitled to benefits and if there is room, they can access hostel places which are free – or, rather, paid for by housing benefit.

The conditions are no doubt more sanitary than in Mayhew's day, but hostels are still regarded as unsafe by many of those who sleep rough; seen as places where they feel that they and their possessions are under attack. Their fears are not unfounded. Figures released under the Freedom of Information Act reveal that between April 2016 and February 2020 in Camden Council's contracted homeless accommodation, a homeless person has died on average nearly every month.

Many I have spoken to have voiced the view, like Mayhew's dung collector about the workhouse, that 'they would sooner die on the street' than go into a hostel. When we hear some accounts of people's experiences, we can see why.

Mat: 'Someone told me about No Second Night Out and I could get a hostel place so I thought, fuck it, I'll give it a try. I got into a hostel in Brixton, one of the worst hostels in London. It descended into chaos, there were about thirty people there, living in a five-bedroom house. It was just awful. I got stabbed twice in there. So I used to spend nights out, it just wasn't safe. You could lock your door, but I got rushed in there a few times. Only one of them was properly housed there, and he got thrown out the next day. That place was awful, it really was.'

Having got himself clean, there was no way that Lee would go back to hostel life:

'I used to live in a hostel that an outreach worker got me into, but the hostel was full of drugs, which I've dabbled with a bit in my time, but in the end I left to go back on the streets, because it's a cleaner life for me, basically, you know, and that's why I'm out here because I don't want to fall back into the drinking and drugs circle, so I thought it was better to come and rough it out here for my own sanity.

'And, you know, up until that day when I used drugs I hadn't used drugs for eight months or had a drink. But I done it in that hostel; if I was still there I'd be still doing it today. Since I left I haven't touched a drink or any drugs, so I'm better off where I am at the moment till I find private housing. I'm a recovered alcoholic, I don't need to have a drink now. So, basically, it's safer for me and my sanity to stay here, even though it's cold. Because for me this is therapy, you know.'

Hostels vary both in the size and quality of accommodation offered, with different hostels catering to different needs. Some offer emergency accommodation, as do year-round night shelters, church and community winter shelters and Nightstop schemes. These services are for the most part accessed by referrals from outreach teams and day centres. People can usually remain in emergency accommodation either until they are moved directly to more permanent accommodation or are first moved to specialist schemes or second-stage accommodation prior to a permanent move.

Seventy-three per cent of accommodation projects consist of second-stage accommodation such as hostels, foyers and housing schemes that provide a variety of low, medium or high levels of support. People are usually referred to second-stage accommodation by a professional service like social services or the probation service, or by a homelessness team in the council's housing needs department. They will generally have to prove a local connection going back as far as four years to be eligible to access these services.

There are also specialist schemes providing support for those with specific issues such as mental health, alcohol or drug use, for ex-offenders, or for other specific groups of people such as women or long-term rough sleepers. Only 7 per cent of existing accommodation projects are defined as specialist.

The reality is that there are not enough hostel beds for all the people sleeping rough in London, particularly in Westminster. If someone is not considered to have a local connection or to be sufficiently 'vulnerable', they will first be offered reconnection to their last place of settled accommodation. If they don't accept this offer for whatever reason, they may end up sleeping rough until their condition deteriorates and their vulnerability increases to the point at which they are offered a bed. Nearly four in ten hostels accept referrals from named agencies only. Four in ten require a local connection.

I heard some hair-raising experiences of accessing and living in hostels.

Andy is fifty-three: 'After a year on the streets and occasionally staying on the floor – or if I was lucky a sofa – at various flats, someone told me about No Second Night Out. As far as I know, the service was designed before the 2012 London Olympics to clean up the streets before the Games. Anyway the idea is you plot up somewhere on the streets, call them and wait for them to pick you up. I waited for a week before I called them again, only to be told that the place I was bedding down was behind a gate. I was in a factory, sleeping in an old van with a couple of dogs that belonged to a pal of mine and that meant I wasn't homeless, is what they said. But they didn't tell me.

'After another week I was still on the street and was about to give up when a friend gave me the number of someone who worked at No Second Night Out – someone who had helped my friend before giving him this number for any of his mates. In this case that was me. I called and told them I was plotted up on the steps of the big church in the middle of Brixton. A few nights later two outreach workers found me on the steps there and asked me questions. Was I on benefits? Did I have a local connection? And the big one, of course: Was I actually homeless? I passed their test and they put me into a van for a trip down the Brixton Road heading to LACS.

'Here I spent the next six weeks, being watched and scrutinised by case workers, doctors and anyone else who thought I needed to be interrogated about my health and capability. Despite a serious drug addiction and collapsing mental health, I was classified as low support needs and moved into a shared house known as supported living.'

Raymond, a volunteer trader at a market, is fifty-nine, a big Afro-Caribbean man with a smooth-skinned face and small moustache. He told me: 'I wasn't homeless, but they put me into a hostel. But the hostels back in them days weren't what they are like now, we're talking about twenty years ago. The hostels, they were manky, they weren't kept properly or like how they are now, where it's all modern, where they've got pool tables, areas where you can meet, and so on and so on. Not like in my time where you only had eggs, egg and a piece of toast, and that was it, that was bed *and* breakfast. It was very lonely, because you were one in a room. So there was no community areas where you could sit down and talk to other people. You were always put into a room on your own. It was very isolating. It was like being in a cell.'

Formerly homeless, Mark is now working in outreach. He told us of his experience of Myriam Lodge:

'It's about four or five floors so it's quite a big hostel. It's in Forest Hill. It's a short-term-stay hostel. It was chaotic sometimes but I kept myself to myself. I was drinking but I was in there with addicts, drinkers trying to be your friends. Even though they had activities and I was slowly starting to go through recovery, being linked with CGL in Camberwell, which is the drug and alcohol service. I got with them and did smart recovery. That helped me get off the drink.

'After Myriam Lodge they put me in Keyworth Street Hostel.' This fifty-person unit in Elephant and Castle is what's known as a wet hostel, he explains, catering for drinkers and other drug users. 'I kept myself to myself again 'cause I don't want to know anyone else. I'm not their friend, I'm not their buddy. I don't trust no one. I'm still like that now. I'm in Catford now in a one-bed studio with a shared kitchen. The only issue I have with that is that I've been there for over a year now and other people are signposted from other hostels to there, so I'm still living with people who have drug and alcohol issues.'

Tim, who went from a high-salary job to being on the streets, talked of his experience of trying to continue to work. 'I did have access to a bed at my mum's place in Suffolk but I had to try and work in London, so staying there wasn't an option at all during the week. People have accused me of being a poverty tourist, but I was trying to do very difficult freelance work and sleeping on the floor of a hostel at night. I was having to get up early, go and meet people in the Foreign Office and boardrooms and having to put on this mask, and I had to dig incredibly deep to get through it. My friend I was staying with helped in that respect. If I had a big meeting, he would give up the bed so I could get a decent night's sleep. The mattress was awful but still it was better than the floor.

'There were other things as well. At one point I thought I saw loads of apple seeds on the bed covers and then they started moving. They were a very exotic and angry form of bed bugs. You can't get rid of these damn things and it got worse and worse and eventually we got it fumigated. We treated the floor and the bed and they all started migrating in columns up the walls.

'It was almost like borstal or prison, with people having no locks on the place. People started to create their own clans and violence started to erupt as crack users and dealers moved in. At one point there was over twenty extra people in a five-bedroom house. A really bad apple came in, he was definitely a crackhead. Things went missing, accusations were thrown and it's quite incredible how a place can change from a degree of conviviality when it goes well to eruptions of really extreme violence.

'It felt very vulnerable. Look, this was a house where there was a different currency. Hand jobs for crack, stolen goods for drugs. I was always aware that things could turn on a sixpence as well. It was interesting to see that when there was no structure, there was the capacity to break the rules and once this bad seed had come in, it suddenly became really dangerous.

'At one point the case worker assigned to the house wasn't allowed to come in because it wasn't safe for her, and it wasn't. It was a very free and trusting environment in the middle of Brixton, and once that started to be abused, nobody seemed to step in, and then suddenly all these bad people appeared. I mean, I would be making a cup of coffee in the kitchen and someone would just walk in and start smoking crack.

'And people were scared to report it. You know the old saying. Snitches get stitches. I think there was an atmosphere that put me in the firing line because if there was a list of people who might grass someone up, because I was the posh git, there was that, Oh, is he a plant? There was a bit of that going on as well.

'There was a time in there that the toilet blocked up and the plumbers left the contents of the macerator unit on the floor of the toilet for the weekend. A macerator is a box that sits on top of the toilet chopping everything up so it can pass easier through the plumbing. So they literally left a pile of shit on the floor of the toilet. Because they were coming to a hostel and it wasn't high priority, they left for the weekend and didn't come back. We had to clear it up. I just thought how little respect can be offered from one group of people to another. It amazed me how, the closer you get to people who society have pegged as worthless, just how badly they are treated.'

Mark's comparison with a prison finds an echo in the experiences of one of the homeless people interviewed by Mayhew: 'This was the first time I ever asked for shelter in a workhouse in my life . . . Oh, I felt then that I would much rather be in prison than in such a place.'

As Mark identifies, at the root of many of the problems experienced by people living in hostels are inappropriate referrals. 'I think they should have been more careful about who they put into those places. Some people were really used to that system and some people really weren't, and I worry about the people who come into that situation and don't know how to handle it. It must be a real shock to them. One interesting thing is that the corporate world that I work in isn't completely dissimilar in that there is no thoughtfulness or compassionate or soulfulness in that world either, and the psychopaths invariably end up at the top.'

Sara, now a project worker, talked about her experience at Lambeth Assessment Centre while homeless. 'It's probably about eighty or a hundred beds, loads, I think it's five or six floors, it's really really massive. They have cameras in there, you are not allowed people to come in, you're not allowed guests, you're not allowed nothing.

'I got moved to a low-support unit under Look Ahead down Crescent Lane in Clapham, where one of the women was attacked. Yep, it was domestic violence, like they would literally batter her. One time I stepped in to help her and I had a taser fired at me by one of the guys. It missed me by that –' She gestures. 'We got absolutely no protection. I had to do a safeguarding referral myself for her and for myself because Look Ahead were . . . you know, I used to call them Look the Other Way, because that's exactly what they were doing.'

She tried to report the incident 'literally hundreds of times. After the taser was fired at me I took the hooks and the string, the taser discharge, to the Look Ahead office and said, Look, I've nearly been killed, I'm not fucking around, this is the taser, this is what happened last night – I've come to the house, she's battered, she's bruised and that could have been me. You're not doing anything to safeguard her and you're not doing anything to safeguard all the other vulnerable women in this house.

'I made a formal complaint against Look Ahead and against the council and they came back to me and said the organisation running the building was a housing association and that was separate. Look Ahead just provided the support, the building was owned by the housing association. Apparently the housing officer who was in charge of the house was on long-term sick, so instead of getting someone to cover her, they just didn't bother.

'It was shit, you know. You just had a small room, some shelves up, a sink. You had to share a bathroom, you had to share everything, there was no community, everyone would just keep to themselves. Another girl came who was in a gang, and there was stabbings, and I've come out of my room before and the living room was splattered with blood and I literally think someone's been killed – they weren't killed, but they were seriously injured.'

Sara could see how people prefer to stay on the street. 'Yes, absolutely, of course. And then at the end of it, what are you guaranteed? You are not even guaranteed decent housing, are you? So it's a bit pointless really. I mean why get involved in that process and inflict all this harm on yourself? Because it is. Being around domestic violence, severe crack use, exploitative males isn't beneficial for anyone, let alone people who are in that place trying to get their housing resolved.'

As she pointed out, another major problem is the inexperience and lack of training of a poorly paid staff.

McGinlay reported that 'in the hostels and in squats it would get so dangerous and chaotic with people fighting and shouting and hearing voices in their head because they're having a bad ketamine trip, that they're charging towards you with glass bottles and shit, so myself and a few other people who also had hidden disabilities, we would like hide out in parks'.

And she picked up on a serious problem of another kind. 'It's constantly said that the information we share is confidential but none of it is confidential. I've got a note where it had a list of people's stuff, confidential stuff, including my own stuff, and it was really really personal, but on the other side it was used as scrap paper. There was a staff member that wrote a note to another client and the client came up to me and said, "You might want to see this." I was devastated. Nothing I said was confidential, which undermines any faith you have in that person and the system or anyone else, even the decent people that are trying to help you within the system. There's no boundaries. It is so chaotic.'

She likens it to the institutionalisation that often affects people leaving different kinds of accommodation.

'I've heard other people say this. When they come out of hostels, when they come out of prisons, when they've come out of care. You put so many barriers up I think you shut something in yourself off. I got to the point where I became so emotionally numb that I found it difficult to cry, like I literally felt like a zombie. I couldn't relate to other people's emotional stuff because I'd already gone through so much myself that I felt completely disconnected. I didn't feel like a human being.

'I had no sense of who I was when I came out. I was wandering around, lost. It was the hostel that did that to me. I remember when I went into the hostel, my short-term memory was quite sharp, and I think because of all the trauma and the stress of not sleeping, insomnia, my adrenalin was so high at one point that I'd been awake for five days in a row without any drugs. It was the adrenalin and stress and fear of being there that kept me awake, and I believe that not having enough rest and time to process things affected my short-term memory mechanism in my brain. And I don't think that's me just getting old. I distinctly remember how my mind was functioning beforehand and afterwards. And I've heard other people say that as well.'

Moving on

Over the past twenty years, hostels and night shelters have developed considerably from what have been described as large doss houses. The modern hostel system has a more holistic approach to homelessness. But the system is far from perfect, especially because, as the result of a severe shortage of social housing, there is nowhere for people to move on to. After spending a few years (now as long as five) in the hostel system, people are moved into either private rented flats (with the recent benefit caps, there are very few that people can afford) or housing association flats with fixed two-year tenancies. From there they are moved back into the private rented sector or, if they are lucky, into a small studio flat with a secure ongoing tenancy. Those who end up in the private rented sector are often made homeless again when landlords try to put up the rent. Often people will already be topping up their housing benefit to pay their rent from the £60 a week they get from the DWP, and they can't afford to pay any more.

A woman who has been a case worker for eight and a half years gave a professional view of what's been going on during that time. She said that funding has been cut, so there are fewer hostels to serve the same level of need. The budgets of drug, alcohol and mental health services are being slashed, so people desperate to access rehab or detox can't do so. Case workers are expected to move people out within two years of starting to use the service. Many simply aren't ready, but even if they are, the private rental accommodation that they have to use is, she said, 'literally terrible'. After all the work that has been done both by the professionals, such as drug workers, probation officers and mental health workers, and by the client, people are moved away from somewhere where they have support and are making progress to an expensive and substandard one-year tenancy in a borough on the other side of London. If people don't accept it, they are told they'll be making themselves intentionally homeless and get no support.

She blamed the private rented sector, the high rents, and the fact that a private landlord who can charge £2000 a month is unlikely to want only £900 from someone on benefits. A holistic approach to recovery, taking time to build relationships and boost people's self-esteem, is, she said, simply not compatible with the government's policy of 'take it or leave it'.

Jumping through hoops

Many people reported to us the barriers that were thrown up in trying to access commissioned services. One was about geography. Lyobimir, who is Bulgarian, told us:

'I tried to find a network through different organisations which could help me for my mental and social issues and I found something, somewhere in Camden. I looked up the address, I went there, I talked to a really nice gentleman. His first question was, "Where are you sleeping now?" I said I was sleeping in St James's Park. He said, "Oh, you're not in Camden?" I said, "It's OK for me, it's no problem, I can come to Camden but I need mental help."

'"I can tell you're not British, this will be difficult for you." Why? And he started explaining. "You can go to Jesus Centre, you can go to different day centres." I said to him, "Sir, I'm looking for real mental help. I found your network, your address, you're open for everyone. Why not for me?"'

He laughs. 'These people, they specialise in mental health and they promote on their website that they work with everyone. They have different centres, different points around London, but this one was closed to me.'

Councils often try to move people on to someone else's territory, so that they don't have to take responsibility or spend the money. Safiya told us how a homeless man near her flower stall on Tottenham Court Road was told, 'You can go and sit there, that's Westminster. But not here, this is Camden.'

Tim discovered that his educated background was actually a barrier: 'When I did try to access services, I wasn't encouraged by what they said. When I put myself forward, it's almost like what I looked like and came across as didn't match any of the cases they had had before. It was some form of inverted snobbery. It was almost like they were saying, I don't believe this guy with eloquence and charisma is actually in need. At the end of the day, when I tried to access services I didn't get any warmth back. I always got comments like you must have rich parents or a rich sister somewhere who can help you. What I'm learning is that they do this to everyone – for different reasons, maybe, but they try and put everyone in their place.'

The Westminster Reporter, published by Westminster City Council, offers advice to local residents about giving money to homeless people. In the statements it makes about what it can offer, everything is hedged with the phrase 'people who are sleeping rough and *willing to engage with our services*' (my italics). That's the rub. Some are unwilling, or unable, to do so.

Ishwari said: 'I tried to engage with DIP, the drug and alcohol place, but it's like they want me to jump through hoops. You have to attend this appointment, you have to attend this group and it's like ... I can barely function and manage to keep an appointment, you know? You're very flexible and I was able to change ... but they're not, and it's like, you've got a problem and they make it even harder. But you need help. You're screaming out for help. And they're saying, Fit through these boxes, and these shapes, and maybe then we'll help you. But it doesn't work like that because each case is unique and needs extra nurturing in its own special way.' She had had no offers of help from anywhere else.

Punitive measures

Sometimes councils, in an effort to reduce rough sleeping, resort to draconian methods, to an extent not far short of cruelty.

In 2007, Operation Poncho, an initiative designed to reduce 'vagrancy', was introduced in the City of London. People were woken early each morning and told to move their belongings so that their sleeping place could be washed down, though apparently all the doorways targeted had been washed already. Disrupting people's sleep, moving them on in the middle of the night, only served to increase their fear and lack of self-confidence; it did nothing to help house them.

Ten years later, in Islington, the town hall was accused of a 'heartless' approach to dealing with homeless people after throwing away mattresses and sofa beds belonging to rough sleepers in Finsbury Park. A local paper reported that an Islington Council rubbish truck, backed up by police officers, cleared the area early in the morning, at a time when many of the homeless community were not around.

Another ploy is the introduction of so-called hostile architecture, most typically associated with 'anti-homeless spikes' – studs embedded in flat surfaces to make sleeping rough uncomfortable and impractical. Other measures include sloped window sills to stop people sitting on them, benches with armrests positioned to stop people lying on them, and water sprinklers that 'intermittently come on but aren't really watering anything'. Most famous was the Camden bench, named after the local authority that originally commissioned the sculpted grey concrete seats found on London streets. The bench's graffiti-resistant sloping surface is designed to deter both sleeping and skateboarding.

For a few months at the end of 2019, a group of seven or eight homeless Roma people formed an encampment near the Angel Islington station, under the overhang by the bank. It was, said one resident, almost a village, with a sofa, double-layered bedding, chairs, even a coat hanger. But just before Christmas, the encampment was gone, replaced by large metal plant containers nailed into the ground. Sometimes when councils express their concern for homeless people, they speak with a forked tongue.

In *London Labour and the London Poor*, Mayhew criticised the Poor Law Commissioners and masters of workhouses for their lack of sympathy, especially for those who he said were driven to the streets by lack of capacity or opportunity. We might take note.

Church and community

Apart from the big charities commissioned by local authorities, dozens of organisations offer support to rough sleepers. Some, like Go Dharmic, give out hot food. There are a number of hubs of activity, where homeless people know they can access help. St Giles Church in Covent Garden is one. The Simon Community provides a weekly street café outside the church every Saturday and Sunday. On Saturdays the mobile library from Quaker Homeless Action visits St Giles to offer its lending service to people who would otherwise not have access to books. Street Storage provides a facility allowing homeless people to store their possessions, which might otherwise be at risk of theft. Green Fields provides haircuts and advice on wellbeing. Alcoholics Anonymous and Narcotics Anonymous hold various meetings at St Giles every week.

While everyone would agree that the ideal is to help people off the streets and into safer surroundings, some organisations will offer unconditional assistance to those who find it hard to engage with public services, or who are in need of immediate help – in a way usually criticised by government services as 'encouraging a dependency culture'. 'Sticking plaster' it may be, but in compassion, in recognition of our shared humanity, sometimes sticking plaster is what is required.

For many years the focus of much charity and community work has been the Christmas period, when the contrast between consumer frenzy and the plight of rough sleepers is particularly acute. It is still a time when most shelters open, when thousands of people volunteer to help, often the first time they have engaged with homeless people. The biggest, Crisis, runs six centres across London, providing hot food and drinks, advice, support and bed spaces where available. There are specialist centres for vulnerable women and those with high dependency needs, and one centre that accommodates dogs. All their residential centres are accessed by referral only.

Some rough sleepers refuse to go to a shelter. *Big Issue* vendor

Darren won't go inside. When I asked him what he was doing for Christmas, his response was: 'Standing here.'

'Why don't you go to a shelter, get warm?'

'They're full of homeless people.'

'There's a small one at the American Church [on Tottenham Court Road]; you can just drop in, get a meal.'

'I don't need food. I live off sandwiches.'

Race feels much the same: 'When you go to sleep, it's a very private thing. It's got to be someone you know, not with strangers. I couldn't sleep with strangers. Tried it at Crisis at Christmas, half of them snored and the other half talked in their sleep. It doesn't work for me. I like being on me own. Or in the woods with the squirrels and the foxes.' He laughs.

But for many the shelters are a lifeline at one of the hardest times of the year. Quaker Homeless Action, a much smaller, more intimate affair than the Crisis shelters, has an open access, self-referral policy. Feedback from some of the guests in 2019 gave a snapshot of those who come: some now have housing but feel isolated and don't like being alone at Christmas; some are sofa-surfing or staying with a friend; some have just been made homeless or have been homeless for years; others live on and off the streets.

When asked why they like coming, the responses included enjoying the warmth of the welcome, the food and the non-judgemental attitude of the volunteers. Others mention more practical matters, such as seeing the social worker or getting a haircut. In the words of one man: 'We've had a beautiful Christmas we will always treasure and remember. Peace, harmony and friendship. And I have had my teeth sorted and can kiss my woman again!'

Ruby is in her eighties, very slender, with a deceptively fragile air. She spoke of her ten years of volunteering, serving food, friendship, making people feel they matter. 'At night some sleep, some read or play cards. Some, who are used to being restive, walk about.

'Their gratitude, it breaks my heart every time,' she says. 'I am reminded of the slippery slope that is there for all of us. It puts things in perspective.' When a new volunteer asked her if she had ever felt scared, Ruby's response was: 'Never, never have I felt threatened; this is a fraternity which will surround you protectively if you feel threatened.'

Increasingly, both Crisis and church groups, recognising that the need extends far beyond Christmas week, have extended the opening of their shelters. Every London borough except the City now has a coordinated church and community shelter project. Each runs for between three and six months, operating from usually a minimum of seven different churches, each doing one night of the week. Housing Justice, an umbrella organisation for church-based homelessness organisations, provides training and other support, including accessing and distributing funding.

A period under cover provides an opportunity to help rough sleepers move on. The Islington Churches Cold Weather Shelter, for example, reported that in 2019 they helped 76 per cent of their guests to move into alternative accommodation.

Resettlement

As we saw from the QHA feedback above, resettlement doesn't always work. People get used to being outside, and they miss the community that they have had around them. Considerable support needs to be a part of any housing initiative. Maureen Crane's survey of older homeless people found that just over half of the respondents who had been resettled became homeless again because they could not cope inside. Others stayed on the streets all night although they had accommodation. Irish beggar Mo told us in his interview: 'I've had about three flats, it was just being inside, I couldn't handle it. I just wanted to get out of it.'

A police officer told us a story:

'There was a girl at Waterloo. The local council got her a flat and it was outside of London, I think it was down near Dartford or somewhere like that. That took her away from her friends who she used to hang out with at Waterloo on the street. She gave up the flat, she came back to Waterloo, got back on the streets again.

I said to her, "What are you doing?" And she explained to me, "I miss my friends, I've got no purpose in life, I was just really lonely." She said, "I actually felt worse being in that flat even though it was nice and warm and clean and everything, it was just not for me."

'I had a chat with her, one night she was really upset, and I said, "Where are your family?" She said, "They're from Brighton." I said, "When was the last time you went to see them?" "Oh, I've not seen them in years." "You keep in touch?" "Yeah, we just speak on the telephone." I said, "Why don't you go to Brighton and visit your family?" She goes, "I can't afford it." So I got her a travel warrant to go to Brighton to see her family and she did. And she never returned. She must have stayed there.' Thanks to his compassionate intervention.

A new model?

Massive efforts have been made over the years, both by commissioned services and church and independent groups, to make inroads into the curse of street homelessness – and yet the figures rise. As we have seen, it will take fundamental societal change – in social housing and a better monitored private rental sector – to make that happen, but maybe it can be helped by a different approach.

Groundswell, an innovative organisation based in Brixton, has changed the way in which homelessness services are delivered by using people with lived experience of homelessness to design and deliver those services. Peer advocates, peer researchers and peer journalists are the engine of an organisation that prides itself on turning the shame felt by people who have been homeless into empowerment. Other organisations are now looking to Groundswell to inform and help design their own peer-led projects. As we will see, it seems to be a mutually advantageous role.

All things considered, therefore, we cannot be very far from the truth, if we assume that the sums voluntarily subscribed towards the relief of the poor equal ... the vast sum of fifteen million pounds per annum in mitigating the miseries of their less fortunate brethren.

But though we give altogether fifteen million pounds a year to alleviate the distress of those who want or suffer, we must remember that this vast sum expresses not only the liberal extent of our sympathy, but likewise the fearful amount of want and suffering, of excess and luxury, that there must be in the land, if the poorer classes require fifteen millions to be added in charity every year to their aggregate income, in order to relieve their pains and privations, and the richer can afford to have the same immense sum taken from theirs, and yet scarcely feel the loss, it shows at once how much the one class must possess and the other want.

20

Commemorating those who die homeless

Dead, your Majesty, Dead, my lords and
gentlemen ... Dead, men and women, born with
heavenly compassion in your hearts. And dying
thus around us every day.

Charles Dickens, *Bleak House*

Each November during Remembrance Week a commemoration service is held at St Martin-in-the-Fields for all who have died homeless in the capital. People with past, or in some cases current, experience of homelessness come together for the service with staff and volunteers from all the many organisations, large and small, funded and voluntary, that make up London's homelessness 'sector': hostels, day centres, outreach and health services, church and community groups.

The heart of the service is always, profoundly and movingly, the reading out of the list of names of all those who have died in the previous year. In the weeks before the service, London's homelessness organisations provide the names of all who are known to have died in the past year. They include not only those who died homeless on the streets, but also many who were in some form of accommodation but still reliant on homelessness services for various reasons.

Between 120 and 150 names are read out every year. In

November 2019 just over 130 names were given to the organisers, perhaps because fewer people had died, but this seems unlikely as there are more people sleeping on the streets than at any time since 1992 when the Rough Sleepers Initiative was set up.

The service is organised by a small team from St Martin-in-the-Fields church, The Connection at St Martin's day centre and the national ecumenical charity Housing Justice, as well as musicians and an artist who was himself formerly homeless.

The service is always led by a minister from St Martin-in-the-Fields; since 2008 this has been the Reverend Richard Carter, who has led the development of a number of initiatives to support homeless people, including the Sunday international group in the day centre, serving the needs of people with no recourse to public funds. Vergers from the church and staff from The Connection also take part in the planning and organising of the service, as well as the reading out of the names.

Since the borough of Westminster, where it is located, has the highest concentration of rough sleepers in England and Wales, St Martin-in-the-Fields is the natural church to host the service. The church has been supporting people who are homeless and vulnerable since the First World War, when the then vicar, the Revd Dick Sheppard, opened its crypt space to soldiers travelling to the trenches from Charing Cross station. The church continued to open its doors to those returning from the fields of battle, many shell-shocked and broken in body and mind. Those who served in the First World War and struggled to reintegrate into society became the 'tramps' of the 1920s and 1930s of whom George Orwell wrote in *Down and Out in Paris and London.*

The 2019 service on Thursday 14 November had as its theme 'Lord you search me out and know me'. The centrepiece at the altar was a cross with a sleeping bag nailed to it. Also placed around the altar were items or artefacts representing homelessness, recognisable to anyone living in London: an old suitcase, sleeping bags, newspapers and tents, one of which belonged to one of the people we were remembering in the service, 'Sparky' Anthony Borrett.

As well as the reading out of names, the service includes uplifting performances from two choirs which work with homeless and formerly homeless people. In 2019, The Choir With No Name sang 'This Is Me' from the West End production *The Greatest Showman*, and Streetwise Opera performed a piece created by the performers called 'The Journey', inspired by the Philip Glass opera *Orphee*. In 2018, the composer Gavin Bryars and his ensemble took part, leading the church in a moving performance of his piece 'Jesus' Blood Never Failed Me Yet', itself based on a 1970s recording of a homeless man singing this now forgotten hymn during the making of a film about the tent city in the Waterloo Bullring, where the IMAX cinema now stands.

Although the number of homeless deaths has over recent years received more media attention, it remains high. Street counts of rough sleepers suggest that on any one night there are almost five thousand people sleeping rough in England; Crisis estimates that the true number is closer to eight thousand.

Pam Orchard, Chief Executive of The Connection, said in an article in 2019:

> It's incredibly important that we take time to remember and honour those who have died on the streets and this service provides the opportunity to do that. It is appalling that homeless people die in today's Britain. Having a safe and secure home is a basic human need, and yet it is something that far too many people are going without.
>
> The service acts as a reminder of the scale of the work that must still be done to ensure that all homeless people are supported on their journey towards recovery. However, it is also hugely uplifting, as it brings together people who have been homeless, or are still homeless, with those who support homeless people in a celebration of life, and reminds us what we are capable of achieving if we all work together.

21

Sex work

The treatment of the subject of prostitution in *London Labour and the London Poor* is problematic. Partly this is because of the Victorian tendency to call any woman having sex outside marriage a 'prostitute', but it's also because not all those parts of the book were written by Mayhew, and they have a different, somewhat moralising tone. Even the statistics are unreliable. In one essay, Bracebridge Hemyng mentions the difficulty of getting accurate figures. 'While the Bishop of Exeter asserted the number of prostitutes in London to be 80,000, the city police stated . . . that it did not exceed 7000 to 8000'. Prostitutes at the time were, for the most part, street walkers or housed in brothels, 'houses of ill repute'.

Both of these were still apparent in London within living memory, particularly in Soho, an area renowned for sex work since its first brothel opened in the eighteenth century. Even in the 1970s, women could be seen hovering in doorways. There followed a phase when sex workers advertised their wares in phone boxes, but now most of the phone boxes have gone and trade is largely conducted through word of mouth and the internet. Prostitution itself is legal in the UK, but a number of related activities, including soliciting in a public place, or owning or managing a brothel, are not.

There is a wide spectrum of reasons for going into sex work, and attitudes to it. For some it is an activity of choice – a way to make a living in hard times; for others it's a hated activity at times of desperation; and some are forced into it, often by traffickers.

In 2018, the *Evening Standard* on 17 April reported an interview with a sex worker who said: 'I only do this kind of work because I choose to.' She operates out of a brothel in a two-bedroom flat in central London. Its owner, a former detective, told the BBC's Victoria Derbyshire programme that 'police are choosing to allow some brothels to operate if they offer a safe environment for their workers'. Louise, who has a diploma in marine biology, said she wants to challenge the stigma around sex work. 'I don't want people to think I'm on drugs or that I've been forced or coerced or trafficked. I'm just here as a normal person who wants to make money, secure a future for myself and do this kind of work because I choose to.'

Not all women working in this field have control over their lives; those working with pimps are often abused, and most of the people we talked to felt pressurised into sex work by others or by circumstances. One, however, did for many years make a good living out of more criminal aspects of the work.

'I became homeless at about sixteen, after leaving Germany. My dad was in the army and there was a family breakdown, so I left and I came to England at sixteen and a half. I stayed with my sister initially, but she couldn't look after me so I ended up on the street.

'I made loads of friends, obviously, out on the street as a young girl. And I ended up clipping, which was getting money out of gentlemen who were looking for a good time. I'd hang around in doorways and ask, "Oi, are you looking for a girl or a good time or something?" Yep, cool, I'd take the deposit off them, of like thirty quid or something, and run round the corner. And I'd say ring that bell and obviously it wasn't the right address and there was no one there. I made a living out of that and it was a very good one. At least ten a day, ten in an evening, so that was like at least three hundred quid a day, and that was a lot of money in those days.

'It did come back on us. I did get a few who would come and look for us. And we used to run off. We got chased by police a lot, obviously. They were always on the lookout for us. And we used to get arrested but we'd only get charged with loitering.' Of course no one wanted to press charges. 'So instead I ended up with about twenty-three convictions for loitering, for being on the street and doing naughty stuff. They'd charge you for loitering and they were quite heavy fines, between thirty and fifty quid.'

'Were you scared?'

'I was, but not for very long. You had to grow up pretty quick out there, and there was lots of us. There was a group of us, five or six, and we used to squat as well. We weren't always on the street. We ended up squatting together in all different squats and we ended up moving around together quite a lot. That was our way of surviving.'

'Did you see the people you were scamming as fair game, the people you were ripping off?'

'Oh yeah. They were very gullible, but then I progressed. We actually knew where all the working girls were and I ended up being a maid. I answered the phones and I got paid for that, and I got a commission for all the customers that came in if I talked to them on the phone properly and dragged them all in. That was on a percentage basis. That was in Soho I done that. I done that for quite a few years. The takings at the end of the day, we used to get a percentage, twenty per cent or ten per cent, it depends on the take home.'

'Did you get to know the customers that came in there as well?'

'No, 'cause it was just like quickies. Five or ten minutes in and out. It was like a conveyor belt. Very busy. A majority of them were walk-ins, not tourists but regulars that came back, but I didn't really get a chance to talk to them. No one did. Not even the girl did 'cause it was set on a timer. Wham bam thank you ma'am.

'I did that, got a bit of money, I went on holiday to Jamaica but unfortunately I came back with tons of weed and got caught. I was just under nineteen.'

Dena ended up going to borstal, then spent several years in prison for drug running, where she became addicted to crack cocaine. She was nearly forty when she came out and her daughter nearly eight.

'I got into running brothels. Initially in Chancery Lane. I got into that from being in that industry all those years. You just know these people. It started with the clipping and I ended up being a card girl. I was putting the cards out for other brothels in the phone boxes. It was a lot of money and I started thinking I may as well run some. So I opened up a few while I was doing that but then it was easy money. I would always have one girl in a flat, I would never have more than one, so I had three flats at one point, with one person in each flat, and then we expanded and went to Crystal Palace and Tooting. We'd have a guy there in each place as security looking after them. And they were busy all day.

'The card thing stopped in 2003; it became illegal. And that's why I had to stop. I would quite happily have continued doing that. It was good money. It was a few hours a day. It was quite a good job. I got arrested for that you see and I didn't want to go down that road again.'

'Did banning the cards in phone boxes force girls back on to the street?'

'I think so, yeah. Especially people who were addicted to drugs, because they just couldn't keep up with going to a flat and working for someone else. I think that's why so many of them are on the streets when they are on drugs.

'Eventually the internet took over. I never been arrested for running a brothel. I got arrested for putting cards out and when I went to court, he said, "You are quite lucky you are not actually a madam." I said to my solicitor, "Well, I actually am," and he said, "Let's just get you a fine for putting cards up." After I went back the next morning, they had raided my flat, to see who was in there, but I wasn't in there, so I closed it.'

After a health scare, Dena gave up drugs, changed her way of life, and got her daughter back. 'She's a part of the reason for me getting myself sorted and clean. She's had to recover from it all, not just me.'

*

For many homeless women, especially those with a drug habit to feed, there are few choices: begging, shoplifting – or, usually as a last resort, prostitution. Women begging on the tube will sometimes make an offer, seemingly as a joke, but with the force of desperation behind it: 'If you want a blow job ... '

Ishwari, whose shoplifting exploits we heard about earlier, was quite nervous, and laughed a lot at different points during the interview.

'Begging is something that ... it scares me sometimes because people are like, if I give you something, what are you gonna do for me? It's not so much like I want to or I choose to, in fact I hate it, I hate it so much. But when you're sick and stuff, and you haven't got a choice, you think right, within a certain amount of time, the time is ticking, it's like a ticking time bomb and I'm gonna start feeling the symptoms ... you know what I mean? I've gotta get myself better. And the guy's saying to me, what can you do for me? Really I wanna poke his eyes out and punch him in the face but you know ... There's been times where I've tried to pickpocket and run away and things like that, and it's turned into a physical thing so it's not always as straightforward.

'Minimum is like twenty quid. And that'll be for, like, oral sex. And then sometimes I have got as much as two hundred pounds for an hour or so, so it just depends. But with me it's a psychological thing, I just hate doing it. I won't accept that, in fact I'm in denial, really. So I try and work as much as I can in the hours at the supermarkets' – shoplifting, in other words – 'and it's only, say for example all the shops are closed and I still haven't got enough, and I'm not gonna be better ... then I have to consider it.'

Sometimes she was asked to deliver drugs, which felt like a relief. 'I feel quite grateful that I don't have to sleep with a person, 'cause a lot of the time, being female, that's the other kind of exchange currency. That kind of gets you where you might wanna go.

'Basically, at the moment I'm staying on a sofa in a person's house who has been very kind. He was homeless himself, so he's been through the route of hostels etc. So for once I didn't have to feel I had to compromise being female for a place to stay as an exchange. It's a sofa, it's nothing much, leather sofa, quite comfortable, so here for a little while. Especially now 'cause it's freezing.'

The pressure to get involved in sex work even seeps into the support system. Sara expanded on her experience at the Lambeth Assessment Centre.

'I was only there for about two weeks. It was terrible. The first night I was there I got offered heroin and crack and to work as a prostitute in Stratford. All in one night.

'I think there was me and one other female there. She got kicked out for threatening somebody, a lad with a screwdriver, because he had been harassing her. Because it was just like me and her, let's just say that we had a lot of men around us. We were the only women in the whole place.'

From there Sara was moved to a low-support women's hostel in Clapham, but that did not keep the men out. 'That was six beds, just girls, no staff, but the girl in the room across from me – I was on the top floor up the stairs, I was room one and she was room three – she was not low support. She was working as a prostitute, she was heavily addicted to crack, so there were staff coming in all the time. When there was no staff, there was no one to prevent what was going on so she was getting massively sexually exploited. The whole house was getting used as a crack house.

'She would do things like knock on my door at three a.m. for a Rizla. You would try and reason with her when she was off it again and say, could you please not be waking me up at all times of night. So I went through that with her and then I went to rehab, but before I left I spoke to the staff and said, look, this is really, really bad, I'm really concerned. Because it wasn't just that they were exploiting her, there was a lot of violence as well. It was a typical crack house mentality. You know, everyone was cool until the crack went and then you know there would be issues. There was always two or three dudes loitering, hanging around community areas, which meant that none of us women could use it unless you wanted to deal with that.'

For McGinlay the problems began as a child. 'I came out of foster care and lo and behold, Westminster social services, whose care I was under, they decided to put me in the red-light district of Paddington, in Sussex Gardens, as a sixteen-year-old female just finishing secondary school, starting college, starting part-time work, with a £30 [a week] allowance and knowing fully well that I was a victim of child sex abuse.

'Yeah, at sixteen that was a shock to my system. I was targeted by gangs. People were spiking my drink on a regular basis. I was then exposed to further physical and sexual abuse ... Errmm, I fell pregnant and lost the baby.' Again, it was a female hostel, 'but there were girls in there who were involved in activities that were quite risky, and wanted me to get involved in it as well.

'Just for the record, I've never sold my body for money, but I've always been a target for people who've tried to groom me into those kind of activities. And it usually starts out ... look, it's not as if they come up to you and go, hey, I'm a creep and I want you to join my gang. It's usually a group of people who will come across as being your friend and offer you loads of drink and drugs and what have you, usually at someone else's house, like a house party. They can see that you are vulnerable and that you're alone and it's like, we're your friends, it's all right, you can hang out with us. That's how it all starts. And when you don't comply with what they're expecting of you, that's when you get physically targeted, that's when it gets nasty.

'When I was sixteen they tried to get me on to crack, that's how they tried to groom me into sex work and get me on the game. I didn't know what crack was, even when I was taking it. They just said to me, if you're struggling to get to sleep at night, try this.'

A woman working with victims of modern slavery told us: 'We know there is a Romanian gang operating in Victoria and they open squats and then they wait for their fellow Romanian people to arrive from the coaches and they offer a bedroom in exchange for money, for sexual services.'

But victims can be from anywhere.

'We had a case of an American girl who was taken. Her mother had severe mental disabilities and she agreed for this gang to bring the girl here. She came to Europe from the States. Sexual exploitation since she was twelve. She escaped when she was nineteen or something like that. She has lots of physical problems because of being sexually abused. She was drugged from one client to another so she wouldn't move in the car. She's not an addict but she has drugs in her system. Now she's reacting as a child. She's saying, No, I don't want to go there. No, I don't want that accommodation. Once she understood that we were here to protect her, that she felt proper protection, then she would let the child in her get out a little bit more. Very challenging for everybody.'

There are organisations to support women and men caught up in prostitution, including the International Union of Sex Workers, campaigning for the human, civil and labour rights of those who work in the sex industry, and Street Talk for the most vulnerable.

Self-expression, desperation or abuse: the oldest profession in the world.

22

Three stories of drug dealing

The general public tend to stereotype those who deal drugs: they have an image in mind of a ruthless, exploitative man, in it to make money.

Here are three very different stories. The first, perhaps, is nearest to our preconception.

JJ's story

We talk in his car, parked on the side of the road on a crisp sunny morning in Bermondsey. JJ is part of a small criminal syndicate that provides heroin and crack cocaine in small £10 deals to a network of addicts in and around Bermondsey and Rotherhithe in south London. He has been doing this in one form or another for the last twenty years and he makes a lot of money.

It is 7 a.m. and he is just about to start work. He is thirty-three, and from an estate on Brixton Hill.

'What do you do for money?'

'Dark and light.'

'You mean heroin and crack? You sell rocks and H, right?'

'Yeah. There's two of us. My cousin, and we use another guy from round the estate so there are three of us. We do one-one-one [working in a shift rotation]. Each of us covers an area and we work seven a.m. until midnight seven days a week, 365 days a year. We take breaks every now and then and the other two will cover the route. We work hard, we take risks and we earn.' They take it in turns to deliver. 'We each cover a few blocks and we work with a few other firms, swapping customers with Brixton, Camberwell. We cover these ends.'

'In a car?'

'Yeah. We have a guy on a push bike who helps when it's busy and a few spotters for police checks.'

'You don't find this easy to talk about, right?'

'No. It's OK though. Just make sure you delete this. OK? OK?'

'Don't worry. I will. How long have you been doing it?'

'Since twelve, thirteen, but I used to help my uncle. Run for him back then. After 2000. He was big then but ... He's passed now. Let's leave it at that.'

'Have you been caught?'

'Yeah.'

'What happened? Have you been to prison?'

'Twice. One year then three.'

'So why do you keep doing it?'

'Money, man, the paper. It's always the paper.'

'Do you want to do something else?'

'No. Like what?'

'So you like it? The life?'

'For real. Always.'

'Do you make a lot of money?'

'Yeah.'

'How much, a week say?'

'*Me* ... you sure you gonna ... you know ... emm, twenty' – he means £20,000 – 'a week after cost. We have three girls wrapping for us. They do that for this.' He gets out a black camera case and holds up a rock of crack cocaine – he has about forty of them on him.

'That's white, yeah?'

'Yep, the females love this shit more than us. It's easy getting people to work for you but you gotta be careful. Only use people you know for time. They know you and they know if they fuck you they get theirs.'

'So you have to scare people, yeah?'

'If people think that they can just rob you and nothing happen then it would happen every day. It has happened, but people know not to mess.'

'Have you ever been robbed?'

'Yeah, but not for a time now. People see you making all this and they want it. The last time they took the phone and tried to steal the business. They called everyone and were serving to them for a few days before it got sorted. We waited for them and beat them. You have to make a lesson of it or it will happen again and again. It's a lot and people want it. They will try and get the police on you so you have to think about it always. I think more about the thieves than the police – that's where the trouble will come from.'

'Does it make you feel guilty? Like some people would say that you are hurting them?'

'Who we hurting? People want it and we give them what they want. It's a business. We take the risk and we get the paper. What about the bar ... they do alcohol there and nobody say anything about it. It's against the laws but how is that wrong? It is a jungle on the streets and people don't know it, how can they talk about it like they know it when they don't know shit? You take risk, you get the reward, that's all.'

'Look, it's not me saying this. I'm asking you if you feel bad because some people think it's wrong to sell drugs.'

'That's their problem.'

'You mean they hurt themselves. It's their choice and you give them what they want.'

'We all doing what we need to be doing.'

'How would you feel if your kid got on to heroin?'

'He's six.'

'But later, if he did?'

'He wouldn't.'

'OK. Have you ever tried it?'

'Light, yep, but not the dark. It's a mug's game. It stops you doing stuff. You can't even be a man with that.'

'But do you like the life or do you just do it for money?'

'It's always about the money. I work for this. You can get jail or you can get robbed. I don't want that. I want the money.'

'But what about the excitement? You see that in the movies, you know, the outlaw life?'

'That's for kids. I'm no youth. I'm not fearful of shit now. I want the money. Simple.'

'So how does it work, how would I go about getting things from you?'

'You call the number and I come.'

'Soon come, right?' 'Soon come' is a common expression used by street dealers – it nearly always means that it will be a little bit longer than usual.

'We will come near your ends. We do .2 10s on the b [heroin], and the white [crack cocaine] depends. I come quick. Some of these fools look bait. If someone see the same man over and over waiting they might make a call, so we try to be stealth.'

It's now 7 a.m. and the start of his day. As he's speaking, he turns the phone on and it immediately begins to ring. As soon as that call ends, the phone rings again. He drives towards my house but pulls over after two hundred yards and someone jumps into the back seat. He sorts the guy out with two bags of heroin and two of crack and the passenger hands over £40. A few minutes later we pull up near my place. As I jump out of the car, another customer jumps in.

Ducking and diving: K

In many ways the world we live in is more tolerant and accepting than it was thirty years ago. Laws have been passed that have out-lawed racial discrimination, while same-sex relationships have been decriminalised and hate crimes outlawed. In 2004 the minicab industry was regulated, making it safer for women to take cabs late at night. It's made this country safer and created a more positive professional and social environment for women and minorities. But for some there is a downside.

It's harder now for people at the edge to earn a buck and survive. For someone who is used to surviving in the informal economy, things have become increasingly difficult.

K is now living in a pretty broken-down house. His first priority is to sort himself out with a hit so he can function. I give him the money for the interview beforehand so that he can do that. I go with him to an alley behind the house and we wait for five minutes until a guy pulls up on his bike and dumps a couple of wraps in his hand. We make the short walk back to his house, collars up against the driving cold, and I watch while he goes through that ritual of getting out the foil and running the gear into dirty brown strips. K smokes heroin now as his veins have collapsed. Once that's sorted, we get the interview under way.

K's history is a long and involved relationship with the streets of London. He's been a dedicated squatter at the heart of the squatting community. He's a very good DJ, known for playing funky techno. He's hosted pop-up raves in squats, sold drugs at them and on the streets. He's shoplifted, begged and driven illegal cabs. In 2014 he got away from dealing on the streets by starting to sell drugs online through the now infamous Silk Road, the open online marketplace on the dark web.

K is someone who lives on his wits, surviving outside the system by trading on and around the streets. People like him are invisible to most of Britain, and when they are reported on they are vilified for selling drugs (poisoning kids), squatting buildings (invading someone's space) or driving illegal cabs (raping women). The truth is not so binary. K is a character and while he takes no shit, he's warm and engaging. He's very intelligent but also has that highly developed social acumen that comes from having to work with people, ducking and diving to survive.

K is fifty-eight and from Preston. He arrived in London in 1984. 'I came down here to do a music degree. I play saxophone. I was a trumpet player but it was too hard.

'I was into squat parties, I was doing all right DJing. Find an empty building, put a rig in there, fill it full of people and kick it.

I was part of various different crews. I won't mention names 'cause I really don't want this coming back to me. We were pioneers. Making it up as we went along. We made that scene and it changed this country. I was squatting places to live as well.' He talks fondly about the last place he squatted in Finsbury Park. 'Eight years ago I got given that flat around the corner. Squatting you can't really do now unless you're doing industrial units, which you're only getting a few weeks in, so there's no point in doing them really. I used to love doing the parties. They were proper fun. Meeting people, making connections and getting off your face – that's always good, innit!

'Look, if I've got something I want to do, I will do it. From when I was doing dark web. It was a little idea at first but it could have been a multi-million-pound business if I'd been able to save a bit of money. Simple fact of life. Bitcoin was £29 a bitcoin.' (It went higher than £20,000 per bitcoin at one point.) 'I did fifty-one pages of trades on my local bitcoin, fifty on each page, so I've done 2500 trades in bitcoin over two years. That's a fuck of a lot of money. I was doing it from 2013, 2014 until earlier this year.

'It was a great thing that, because it took my dealing off the street. Everything was undercover. My main delivery system was the British mail and I used to send stuff all over the world. I sent 2500 parcels and I had one pinched in Helsinki and that was it. It all worked as a feedback system, which was on the dark web and the feedback was about the quality obviously and how quick you sent 'em and how good you were at messaging these people [the customers] and keeping in contact with 'em. I did all right. I could have done a lot better but having a habit makes it difficult because you've got to draw money out every day. If I could have supported my habit then by carrying on street dealing I'd have been a multi-million-pound business. I want to get back on the bitcoin thing but my teeth are a mess and I have to sort them out. But I've got people who want to put money into it. People would pay me to be going down and teaching 'em how to do this.

'But while people talk about the evil of the dark web and Silk

Road, they don't see the other side of it. The fact that it gets people off the street so when they go to buy drugs they are not put in danger. The drugs just drop through the mailbox. And the bullshit of people ordering assassinations up on it – that's not true. It was just a way of the FBI getting the backing to take it down.'

'So when you were working on the bikes, describe what your typical day looked like?'

'Get up, sort meself out' – have a hit so he could function for the day – 'then wait for the phone to ring. Then just ride around dropping the shit off. We had about ten customers for white and brown a day. That was enough to cover me and him, to keep us in gear. That was around Finsbury Park and Manor House. The customers were low-level junkies, shoplifters, people who used to live hand to mouth. Get their twenty or thirty quid together, give us a ring and we were doing the best deals at the time. If you're doing the best deals you're gonna get the custom. And you only need ten customers 'cause they spend every penny they get with you. They'd offer us all sorts for gear as well. Meat, all sorts, everything.

'Look, it weren't for money at that point. Any money I got I gave to Ted and he would cover me. It wasn't a great way to do it. It's stressful. You've got people wanting to take the things off you. I've been dealing on and off for thirty years, but actual robberies I've been robbed four times. The one that happened in Brixton – I'd lined up a deal for some skunk. It was half a key – three and a half grand, something like that. I've done work with these people before as well, they've gone dodgy since, so I've taken half a key down and next thing we're being pepper sprayed from here and there. I was fighting to keep hold of it and I was doing all right.' He thought one of the others had gone off 'to get some backup but he'd just run off to wash the pepper spray out of his eyes. So he just left me to it. And that came back on me. He blamed it on me and tarred me name.'

'Do you find that to be a problem when you do gear? You know, that people don't trust you?'

'Yeah, straight away, people think you're dodgy and if anything goes wrong, you're the first person they blame.'

'So how did you deal with the Old Bill, because you had a profile with them, didn't you?'

'When things were good I was doing everything. Hash, weed, brown, white. Basically they knew me and Stu [one of his colleagues], and he put it on top for me – you know what I mean – and then they had me marked, and every time they used to see me, two of them used to jump on me. And then one time I had a fight with one of the coppers and he tried to nick me for theft by finding a bag of gear – which is personal. They knew I was at it, but they couldn't get me. The secret of street dealing is not to keep punters waiting, 'cause then you get attraction, if they see people waiting they . . . '

'As far as dealing goes, you've been involved in just about every level of it, right?'

'Yeah, big stuff, small stuff and every type of drug there is too. I got into dealing through the party scene and Ecstasy. If you can make money from it and you're good and making money from it then you're going to do it, aren't yer. You're putting on a party and you've got all these punters wanting something, so you're gonna help 'em out. It makes sense, innit. And then it's hard to get out of it. Especially with a habit, because it's easy money at the end of the day. It's hard money, but it's easy money. Hash and weed were my main things. My first nicking was cultivation in 1982. I got community service for that and a fine. This was up north. I was trying to get on my music degree then, but the party scene kicked off. Then it went a bit wonky. It was such a lot of fun. The people I was meeting and the time I was having, I just couldn't do school then – I just couldn't do it.'

He first came across gear in 1994. 'My missus had a habit and I didn't realise. She was pilfering off the top of my hash business – for six months, getting a bag of gear every day. I wasn't into the gear then but obviously she's doing it and it was my missus, and so I thought let's have a go at it. It can't be that bad. Everything started to go downhill. I can't blame her. It's my own fault, really.'

'How many people were you getting at parties?'

'It depends. A couple of hundred sometimes, sometimes five

hundred, and occasionally at King's Cross we got a couple of thousand.'

'When you worked for the guys in Essex, that was a proper professional organisation?'

'Yeah. They headhunted me because they knew I wouldn't stop if the Old Bill pulled us and that would give the lad a chance to get rid of the drugs, you know by plugging them [putting them up your prison pocket]. There was two of us, you see. They headhunted me because I wouldn't dob 'em in. It was a cash job. They used to pay for our hotel and it was a hundred and twenty quid a day but it was for twelve hours. Shit money really because of the risk you're taking and you're driving around for twelve hours.

'So I was getting me drugs. I'd get like an eighth and that would last me three or four days, go out driving, so the money I was earning from that, six or seven days a week, was going in my pocket. Hotel was paid for, food was paid for, cheap drugs and cash in hand. They knew I was using but they still trusted me. You see, that thing of people trusting junkies or not, it's about what walk of life people are coming from.

'It was a professional set-up. I met them in north London but they had a set-up that ran in about ten towns. Rented cars, hotels. I knew the top man, a local north London firm. I was taking 3k for them a day and I was one of ten so they were taking 30–40k a day. About half of that or more was profit so they were pocketing 15–20k a day at least. That's a couple of guys. And they're bulletproof.

'We got nicked once driving for them but I got my solicitor on it and it got kicked out. I was working with this real idiot and they found the drugs on him and that's it: all hell breaks loose. I was the one driving the car, so I said I was just giving him a lift. He had about thirty bags on him. I used to check online to see where all the cameras were, so I used to weave about on my route. I used to meet people on the street and they'd just jump in the car and score, and I'd drop them off round the corner. I did several places. I'd had enough of the hours, and to tell you the truth doing that job gave me a kick-start again. Just before I started doing that I got robbed for a key of MD [Ecstasy] that was for £7800 – someone's turned up with guns, put a gun in my neck and one in my mate's gear. If it'd been me on my own, I'd have said fuck off, but there were two of my mates there so I just let them take it.'

'The police round here had a real problem with you. Why was that?'

'They had a hard-on for me for ages. Robocop, especially. The first time I've gone out of Tottenham into Finsbury Park in a car. As soon as we got to Islington we got pulled over. One of them was my last nicking in Islington. I was trying to keep my head down when he shouts out my name, "It's K, innit." I was oh . . . for fuck's sake. He was like, we've been looking for you. And that's the first time I've been into Islington in six years. It's shit because at the end of the day I'm not a high-profile criminal. All I'm trying to do is get by and I'm not harming anyone. They've got a job to do, I suppose, but fuck it.

'I'm open about my habit. I do it and I pay for it. But it's horrible having to lie about it or try and cover it up. People do force you to lie about it and then tell you off for doing that. It's fucking annoying. People ask why you're hiding it, but some people when you tell them will stop working with me, and that's happened to me a lot. Look, I've never robbed anyone, it's just not me.'

'Maybe we were decoys'

As we heard earlier, Dena was involved in the sex trade. She also got caught up in the drug business. 'We went on holiday and there was four of us. We had a couple of villas between us. We were told that we were only bringing a bit back and we thought, why not? That was someone we met in London who set it up. We were quite gullible, obviously.

'So we went on holiday for a month, all paid for by them. We went out the night before we were coming back. We packed our suit-cases, or so we thought, and we came back drunk and everything and next day they dropped us off at the airport with our suitcases and when we got to London we got caught. We got stopped at the airport, all of us, and when they opened our suitcases, there was nothing in there but weed. So we ended up with eighty-four kilos of weed between four of us. It wasn't even hidden. But as we were getting caught, another person we were on holiday with who was flying through and somebody shouted, "What about her?" So they caught her as well. So I think that maybe we were decoys in that one.'

'Could you explain what a decoy is?'

'A decoy is where you are set up to be caught so they don't take notice of the other person, they just casually walk past as you are getting arrested. It's easily done and they probably have a suitcase full of cocaine that is worth a hell of a lot more. I gather that is what happened.'

'And what happened to you as a result of that?'

'I ended up getting borstal, because the law had changed. It wasn't six months to two years, I think it was up to three years, and because I was nearly nineteen I ended up doing nearly two years in borstal for that. I felt bloody stupid really. I thought, how the fuck can that happen? But I was pretty young and you don't have any conception of consequences at that age. You get greedy, and I'd rather not go into this but I did it again. I got caught a second time later on.

'I did a number of runs and it was quite easy money. That was for someone I knew, when I was homeless. 'Cause obviously when I done borstal I came out and I was homeless again. I struggled, as you do . . . my daughter was three, I was on the street and I needed the money. I could never get work because of my record, it was impossible. So I said, why not?

'So I done the trip and I thought I was on my own. I thought, this is great, yer know, I'm not going to get caught. It was to Jamaica again. But obviously someone else had bought the ticket and when I went to pick up the drugs, it was in a plastic bag, it wasn't even wrapped up. and I thought, oh my God. I had to take it on my own all the way through Jamaica and pack it myself to bring back to England and I had to leave some because there was too much. There was about one and a half kilos of cocaine. So I ended up taking just over one and I had to phone someone else I knew and say, "You're gonna have to take the rest because there is no way I can do it." So stupidly I started panicking and thinking there is no way I should be doing this, but I still went ahead and done it. I knew I was going to get caught, but I still went ahead and done it. It was just autopilot, it's just crazy. So I got caught and they got caught, and the person who bought my ticket got caught. Everyone got roped in and everyone got sentenced. And I got seven years.'

'How was the cocaine hidden?'

'It was in my corset. I was on my own. I had to do it all myself. I was strapping myself up, it was awful. It was horrible when I got caught. They were expecting me to have weed and they were very surprised to find me with cocaine. In other words, they probably had me marked already. I got seven years and I did four years eleven months. It's quite a lot really. I didn't get parole or anything.

'When I came out I got my daughter straight away and I went to see the MP because I had nowhere to live and I refused to leave the office until they housed me. I said I haven't got anywhere to go and my daughter's in care and it was a few days before Christmas and I wasn't going to allow them to keep my daughter, so I ended up getting a place. On that day social services stuck me in a flat in Tooting, and after Christmas I got offered a flat in Balham that the MP had obviously sorted out, so it was really good. The problem was, though, I had come out of prison as an addict, 'cause I started taking crack cocaine when I was in prison and that's where I got a habit. That's where I got a feel for it. I had never tried it before. Because I was struggling, I was gradually doing that every day. And that's where my addiction started. It took me quite a lot of years to get back to reality, really, I was bang on it for seven years every single day.'

'And was that the end of your criminal enterprises? Have you still got any contacts you are still in touch with from that world?'

'No. No. None whatsoever.'

'And do you see that as part of your recovery, staying away from those sorts of people?'

'Yes, definitely. Earning that sort of money wasn't doing me any good, was it? 'Cause it was easy come, easy go. I was spending it on whatever I wanted. Not only that, I just stopped taking stuff. I thought, that is it now. I'm going to give up the flat, I'm going to give everything up and I'm not going to do anything else. And then I woke up with a wonky face. That was 4 December 2002 actually, and I went straight to the hospital and they said, "OMG, we think you've got Bell's palsy," but then my arm went and I couldn't move and they said, "OMG, we think you're having a stroke." So I've probably had a mini-stroke and it's probably taken about ten years for all my nerves in my face to come back. So that on its own has probably stopped me taking anything because it scared me.'

'So when did you get your daughter back full time from care?'

'The day I came out of prison, I got her back. I went to the foster carer and I took her back. They couldn't say anything.'

For organised crime, the illicit drug trade has replaced armed robbery as the main source of cash flow. These interviews demonstrate the way that drugs shape a part of what goes on on our streets and the hold that drugs currently have over people, from dealers to users. They may also shine a bit of light on why people end up selling them and why they end up taking them.

V

My Time

23

Coming through

Trafalgar Square is a good place to sit, especially on the first warm day of spring. While tourists mill about the square, others sit on the perimeter walls and open up more readily than usual. Two men, unsolicited, told me their life stories. One made little sense, talking of how Johnny Depp had stolen his pirate ideas. But the other told me in a broad Scots accent he had been homeless, a *Big Issue* seller for a couple of years, but that he now had a job. The *Big Issue* had put him back on his feet. He was now attending a course on politics and current affairs and was hoping to take up politics: a councillor to begin with, then maybe an MP. So good to hear hope.

Stoicism and resilience were the keynotes of many of the stories we heard from people who'd gone through appalling experiences or were even now living in the most difficult conditions. Most had had dreams, as children or when leaving school. 'Ideally, in another world, I'd like to be a movie actor, but unfortunately that's probably never going to work. So I just have to hand out leaflets. No, that's just a dream I have.'

A casual labourer in his twenties scoffed at the very idea: 'Dreams? No, I'm not that way ... I've never really been one with many dreams. I mean when I was little, I wanted to play for England but that career certainly isn't going to happen!' He was not the only one to mention football – and one nearly made it. Dave, a trader in his fifties, recalled his early ambitions: 'I was going to be a footballer. But unfortunately I broke my leg in two places, and I didn't get a contract. My dad had a big contract with the oil firm, and I just went on to work for 'im. But, yeah, I was quite a good footballer. Till about sixteen, seventeen, when I snapped me leg. That put an end to that all them years ago.'

Food sellers talked of plans to expand their businesses; buskers of their ambitions. Sebastian, the Argentinian busker, said: 'In the future I would like to see myself doing shows, having the idea of putting projects together with my own music. I would like to do more of that and less of this. I like this but something that I don't like about it is that a lot of people ruin your set on purpose ... You've been waiting there for four hours and then some selfish person that's really angry with everything, it kind of gets to you after a while, you know.' He laughs.

Eric, who has been fundraising for years, told me rapidly, in a Scots accent, about his experiences and of his plans for the future.

'I've been homeless. Quite a few times, it's quite a strange one, actually. About two years ago now I was living in a hostel in Peckham. I was having a lot of mental health problems over the years. I was working at the time, depression came back, and so I had to take some time off, and that cost me my job, and that in turn cost me the roof over my head. I had to declare myself as homeless. I was offered a place in a hostel. I was in there for about six months, I er came back to work ... '

'You found it easy to get a job? It can be quite hard from that position.'

'It can be. But I mean, this is the thing with fundraising. It can be a difficult job, a lot of people drop out of it. But for good fundraisers, which I consider myself to be, because I've been doing it so long, you can get a job anywhere in the country. I started working in 2018 and I've been back at work ever since, really, so it's very valuable for me. But *now*, I've done some training with people who are vulnerable in a hostel, and hopefully in the New Year, I'm going to become a support worker. Working *in* a homeless hostel, so giving a little bit back.'

A newly homeless man kept up his optimism: 'You know what, at the end of the day, I'm a grown man. You've got to get up. No point moaning about the past, you've got to think of the future now. And the future's bright, the future's orange.' We both laughed. As I gave him the donation, 'That's made my day. I'll have a really good meal with that.'

And for some people the future is bright. They have come through, have emerged into a better world. Even if life is still a struggle, it's better. Ben, whom I met at the car boot sale in Kilburn, made it sound simple.

'When I left school, I was a bit of a bad lad, and I didn't really have many ambitions or want to do anything. So I just went from labouring jobs and stuff like that, and factories. I was a bit in with a bad crowd, did a lot of things I wasn't proud of.'

'So what changed?'

'A woman. I met a good woman and I moved to England, and I stopped doing everything that I was doing that was bad. I was twenty-three when I moved here. In Scotland I was a really bad lad, as I say, getting into crime, doing drugs, drinking, stuff like that. Met a good woman, moved to England, to London, and stopped everything. I don't drink any more, I don't touch drugs, I sorted my life out, yeah. That was all for the love of a good woman.' He laughs.

Michael moved from a life of homelessness and drug use to becoming a busker and artist. 'I got this flat in Broadway Market in 2006. Things did go very pear-shaped. I used to be a drug addict. Because I used to work with a guy who was addicted and we just kind of clicked musically and every day I started busking with him and every day it was like, We gotta get twenty quid, man, we gotta score. I was kind of a giro junkie at this point and then the next thing I know I'm doing it every day with this geezer. So I got a habit for a few years and then I ended up in the hostel system.'

'Have you been able to get off that? You're clean now?'

'Yeah, yeah. I use a bit of weed. Last year I was Humpty-Dumpty in November. Now they're having to get strict because I think the government's told them they can't keep giving loads of money to people unless they're on tax credits. If you're getting full benefits you're not allowed to earn money. So it's getting a bit hard for people, which is why I get a lot of gigs when they need some paintings. They can rely on me, 'cos I have to earn money.'

'So are you doing the things that you really love doing then? Your art, your music ... are these your passions? Have they always been part of your life?'

'Well, I didn't think I could even draw a thing until I met this great teacher at Crisis. He took us through baby steps ... you know, this is how you paint, you put the brush in there, then you do that, and then you go on that one ... really like, back to beginnings. And that kind of got me going. 'Cos I would have just made a mess and just thought I'm no good.

'In five years? I'd like to just be doing what I'm doing now but be more successful.' He laughs. 'Well, to be able to sell. I'm not worried about all the nonsense, fame, but just ... maybe be able to completely stop the old benefits. And be independent. I've got two kids in Germany. Which is another reason why ... I don't see them 'cos they're in Germany but I would like to create a legacy of some sort for them.'

When I met Raymond at Ridley Road Market he was standing, smiling, chatting with a group of black women at a vegetable stall. We went over to a barrow and sat on it and he told me his story in a calm and measured voice.

'I live in Sandringham Road, just across the road from the market. I've been working on and off in the market for, yeah, over ten years. So, what it is, I do voluntary work. I don't really get paid. I do things out of the kindness of my heart. Obviously because I'm on certain benefits, this is my way of contributing to society.' He's had an up-and-down life, quite affluent at one time, could afford to travel. 'Yes, nothing stays the same. I've seen billionaires lose everything, and they're not good. I don't let it get to me. I like talking to people, listening to other people's stories. The difference is my spirit.'

Second time around

In Britain and other Western countries, we live in an age when it is no longer expected that people will continue in one career for the whole of their lives, get a gold watch, retire and drop dead. Many people, living longer, change their lives in middle age or later, and continue in quite another direction. Some are forced into it.

Chris went into dog walking when he was sacked after thirty-eight years as a dental technician – and found his vocation. 'I love dogs passionately. I have a massive, massive passion for dogs.' For Delia, it was a series of accidents in her fifties that changed her life. Giving out free newspapers is how she pays for her law studies.

The most extraordinary transition that I came across was in the career of Ellie, at the Kentish Town fruit and veg stall. I asked her how she had come to do this. 'Because I closed my previous business, and he's a friend of mine, and I used to come past every day and used to help out in the morning, and then came for a couple of hours, that's fifteen years ago now. It wasn't ever intended to be a permanent job.

'I would come early in the morning when he was still setting up and he'd say, "Can you hang on a minute, I've just got to get something out of the van." And then someone would come and just want one banana or whatever, that's quite easy to deal with.' Then, when she was closing her business, 'I would stay longer and longer, and when I said, "I'm closing the office now, I won't be coming back," he said, "Do you want to come and work?"'

'And had you done this kind of thing before?'

'No, no, I was a solicitor. Nothing like this at all. I'd never worked in a shop. That's part of the appeal. Generally, you know, as a Saturday job you worked in a shop. I'd never worked in a shop. One of the attractions, as well, is the lack of responsibility comparatively. You know, getting sued for overcharging someone, that's the worst you can do, really!' She laughed.

'Do you miss your old life?'

'Yes and no. Yes because of the responsibility and the excitement

of it – it can be exciting – and . . . you know, just the human interest of it. On the other hand, I think I'm glad I got out of it when I
did. It is so regimented now. Especially as I was a sole practitioner,
I couldn't do it any more, because you have to do all these things
yourself, like money laundering, consultant compliance. The insurance companies insist that you fill in dozens of checklists now, and
generally the number of regulations, all the courses you have to go
on, and the accounting records . . . I mean you always had them to
an extent, but it's more than doubled. And if you're the only person
doing that, and you don't get paid by clients for doing that directly,
that's why . . . I don't know if you've noticed, but there's hardly any
solicitors left now' – to a customer – '29p.'

Many come to a time in their lives when they feel they need to
fulfil a long-cherished dream, to leave the day job, and even if it
means making financial sacrifices, to express themselves more fully
in what they do. This can be seen as the privilege of the affluent
middle classes, but in fact those making that kind of decision come
from all sorts of backgrounds.

'This is my time'

Rhoda pays £10 a day for her pitch in Lower Marsh Market. 'I do
African-frame linen dresses, hand-made stuff, all I have in my stall
is mostly hand-made stuff. By me and by my sisters. Yeah, so I'm
more designer. I design lots of stuff, and get them to make some
of them. The ideas that come to me, I pass it on to other people as
well, so that it's not just about me, there are other people that are
part of my business.

'It's been a year and seven months I've been here. Before then,
I never used to do fashion. I'm actually a minister. I minister in
song. I'm a believer, I'm a Christian, I'm born again. So I used to
do that. I do my community work, I've been bringing up my two
sons, that are now in university, so this is giving me the opportunity
now to come and really expand my business more. I used to do my
business for friends and family, but now I wanted to reach out for

other people. So here I am in Lower Marsh doing this. And I really enjoy it.'

'Do you make enough money?'

'For my needs, yes. Because now I am over fifty, this is good for me now. My last son has just gone off to university, so I have all the time in the world to do this. I could stay at home and be on benefit. I don't want to be on benefit, I wanna work for my money, so I'm here. So the time come when I've sold enough, I've worked enough, to pay my bills, so I'm good. And I don't have to work all day. I start at nine, and by two thirty, three, I've gone home. Except when we do late nights.

'I am still a minister, yeah, part time.' She laughs. 'Sunday, yes. Saturdays and weekdays I do counselling over the phone. As I said, I finish at two thirty, so most of the time by three o'clock I'm home. So I have time now to deal with other things.

'I've got grandchildren, they fill my day as well, so I make time for everybody. Before, well, my sons took my time, because of all the issues and all that, but now that they're away in university, I'm able to do my thing now, so this is my time. A lot of people say life begins at forty, but I think life begins at fifty because you have a clear mind. I feel that any mistakes I've made, I've made them already, so now that I'm over fifty, I have a clear mind of what I want to do.'

Robin, the dairy stall owner in Berwick Street, is a former art director in an advertising agency. Having been involved in urgent political battles around coffee production and rainforest initiatives, he feels now that trying to save one of the 'beating hearts' of Soho is where he can make a difference. 'I need to feel that I'm doing something. I need to see that it's having an effect. I have done it in the past, throughout all the things I've worked in, but they were all small scale at the time; they are big scale now and there are fifty million people looking after that issue; no one looking after this one. So that's kinda why I chose this street at this time.'

Tashomi busks outside Brixton station. We met at the station, in rush hour in the pouring rain. He took a last couple of puffs from his roll-up before joining me, then we adjourned to Starbucks.

'I'm a full-time musician and decided to quit my day job two and a half years ago and focus solely on music. I've done a lot of things: cake making, youth work, and most recently the day job was IT management, software development, so I was making a handsome buck, doing it nine to five obviously. But music is heart stuff. I was also going through a lot of personal change. I got divorced, left my work, and I had a bit of a crisis. Sax was the only constant in a dark time. Sometimes I'm surprised I'm still here. I've been playing the saxophone for about fifteen years. I've never taken it up as a sort of full-time occupation, so I thought, why not?

'I'm thirty-one. I didn't study music. I had a private teacher for about six months, and pretty much taught myself the rest of the way. The musical ones can hear that I'm not professionally trained. But they seem to like it. I play with a band and will be playing there over the next month. I play for a bar in Soho called Piano Bar and play for a restaurant in Camden. I busk in Bromley and in Brixton and I do weddings and sessions and parties and all that kind of stuff. I come here at about eight a.m. for the early shift and do just soft jazz. Other buskers don't come then. Now that I've stopped smoking weed, I can get up early.

'Enough money? Does one ever make enough money? No, no is the short answer to that question,' he says with a laugh, 'but I've been making more. The more I play, the more I feel doing this, the more I've been increasing how much I make. Anything between two-fifty and four hundred a week.

'Say to a musician, don't give up the day job,' another laugh, 'because it's bloody hard. But I think actually, one of the reasons I quit the day job was love of music. One of the things I didn't appreciate in the nine-to-five grind is the spontaneity of life, and how there's an actual flow of life that you can be a part of if you're available to it. And I think when you're doing nine to five we're not available for life to surprise us. Life becomes too regimented and orchestrated, so much so that your days are already written out for you, whereas being a session musician is being free to explore what I want to do for me. I think I know more what this life thing is all about, just being on this journey. It may not be the easiest financially, but in terms of my way, my spiritual way, my connectivity, with the people and universe around me, music is it in many respects. Yes, it hasn't been great, lucrative, financially, but in terms of what I've learnt and what I've been privy to, I wouldn't go back.

'Deep down, everyone wakes up and thinks, what am I doing here? Really, what's going on? Yes, when you've got a boss who says this is why you're here, it puts you at ease, but it's just an illusion, because when you do that job, you're back to square one, right? I think I really valued the structure because I didn't have to think for myself. And I'd be in a position where you depend on what you're doing, and it's given me a new respect for my capabilities. Without a structure, I had to create my own, I had to really push for it, and it's given me a new respect for sorting my life out.'

Helping others

Many people we spoke to had moved from a life of homelessness, drug use and crime to helping other people make the same transition. After years of drinking, and living in hostels surrounded by addicts, Mark came through. He has been volunteering for some time with the peer organisation Groundswell. He started with homeless health peer advocacy, and said the work has helped him keep clean.

'It's kept me focused. This place is unique in the way that apart from senior management everyone, the project managers and the volunteers and staff and research team, have had some lived experience. We don't employ your average Joe Bloggs and we only really deal with health, which is also unique. I can knock on Stephen's [the CEO of Groundswell] door tomorrow and I won't get that "oh, you've got to talk to your manager" rubbish. From volunteer to project manager you get that togetherness, it's not us and them.'

He has no doubt that the experience of addiction helps with his job. 'Yes, because I can empathise with Joe Bloggs. If their Universal Credit hasn't been paid I can't help them with that, but I can see it for what it is and understand what is going on – what it feels like. You know, I've been through those different life challenges that face people and that's where I will always sit down with 'em and have an advocacy meeting. I want to know them and know what makes them tick.

'Look, before anything else I have to see the humanity first. What's stopping them from getting to their appointment? Is it simply an Oyster card, or is it more? Is it that he doesn't like being in enclosed spaces or he doesn't like busy GP surgeries? If that's the case, I will speak to the doctor and say, look, can we get an appointment in a private room or something we can work with?

'I work across three different projects. One day of the week I'm at King's College in Camberwell, I work with the homeless team, so if you're being admitted to hospital and you're sofa-surfing, rough sleeping, in a hostel, then they give me a handover list – Jane Doe, she's in bed six, can you have a little chat with her and introduce yourself, and let her know how I can support her when she is being discharged. Two days a week I'm the hep C case worker, locating service users, making sure they're taking their meds, doing their blood tests, making sure they're engaging, and a few days a week I'm a homeless health case worker for Islington.

'I think confidence grows on you here, because I had to do a talk at Barnsbury Road job centre to promote Groundswell for homeless health service users. I couldn't have done that a couple of years ago. I know I couldn't because I'd have been like, er, er, er . . . It's OK to make mistakes, it's OK to stumble. We make mistakes every day.'

After years on the streets and some abusive hostel experiences, Sara herself now works with people in similar circumstances. 'My job involves doing research with homeless people, so mainly it's been talking to homeless women about their health needs and their physical and mental health and the impact of homelessness on that. But it could be phone interviews. It's varied because we all work on different projects, but predominantly I've been doing the women's research.'

She does a bit of work for *Pavement* magazine too. 'I like a good old write. That's therapeutic as well. The *Pavement* is a free homeless magazine that has articles to do with homelessness and a range of resources for different services, read by homeless people and people who work in the homelessness industry, but I think anyone would stand to benefit from reading … It's good for me to work with people and be that person I wish I had representing me when I was on the streets. If you can, why wouldn't you?'

After her life as a sex worker, Dena is now volunteering in the homelessness sector. 'I'm volunteering for years, on and off. I volunteer for loads of different charities working with vulnerable people and homeless people. My initial passion was to help people overcome their experience of being in prison and helping them when they come out. But gradually as I went through all these charities, I realised that homeless people includes everything – the after-effects. The criminal justice system, addictions, it's all involved, isn't it? So now my passion is just to help homeless people and people who are facing obstacles and it's also helped me in my recovery. It really has. I find that the skills I learnt and the knowledge I had and the feelings of being arrested and being in active addiction help me to help other people because I can understand where they are coming from. I'm not an expert in anyone else's experience, just my own, but I can get a sense of how they are feeling when they are talking about something. But everything affects people differently.

'I don't think I'm good at it. I just think I'm just being me now. It's probably who I should have been years ago. I'm doing what comes naturally, so I don't know if it's good, or right, or what, but it seems to work. I've got to the point now where I feel blessed to have gone through everything I've been through.'

Now she is a community connector in Lambeth. 'I'm quite good at chatting to people and, if they need any help, I refer them to places to help them with their health and wellbeing and it just comes naturally.' She also volunteers for Groundswell. 'There's some heart-breaking stories but I've realised after listening to them that I don't just want to listen, I want to try and do something about it.

So I want to get more involved and that's why I'm hoping to work for Groundswell in the future. That's my passion.'

A police officer told a story of one young man he helped move on. 'There was one chap, he was homeless and he was sitting at the steps at Exit 5. I'll always remember this young guy, he was crying and I went down, I said, "Are you all right there?" And he goes, "My life is shit, I don't know what to do." I buy him a cup of tea and I took him around the corner to give him a bit of dignity and privacy and I was like, "Tell me, what's happened?"

'So he got kicked out of home because he was doing drugs and stuff, and I was like, "Look, I can help you." But I said, "You need to help yourself as well. I can't take you by the hand now. You need to listen to my advice and what I'm going to do." He was on the street. He had no place to sleep. I took him down the street and pointed him in the right direction, rather than taking him by the hand, because people need to take that responsibility, don't they? I said, "This is your opportunity now." I got him in there' – this was St Mungo's – 'told him about the local soup kitchens, told him about St Martin-in-the-Fields.

'He went, he stayed there for a while, and he used to come back to Waterloo station to see me, to give me an update on how he was getting on, and then he got a job on a building site. Don't know how he did it. I said to him, I said, "Just because you're on the street, just because you're homeless, doesn't mean you can't work. You can actually get a job if you speak to the right people." I said, "Avoid drinking the alcohol," because he was drinking a can when I came across him, "avoid drinking the alcohol because the image that that gives . . . it shows that you're not entirely serious about where you want to carry your life."

'Oh my God . . . he used to come back on a weekly basis. Every time he'd seen me he'd say, "Thank you very much for looking after me." About six months afterwards he came back to me, "I'm actually getting a really good job on a building site and I'm getting my own flat, a one-bed maisonette." He had bought himself a second-hand BMW car from the money he was earning on the building site and

I was like, you know what, this is what my job is about, helping people, putting them in the right direction, giving them a chance.'

Freddie is still on the streets, but has taken a major step in turning his life around. Having been in and out of prison, worries about his mother made him decide to give up the criminal life. 'Feels good to have left it behind? Yeah, it does, because this sentence of forty-five months, it's the longest sentence I've done, and this one killed me. And that's why it's at the back of my mind now. Freddie, remember that, don't go back to that, know what I mean?'

Even those who have hit rock bottom often retain a glimmer of hope, a memory of some distant aspiration. David, staggering with drugs and dipping in and out of lucidity, said: 'I'm going to write a book as well, me. Could I interview you, one of the days? You know, one of the months. We could compare notes and stuff.'

'What would your book be about?'

'Er, I don't know. Life, maybe, about life.'

Carrie, in her thirties and homeless since leaving care at fifteen, talks of suicide. But when asked what she would like, she gives simple expression to what thousands of people in her situation want: 'My dream? I'd like a nice job, a nice house with a mortgage. I just want everything what everyone else has got.'

24

My London

It is striking how many of the people I talked to – both native Londoners and those who had come from abroad – spoke of their love for London. Hearing their stories felt like an overwhelming celebration of the city. Delia, for example:

'Do you like London?'

'Ahh, I'm a Londoner. I am a Londoner.

'I love those people who have left and come back. I say yes, go, and you'll come back. They come back. If you are tired of London, you are tired of life. London has everything life offers – it's so diverse, it's so interesting.'

Zack, giving out leaflets in Parliament Square: 'I was born and brought up in London. I've lived outside of London for a while; other places are nice, you get the peace and quiet, but I think there's nothing like London. It has a certain charm, a certain vibrance about the place. You can walk down somewhere and there's this, you see things happen, there's never a day goes past in London when you're bored. You always see something. Might be something ordinary, something completely crazy, at least there's something there. And that, you know, makes you feel alive.'

Rhoda at Lower Marsh: 'Yeah, I'm a Londoner. I like London. Apart from when I went to college, I've always been in London. I can't see myself living anywhere else, to be honest. I love the people, and this market brings me joy. I'm always happy, that's why I'm here. It's so lovely, with different people from all over the world, from places that you wouldn't think people even live, and I get to meet all of them here. So it's a joyful time for me. They tell me about their traditions, their homes, it might be a few, maybe half an hour, but they all come back during their stay. Some of them stay like a week, and during that week I maybe see them three or four times. They come and talk, they ask me about London, what to see, where can I get something, maybe they don't know, and I'm able to tell them, so it's nice – to meet different people from different places.'

A woman fruitseller in her twenties also left London to go to college. 'When I lived in Lancaster, I never thought I'd move back home and then my grandad got ill and I had to. And now, I don't know, I can't really see myself moving off again. I love London. My family is here, my friends are here. London is home. I think it's just because it's where I've grown up. And it's really nice. I don't know, every time I plan to go away, something happens. So I think it's where I'm meant to be.'

Market trader Dave: 'London? I'm a Londoner, yeah, East End. I've been to lots of cities – Rome, Vienna, lovely, Paris, lovely, New York. People say all cities are the same. They're not. There's nothing like London. I'm fifty-six years old and I've still not seen everything here.' He tells me about a Buddha that he's just discovered in a London park. 'Did you know that was there?'

Viorica, the Romanian cleaner, agrees there's nowhere like London. 'I like London because I have a good life here. And, after that, I like the weather here. Even if it is rain, it is fresh air all the time. I can say, I like London. I have no bad experiences in my work. Sometime a customer complaining but not all the time. Even if I'm old. For example, in my country I can't find work now because they are saying me I am too old, but here, they never say to me, no, you can't work for me because you are too old. For me it is good.'

Livia, selling the *Big Issue*, echoes her feelings: 'Yes. Because in London they are the best, in Romania no best. No good people. No help you. If you, ah, lady old one in the street, other person no. Here, all the people help. Good.'

Daniel, the doorman at the Langham Hotel, spoke of his role as an advocate for London. 'You're the first person somebody sees when they come to the hotel, and you're the last person somebody sees, so in many ways you're the face of the hotel. You present the hotel to the guests as they arrive. Plus you're hopefully an advertisement, a promoter for London in general, and that's part of your job as well. As well as promoting the hotel, you're promoting London. You want people to come back, you want people to have a good time, and you want people to really invest in their experience in London.

'I love London, I do, I think it's the greatest city in the world. And I've lived away, so I'm even more fond of it since I've come back. I was in Ireland for fourteen years, I was a factory manager for Hewlett Packard for a few years, which kinda didn't suit, being inside work, and I was a taxi driver as well in Dublin.'

'So why do you think London is the greatest city?'

'It's not just the history. It's a very eclectic town, I mean all tastes are accounted for. All the cuisines from all round the world are here. You've got the theatre, which is extraordinary, greatest theatre in the world, you've got artefacts from all over the world in the museums – probably the best collection of artefacts across the world. So it's that eclecticism, it's that dynamism, the multiculturalism, diversity, everything really . . . feeds into a renewal. In my business, we get free tickets for theatres, we get to go, we're constantly privy to information about what's happening, what's going on in London. If you work in the concierge, you get free tickets to the theatre, occasionally you get invited to new restaurants, to publicise the restaurants . . .

'You would never see all of London. You would never be tired of it. You would need ten lifetimes to get from one end of it to the other.

'I try to plan out what I do, which is a little bit peculiar to me. I try to go to central points, like originally I went to the British Museum, and then I'll see what's around there. Because there are new things, and I would try to link up . . . Typically when I go abroad, you go to major sites, you see it for a couple of hours, and

then you go, what am I going to do now? So what I try to do for
guests if they ask, or if they're going somewhere and they inform
me, I go, why don't you think of going there afterwards? Two or
three hours of the British Museum, you could go to Star Spa, you
could go to Sir John Soane's Museum, they're all close, so what I
try to do is map out the day for people, because everybody's short
of time when they're on holiday. I try to get them maximum experience of the area they've gone to that day. And er, so I've got all these
little maps in my head, about different areas and different places.'

'You could be a tour guide!'

'A blue badge? A lot of people have said that to me. With the his-
torical knowledge, I could probably do it, but it's a little bit too . . . I
dunno, structured for me. I like the variety. I've met business people,
I've met Nobel prize winners, I've met stars, and if you invest in
the guests, they will talk to you, and they will come back and talk
to you again and you really get an understanding and appreciation
of who they are, and what they do. It's very interesting. People are
very interesting.'

Gerry, a gardener, was 'born in London, University College
Hospital, brought up in London, all my life. Love London, yeah.
I wouldn't want to live anywhere else. I don't drive, and to be
honest I've got everything on my doorstep, I don't have to have a
car. That's London for you, everything's on your doorstep. Where
I live, I've got King's Cross there, I've got Euston, I've got Camden
'igh Street, I've got the West End, twenty minutes from where I
live. Yeah, that's why I love London, and it's multicultural as well,
quite a lot of friends, I've got African friends, all round where I
live. If you don't live in London, you don't experience it. I am
proud to be a Londoner, I really am. I think it's the best place,
the best city in the world. And, yeah, I wouldn't move out of 'ere
even if I could.'

Sameh, from Palestine and now selling fruit juice in Brixton
Market: 'No, I don't want to go back. When you've lived in the
freedom of somewhere like London, you wouldn't want to live in a
racist country like Israel. The best thing? The freedom, something

people take for granted. They don't appreciate it. No one asks you where you are going or where you have come from. I'm a lucky man.'

Anthony, Jamaican caricaturist: 'London? I've lived here all my life. I've got what I've got. It's not much, but London's one of the best cities in the world to live in, you know what I mean?'

And, to end with, the voice of Pat, at eighty-eight still standing outside Goodge Street station, giving out the *Evening Standard*, born in Holborn and a Londoner through and through.

'It's good. It's great. I love being here. I love my London. I do love my London. Everything. It's my home. My home.'

Epilogue

Julie was the first person I interviewed, drawn by her wonderfully stentorian voice calling 'Strawberries, strawberries, two for a pa-a-a-nd.' Nearly a year later, just before Christmas, again she was calling out, 'Blueberries, two for a pa-a-and!'

When I stopped to say hello, she said: 'This is my last day.'

Thinking that she meant before Christmas, I asked, 'When will you be back?'

'I'm not coming back. I've got a new job. In a bank. The AIB, Allied Irish. More money, less hours. And, yes, INSIDE!'

References

Introduction

1 *Let me take you by the hand . . .*: 'Streets of London', lyrics by Ralph McTell. Copyright © Westminster Music Limited.

1 *'Mosaic is a metaphor for bringing together . . .'*: 'Queenhithe Mosaic – a stunning new installation in the City of London', http://missbtakesawalk.blogspot.com/2014/12/queenhithe-mosaic-stunning-new.html.

1 *'fuller of wonders and wickedness . . .'*: Charles Dickens, *David Copperfield* (1849–50).

1 *'the epicentre of the elites . . .'*: Sean Coughlan, 'Super-rich elites making London "off-limits"', BBC News, 22 January 2020. See Katharina Hecht, Daniel McArthur, Mike Savage and Sam Friedman, 'Elites in the UK: Pulling Away? Social mobility, geographic mobility and elite occupations', Sutton Trust, January 2020, https://www.suttontrust.com/our-research/uk-elites-pulling-away/.

2 *These streets that Dickens drew on . . .*: Judith Flanders, *The Victorian City: Everyday Life in Dickens' London* (London: Atlantic Books, 2012).

8 *'Among the street-folk there are many distinct characters of people . . .'*: Mayhew, I.7.

1: The changing city

11 *By the last census return:* Mayhew, *Morning Chronicle*, 19 October 1849.

11 *'The remainder of the roadway is . . .'*: Quoted in Judith Flanders, op cit.

13 *According to a parliamentary briefing paper:* Chris Rhodes, 'Construction industry: statistics and policy', briefing paper no. 01432, 16 December 2019, https://commonslibrary.parliament.uk/research-briefings/sn01432/.

13 *in 2018, 28 per cent of workers:* 'Migrant labour force within the construction industry: June 2018', https://www.ons.gov.uk/peoplepopulationandcommunity/populationandmigration/internationalmigration/articles/migrantlabourforcewithintheconstructionindustry/2018-06-19.

18 *'the riot and tumult of the traffic . . . ':* Quoted in Flanders, op cit.

19 *The stranger who finds himself in 'The Dials':* Mayhew, II.35.

22 *'once an area "improved" . . . ':* Flanders, op cit.

2: Which Londoners?

25 *According to the 1861 census:* See 'Census records', https://www.nationalarchives.gov.uk/help-with-your-research/research-guides/census-records/. See also 'Greater London & Outer London Population and Density History', http://www.demographia.com/dm-lon31.htm.

25 *In 2011 it was 3,231,901:* '2011 Census', https://data.london.gov.uk/census/.

25 *The enormous population growth:* 'London Population', http://www.populationu.com/cities/london-population.

25 *In 1851, over 38 per cent of Londoners:* 'Census records', The National Archives.

3: The world outside

37 *a further 450 km of new routes by 2024:* Mayor of London/Transport for London, 'Cycling action plan: Making London the world's best big city of cycling', http://content.tfl.gov.uk/cycling-action-plan.pdf.

42 *only 39 per cent of inner London households:* 'Roads Task Force – Technical Note 12: How many cars are there in London and who owns them?', http://content.tfl.gov.uk/technical-note-12-how-many-cars-are-there-in-london.pdf.

43 *It was noon, and an exquisitely bright and clear spring day:* Mayhew (ed. Peter Razzell), 'Letter XLVII, 11 April 1850', *The Morning Chronicle Survey of Labour and the Poor: The Metropolitan Districts Volume 4* (Abingdon: Routledge, 2017).

44 *Now of all modes of obtaining subsistence:* Mayhew, I.6, 57.

4: 'People make mess'

58 *Of the different forms of pauper work:* Mayhew, II.245.

60 *That portion of the London street-folk:* Mayhew, II.465.

63 *There are in London upwards of 300,000 inhabited houses:* Mayhew, II.170.

64 *'Of this, only 52 per cent is currently recycled and . . . ':* 'Waste', London Environment Strategy, https://www.london.gov.uk/sites/default/files/waste.pdf.

5: Good morning London

71 *'a perception that a strong and well-managed . . . ':* Quoted in Ed Sheridan, 'Town Hall plans new licensing policy after huge loss of venues', *Camden Citizen*, 28 October 2019.

6: 'And then some are rich'

77 *My earnest hope is that the book:* Mayhew, I.iv.

80 *the epidemiologist authors of* The Spirit Level*:* See Kate Pickett and Richard Wilkinson, *The Spirit Level: Why More Equal Societies Almost Always Do Better* (London: Allen Lane, 2009).

80 *According to the Trust for London poverty profile:* 'London's Poverty Profile: 2020', https://trustforlondon.fra1.digitaloceanspaces.com/media/documents/Londons_Poverty_Profile_2020.pdf.

80 *According to an evidence pack produced by the local council:* 'Household Income 2018', https://www.towerhamlets.gov.uk/Documents/Borough_statistics/Income_poverty_and_welfare/Household_Income_2018_Factsheet.pdf.

81 *According to the* Guardian *in 2017:* Caelainn Barr, 'Wealth and poverty sit side by side in Grenfell Tower's borough', *Guardian*, 15 June 2017.

81 *'It is a place where inequality has become ...'*: Emma Dent Coad, 'After Grenfell: Housing and inequality in Kensington and Chelsea', November 2017, https://justice4grenfell.org/wp-content/uploads/2017/11/364307729-After-Grenfell.pdf.

8: 'All in the family'
101 *Syd's Coffee Stall is a piece of our social history:* 'So Long, Syd's Coffee Stall', https://spitalfieldslife.com/2019/12/21/so-long-syds-coffee-stall/.
105 *My mother came out to the garden:* Mayhew, III.381.

9: Billingsgate then and now
111 *To see this market in its busiest costermonger time:* Mayhew, I.65. An excerpt from a much longer piece.

10: Selling on the street
119 *Each salesman tries his utmost to sell his wares:* Mayhew, I.10.
122 *280 retail markets in London:* 'Understanding London's Markets', https://www.london.gov.uk/sites/default/files/gla_markets_report_short_web.pdf.
122 *'Markets ... are an expression ...'*: Ibid.
124 *Then there are the apple merchants:* Mayhew (ed. Victor Neuburg), *London Labour and the London Poor* (London: Penguin, 1985), 45 and 44.
127 *The principal sale of milk from the cow is in St. James's Park ...:* Mayhew, I.192.
134 *'The first handful of food shops ...'*: Louise Moon, 'Chapel Market: The history behind Islington's most vibrant street', http://islingtonnow.co.uk/the-history-of-chapel-market/.
136 *'I have bought from Dave Jackson ...'*: 'Our top traders', https://islingtonlife.london/discover-islington/blog/our-top-traders/.
138 *In 2016 the* Guardian *reported:* Susanna Rustin, 'Soho's last stand? Inside the battle to keep Berwick Street market independent', *Guardian*, 25 July 2016.
145 *The trade in second-hand apparel:* Mayhew, II.26.

11: Food to go

152 *Men and women, and most especially boys ...:* Mayhew (ed. Victor Neuburg), *London Labour and the London Poor* (London: Penguin, 1985), 69.

164 *The coffee-stall usually consists of a spring-barrow:* Mayhew, I.184.

164 *The trade, I am assured by all, is overstocked:* Mayhew, I.185.

12: Working on the streets

171 *There are, of course, only three modes of economising labour:* Mayhew, II.307.

174 *The so-called 'gig economy':* See 'Organise for Change', https://uphd.org.uk/about/.

175 *Research by the Trades Union Congress (TUC) estimates:* 'UK's gig economy workforce has doubled since 2016, TUC and FEPS-backed research shows', https://www.tuc.org.uk/news/uks-gig-economy-workforce-has-doubled-2016-tuc-and-feps-backed-research-shows.

176 *Let the working man and the employer: Rerum Novarum*, http://www.vatican.va/content/leo-xiii/en/encyclicals/documents/hf_l-xiii_enc_15051891_rerum-novarum.html.

177 *'for all members to receive at least ... ':* As at 'Unions', Freelances Make Theatre Work, https://freelancersmaketheatrework.com/associations-networks/.

179 *According to the Trades Union Congress:* 'UK's gig economy workforce has doubled since 2016, TUC and FEPS-backed research shows', https://www.tuc.org.uk/news/uks-gig-economy-workforce-has-doubled-2016-tuc-and-feps-backed-research-shows.

179 *One in six UK workers:* Rob Moss, 'One in six workers are in insecure, low-paid jobs', https://www.personneltoday.com/hr/living-hours-sixth-workers-insecure-low-paid-jobs/.

179 *'In no country in the world is there such an extent ...':* Mayhew, II.297.

179 *'that vast national evil':* Mayhew, II.323.

180 *'Most workers did not have a single job ... ':* Judith Flanders, op cit.

185 *The evils consequent upon the uncertainty of labour:* Mayhew (ed. Robert Douglas-Fairhurst), *London Labour and the London*

Poor: A Selected Edition (Oxford: Oxford University Press, 2010), 309.

13: 'Can't stop'
189 *The conveyance of goods from one part:* Mayhew, III.362–4.
201 *The metropolitan carriages:* Mayhew, III.357.

14: Entertainers
207 *'The first pitch we made was near . . . ':* Mayhew, III.110.
214 *A spare, sad-looking man:* Mayhew, III.214.

15: Getting the message out
232 *More than one half of the tract sellers:* Mayhew, I.242.
237 *'vast majority of vendors are paid hourly . . . ':* Amanda Andrews, 'London's Evening Standard to become free paper', *Telegraph*, 2 October 2009.

16: No Fixed Abode
249 *According to statistics released:* See Rough sleeping in London (CHAIN reports), https://data.london.gov.uk/dataset/chain-reports.
250 *Westminster Homeless Action Together (WHAT) reported:* 'Results – Westminster Homeless Action Together', https://passage. org.uk/2016/08/05/results-westminster-homeless-action-together/.
251 *now Shelter says that eight million people:* 'Almost half of working renters only one paycheque away from losing their home', https://england.shelter.org.uk/media/press_release/ almost_half_of_working_renters_only_one_paycheque_away_ from_losing_their_home.
253 *Six in ten rough sleepers:* See 'About Homelessness', http://www. streetsoflondon.org.uk/about-homelessness.
253 *'nails their fate to the streets . . . ':* In Eddie Ephraums (ed.), *The Big Issue Book of Home* (London: The *Big Issue* and Hodder & Stoughton, 2000).
255 *'perhaps more so than at any time in the past':* Adam Corlett, Stephen Clarke, Conor D'Arcy and John Wood, 'The Living

Standards Audit', https://www.resolutionfoundation.org/app/uploads/2018/07/Living-Standards-Audit-2018-3.pdf.

255 *analysis by the BBC has shown:* Daniel Wainwright, 'Benefit cuts "have made private renting unaffordable"', BBC News, 8 May.

256 *Maureen Crane's survey on older homeless people:* Maureen Crane (with contributions by Tony Warnes), 'Homeless Truths: Challenging the Myths about Older Homeless People', https://www.kcl.ac.uk/scwru/pubs/pre2000/crane1997homelesstruths.pdf.

256 *The WHAT survey in 2016 found:* Westminster Homeless Action Together (WHAT), 'The European End Street Homelessness Campaign: Learning, Findings and Next Steps – Executive summary', https://whpartnership.org.uk/wp-content/uploads/2020/09/WHATExecutiveSummary-Oct2016.pdf.

263 *A quarter of those interviewed in the 2016 WHAT survey:* Ibid.

266 *Figures released by the multi-agency:* See 'About Homelessness', Streets of London; 'Rough sleeping in London (CHAIN reports)'.

267 *CHAIN report showed:* Ibid.

267 *In 2017 the charity Crisis reported:* See 'Letters: Don't make criminals of homeless people', *Guardian*, 18 March 2019.

267 *in London between 2011 and 2015:* 'Offences, Arrests, Charges and Cautions etc. for "Vagrancy" Calendar Years 2011 to 2015', https://www.london.gov.uk/questions/system/files/attachments/Appendix%20C_63.pdf.

269 *In 2018 the British Legion estimated:* Nigel Morris, 'Thousands of armed forces veterans homeless or in prison', iNews, 17 September 2018.

269 *CHAIN reported that 6 per cent:* See Rhiannon Curry, 'Number of people sleeping rough in London rises by almost a fifth', Inside Housing, 20 June 2019. See also 'Rough Sleeping in London (CHAIN reports)'.

274 *In London, some 11 per cent:* See 'About Homelessness', Streets of London.

275 *According to the Ministry of Housing:* 'Homelessness in the UK 2019/2020', https://www.cornerstonepartnership.co.uk/homelessness-in-the-uk-2019-2020.

17: Hanging on

279 *The first instinct of the well-to-do visitor:* Mayhew (ed. Victor Neuburg), *London Labour and the London Poor* (London: Penguin, 1985), 443.

280 *Almost six hundred people died:* See 'Deaths of homeless people in England and Wales: 2018', https://www.ons.gov.uk/peoplepopulationandcommunity/birthsdeathsandmarriages/deaths/bulletins/deathsofhomelesspeopleinenglandandwales/2018. See also Bethan Thomas, 'Homlessness kills: An analysis of the mortality of homeless people in early twenty-first century England', https://www.crisis.org.uk/media/236799/crisis_homelessness_kills_es2012.pdf.

285 *The substitution of Universal Credit:* Professor Pat Thane, FBA, 'How poverty in modern Britain echoes the past', https://www.thebritishacademy.ac.uk/blog/how-poverty-modern-britain-echoes-past/.

287 *I think a beggar's life is the worst kind of life:* Mayhew, III.381.

287 STATEMENT OF A VAGRANT: Mayhew, III.385–6.

288 *'the majority of the Irish street-sellers . . . ':* Mayhew, I.105.

18: Destitution

297 *The destitution of those whose asylum claims:* 'Out in the cold: Homelessness among destitute refugees in London', https://www.jrsuk.net/wp-content/uploads/2018/01/Out-in-the-Cold_Homelessness-among-destitute-refugees-in-London_A-report-by-JRS-UK_January-2018_FINAL.pdf.

298 *'squalid, unsafe, slum housing conditions':* Frances Perraudin, 'UK asylum seekers living in "squalid, unsafe slum conditions"', *Guardian*, 27 October 2017.

19: The homelessness industry

313 *Asylum for the homeless poor of London is opened . . . :* Mayhew (ed. Victor Neuburg), *London Labour and the London Poor* (London: Penguin, 1985), 440.

313 *London Mayor today announced plans:* Alexandra Richards,

'Shelters for London's homeless people every day the temperature drops below zero', *Evening Standard*, 15 December 2017.

313 *DESCRIPTION OF THE ASYLUM FOR THE HOMELESS:* Mayhew, III.408.

318 *Ninety per cent of homeless accommodation projects:* 'The Future Hostel: The role of hostels in helping to end homelessness', https://www.homeless.org.uk/sites/default/files/site-attachments/The%20 Future%20Hostel_June%202018.pdf.

318 *Figures released under the Freedom of Information Act:* Samantha Booth, 'Homeless person dies every month on average in Camden hostels', *Camden New Journal*, 6 February 2020.

324 *'This was the first time I ever asked . . . ':* Mayhew (ed. Robert Douglas-Fairhurst), *London Labour and the London Poor: A Selected Edition* (Oxford: Oxford University Press, 2010), 314.

333 *The Islington Churches Cold Weather Shelter:* 'Islington Churches Cold Weather Shelter', https://www.carisislington.org/phdi/p1.nsf/supppages/1381?opendocument&part=4.

333 *Maureen Crane's survey of older homeless people:* Maureen Crane (with contributions by Tony Warnes), op cit.

334 *All things considered, therefore:* Mayhew, III.430.

20: Commemorating those who die homeless

339 *It's incredibly important that we take time to remember:* Quoted in Jo Seidlecka, 'Record numbers attend Commemoration Service for those who died homeless in past year', https://www.indcatholicnews.com/news/38333.

21: Sex work

341 *'While the Bishop of Exeter asserted . . . ':* Mayhew (ed. Victor Neuburg), *London Labour and the London Poor* (London: Penguin, 1985), 473.

342 *'I only do this kind of work . . . ':* Quoted in Tom Powell, 'Sex worker reveals what life is like working in London brothel run by ex-police officer', *Evening Standard*, 17 April 2018.